The Orchestra

The Orchestra

MICHAEL HURD

PHAIDON

A QUARTO BOOK

Published by Phaidon Press
Limited Littlegate House St
Ebbe's Street Oxford

First published in the United
Kingdom in 1981

ISBN 0 7148 2170 5

Filmset in Great Britain by
Brown Knight and Truscott
Limited, Tonbridge, Kent
and Abettatype Limited,
London.
Color origination by
Hong Kong Graphic Arts.
Printed in Hong Kong by
Leefung-Asco Printers
Limited.

This book was designed
and produced by
Quarto Publishing Ltd.,
32 Kingly Court,
London W1.

Editorial Director
Jeremy Harwood
Editor
James Roberts
Art Editor
Neville Graham
Editorial Assistant
Jane Struthers
Picture Research
Patricia Elkins

Contents

1. A German wind player of the early seventeenth century.
2. Leipzig cellist Carl Reimers' idea of the demonic force behind the scherzo of Beethoven's Fifth Symphony. Reimers himself appears far left.
3. The first ever printed symphonic score. The work is by Haydn; the year is 1801; the publishers are Leduc of Paris.
4. Stravinsky conducts.

2

The History

The permanent self-governing orchestra, nowadays to be found in every major city of Europe and America, developed during the nineteenth century and has a history of little more than one hundred and fifty years. How this great musical institution came into existence is the subject of the following pages.

3

4

The Early Orchestra

I T IS ONLY comparatively recently in the history of music that a composer could sit down to write a new work, confident that in most parts of the civilized world he would be able to find an orchestra with all the instruments necessary to play it. Before the year 1800, and even for some time after, he would have enjoyed no such assurance. What passed for an orchestra in, say, 18th century Vienna might in many respects have been rather different from a Paris or London group of the same period. Nor was there any guarantee that the orchestral resources of Paris and London would be absolutely identical. Though orchestras came into existence in the 17th century and began to settle into a recognizable pattern during the 18th, it was not until the 19th century that the standard orchestra as we know it today could be said to have become a predictable fact of musical life.

It is, however, clear that musical instruments have been played together in various combinations for hundreds of years. In medieval times they were used to support the voices as they negotiated the intricate polyphony of church music. The instrumentalists who helped out in this way were usually recruited from the small bands of 'town musicians' that began to appear in the 13th century. Such groups were to be found in most cities and large towns. They were employed by the municipal authorities partly as watchmen whose instruments could give warning signals, and partly as musicians pure and simple who could play for important civic occasions, or even hire themselves out for private entertainments. In England they were called *waits*, in Germany *Stadtpfeifer*, in Italy *pifferi*. They played wind instruments, such as the shawm and curtal (the early forms of oboe and bassoon), and were often organized into professional guilds with their own strict rules of conduct.

How the town musicians treated the music they played is largely a matter of conjecture – for instrumental full scores were not written out at this time. The likelihood is that each instrument played whichever notes it could, and that the parts were interchanged at will. For this reason alone we cannot consider these groups to be genuine early forms of orchestra. The orchestra, in fact, cannot be said to have existed until specific instruments began to be used for specific musical purposes and in specific groups or combinations. That moment did not arrive until the beginning of the 17th century, and even then it took many years before any degree of standard practice was established.

The first signs of a truly 'orchestral' attitude appeared at the very end of the 16th century in the music that Giovanni Gabrieli (1557-1612) wrote as organist and choirmaster of St Mark's, Venice. He was one of the first composers to realize that voices and instru-

The use of contrast

Gabrieli, organist and choirmaster of St Mark's, Venice (**bottom**), scored the *Sonata pian'e forte* (**below**) for two self-contained groups of instruments which, as the layout of the score shows, play either antiphonally or together, thus varying the weight of sound and the direction from which it comes. The dynamic markings in this version are modern. Gabrieli himself relied on the changing number of instruments for his 'pian' e forte' effects.

Above: five Nuremberg *Stadtpfeifer* of the sixteenth century. Their standard instruments were cornett, sackbut, curtal, serpent and shawm. In Leipzig in 1595 the town's *Stadtpfeifer* found their woodwind and brass sound challenged by the string tones of incoming fiddlers. The newcomers were given official but inferior positions. The *Pfeifer* would play from the church tower every morning and evening and at Sunday services. **Left:** the *pifferi*, their counterparts in Italy. **Right:** the English *waits*.

ments could be effectively used in contrast with one another. In such works as the motet *In Ecclesiis* two choirs and four soloists are accompanied by an organ and an orchestra consisting of violas, cornetts and trombones. These sometimes merely duplicate the voice parts in the traditional way, but at others provide an independent accompaniment, or play entirely by themselves. The contrast and variety thus available is considerable. He applied the same principle to certain instrumental works. For example, the famous *Sonata pian' e forte* (published in 1597) wholly depends on the contrast

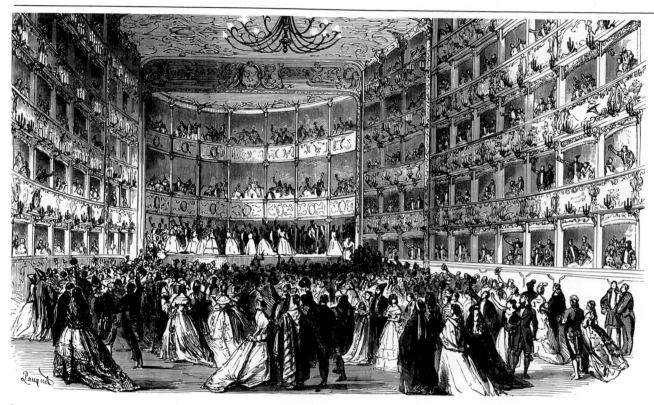

between two instrumental groups: one consisting of a cornett and three trombones, the other of a violino (viola) and three more trombones. When only one group plays the sound is soft (*pian'*); but when both play together it is loud (*forte*): thus giving the work its title, its musical shape, and its effectiveness.

Gabrieli's experiments are part of a general movement towards making music effective as a public entertainment. Hitherto it had been primarily functional – either part of a church service, or to accompany dancing – or for the personal delight of the performers (as in madrigals). Now the swing was towards presenting music to an audience: first a mainly aristocratic one, and then, increasingly during the latter part of the 17th century, an audience consisting of anyone who could afford to pay for the privilege.

The first important form of public entertainment was opera. This was an invention of the last decade of the 16th century, and though at first confined largely to the courts of the nobility its popularity spread rapidly. In 1637 the first public opera house was opened in Venice, and within a dozen years the city was able to support no fewer than four such theaters simultaneously.

By its very nature opera demands not

Since its inception at the end of the sixteenth century, opera has played a dominant part in Italian musical life. The grandure of the major opera houses such as *La Scala*, Milan (**above**) and the *Fenice*, Venice (**top**) reflect the esteem in which opera is held. For the average audience the heyday of Italian opera began with Rossini, Bellini and Donizetti and ended with Verdi and Puccini, but in recent years the significance of earlier composers, in particular Monteverdi, has also come to be appreciated.

only that the singing voices should be supported by instruments, but that its music should describe the thoughts and emotions of the characters in the drama. It is therefore not surprising to find that it is the instruments used to accompany early opera that first begin to sort themselves out into definite groups and patterns, each with a special function – in other words, an orchestra. The process was, moreover, hastened by the rapid spread of opera and the need, therefore, for a degree of standardization in the way it was written and presented.

Indeed, from opera came the very word 'orchestra'. The first operas were written in imitation of what ancient Greek methods of presenting drama were supposed to have been. And since the semi-circular area in front of the Greek stage was known as the *orkhêstra* (the place where the chorus danced and sang), it was only logical to adopt the word for the group of accompanying instruments that sat in front of the operatic stage.

The first 'great' opera was written by Claudio Monteverdi (1567-1643) and produced at the court of the Duke of Mantua in 1607. It was called *La favola d'Orfeo* (The Story of Orpheus). And although we have no orchestral full score to show exactly where and when each instrument is to play, Monteverdi was very specific in stating which instruments he wanted. (See opposite.)

Of the instruments in Monteverdi's *Orfeo* orchestra the most 'complete' group – in the sense that between them they could provide a full range of notes – is that of the bowed strings. Both viols and the more recently invented violins are called for, but it is the violin family that predominates.

Different from viols, both in construction and the manner in which they were played, the violins were altogether more brilliant and extrovert. They could make a 'big' sound that would fill a concert hall and satisfy a large audience. The viols were intimate and quiet-voiced, and thus more suited to small-scale chamber music. Although it seems likely that both types of instrument were used by the early orchestras (for orchestral 'scores' of the period are very sketchy and seldom indicate which instrument is intended), the members of the violin family gradually came to be accepted as the true concert instruments.

Again it is a work of Monteverdi's that points the direction orchestral music was to take. In the dramatic cantata *Il combattimento di Tancredi e Clorinda* (The Combat of Tancredi and Clorinda), 1642, he uses an orchestra consisting only of strings and harpsichord. This was soon to be recognized as the basis for all orchestras. Moreover, this work is the first of any kind to explore specifically 'orchestral' effects. Plucked strings (*pizzicato*), the rapid reiteration of notes (*tremolo*), the repetition of short musical figures, are all to be found in this score, greatly adding to the sense of drama and description in the music.

The central influence of the court

During a century which rapidly embraced the idea of music as entertainment, many different composers in many different countries were to make individual contributions to the development of the art, and it is perhaps a little misleading to single out particular men. Yet individuals, such as Monteverdi, do stand out; and so also does the influence of certain courts and noble households. High among them is the court of King Louis XIV of France during the reign of Jean Baptiste Lully (1632-87) as composer-in-chief.

Among the large staff of musicians which provided Louis with chamber

The Court at Mantua

Monteverdi (**left**) discovered that instruments could have a much more important role in a vocal work than that of merely doubling the voices. The collection (**below**) for *Orfeo* clearly foreshadows the divisions of the modern orchestra. Only the plucked and keyboard instruments stand out as unusual, but they were the means of providing a harmonic background to the music (see p14). It was only through working under a great nobleman in a city such as Mantua (**above**) that a composer could have at his disposal such a large group of instrumentalists.

Wind instruments

Brass instruments

Bowed strings

Plucked instruments

Keyboard instruments

Music at the court of Louis XIV

Jean Baptiste Lully (**below**) came to France from Italy as a boy and rose to become the favorite composer of Louis XIV and arbiter of French musical taste. He developed an orchestral style for his twenty operas which rested less on blending and contrasting color than on a kind of dialogue between the basic string orchestra and the woodwind. The central instruments at his disposal are shown (**bottom**). Charles II attempted to organise his music along similar lines to the French court. **Bottom right:** a score from Lully's opera *Persée*. To have operas printed in score was extremely rare at this time. Only the generation after Lully began to release the orchestra from subjugation to voices.

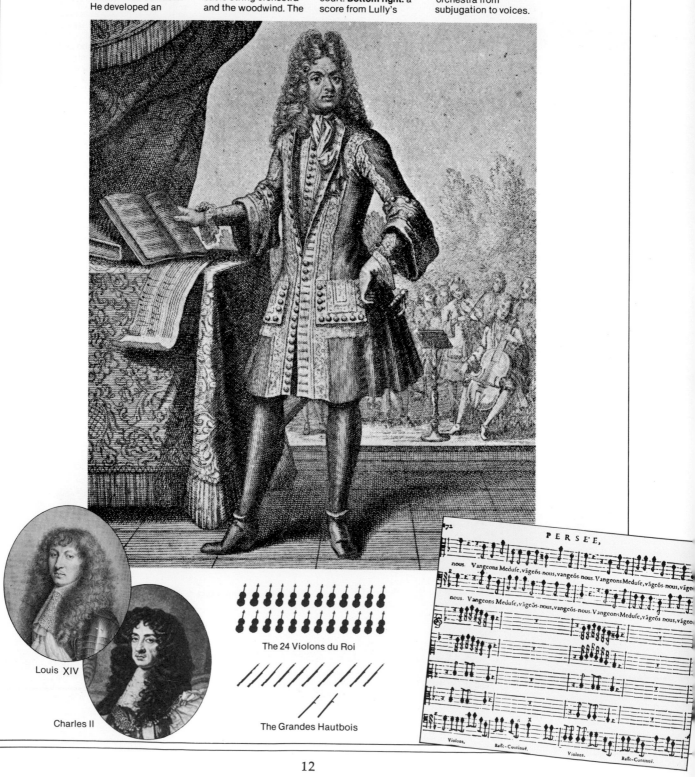

Louis XIV

Charles II

The 24 Violons du Roi

The Grandes Hautbois

music, opera, church services, and music connected with ceremonials, there were two groups of great importance. First, the *24 Violons du Roi*, usually called the *Grande Bande*. This group played as a five-part texture consisting of 6 first violins on the melody, 6 basses (the equivalent of the modern cello) on the bass line, and 4 each of instruments tuned as violas to take the three inner parts. Next to them came the *12 Grandes Hautbois* which, since they were mainly employed in outdoor work, belonged to *La Grande Ecurie* – the Royal Stables, which organized every aspect of ceremonial and not just the horses. This group actually consisted of 10 oboes and 2 bassoons, and could join the strings as reinforcements to the top and bottom lines.

The example of King Louis' *24 Violons*, with or without the *Hautbois*, caught the imagination of his fellow princes. In 1660 Charles II, newly restored to the throne of England, celebrated by reorganizing his music along the lines of the French king's, in whose court he had spent his years of exile. And if other courts could not afford to maintain a full band of 24 violins, they at least tried to find the money for a smaller group. Thus we may say that by the middle of the 17th century the violin family, in its various sizes from double bass to violin, was firmly established as the accepted basis for all orchestras.

To such a basis could be added, as we have seen, oboes and bassoons. Equally available were flutes – both the end-blown recorder type, and the side-blown transverse flutes. In a large court these players would have been drawn from the general music staff. But in a smaller establishment they were often recruited from the municipal town bands. For very special occasions trumpets and drums might also be added. These belonged to the military and ceremonial side of court life, and in earlier days were very restricted in their use – being essentially 'royal' instruments, fit only to announce the presence and commands of a king. By the beginning of the 18th century horns could also be called upon – this time from the hunting field. Trombones, though long available as part of church music, were not yet considered as potential orchestral instruments – the example of Monteverdi's *Orfeo* is somewhat exceptional.

Essential instruments

Thus it can be seen that by the end of the 17th century the main instruments of the modern orchestra were there to be used. But in practice it was to be some time before they all gained an equal acceptance. The center of attention was the string orchestra.

Even so, the strings were not expected to function as a wholly self-contained unit. They could have, had

Trumpets and their partners the timpani had a special elevated role throughout the seventeenth and well into the eighteenth century. Monarchs were keen to preserve their peculiar sonorities for appropriate occasions — that is, for the majesty of their own ceremonies and the holiness of their own wars. Anyone who sullied the sound by employing it on a mean occasion was probably acting most unwisely. Trumpeters themselves were, of course, keen to preserve their privileged status and keep their instruments out of the hands of ordinary town musicians. Their guilds were separate from and socially superior to the other musicians' guilds. They resisted strongly attempts to add crooks to trumpets, partly because, unlike horns, they were unbalanced by them. They also felt their monopoly was threatened as it seemed to be by the slide trumpet. **Below:** part of the 'Coronation of James II' by Sandford (1678). One of the most talented trumpeters of the time was John Shore, appointed by James to the post of Trumpeter in Ordinary in 1688, in which role he joined his two older brothers. It was for him that Purcell wrote his most brilliant trumpet *obbligati*.

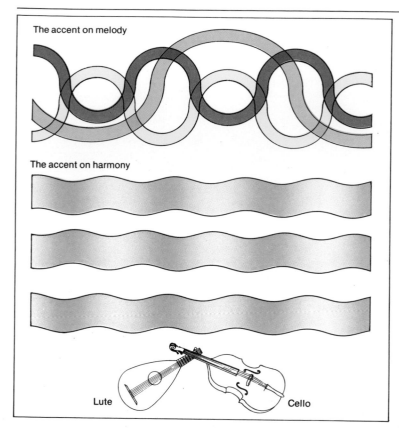

The accent on melody

The accent on harmony

Lute   Cello

it been so desired. But the tendency at this period was to give precedence to the highest and lowest parts – the melody and the bass line – and leave the inner parts somewhat indeterminate. The result would have been a sound with a hole in the middle, had it not been for the use of the *continuo*.

Providing bass line and harmony

The continuo came into existence as part of the change of attitude that came over music towards the end of the 16th century. Before that time music was primarily polyphonic – that is to say: woven from many different strands of independent melody. The emphasis, so to speak, was on the *horizontal* aspect of music; and the harmonies (the *vertical* aspect) came into existence because of the way the melodic lines moved against each other. The new attitude looked at things differently. What now mattered was a firm bass line from which chords could be built up vertically like pillars to support a melody. The inner melodies (the way the inner parts moved) were now less important – they had virtually been melted together into a block of harmony.

Just how fundamental this change of attitude was can be seen in the function

In polyphonic music harmonies are incidental to the interweaving lines of melody (**top illustration**). By the seventeenth century composers had begun to think in rather different musical terms. They were more interested in the way simultaneous sounds blended with each other. (**above illustration**). Probably because it paralleled the range of the vocal choir, spanning three octaves or more from low bass to high treble, the string orchestra became the essential foundation of orchestral style. It did not supply the four-part harmony necessary to fill the range, but took the prominent higher and lower parts. The sound was completed by the addition of a continuo instrument such as the harpsichord, organ or lute, which could play chords, and a bass line from the cello, double bass or bassoon. The presence of the bassoon here was often so taken for granted that its part was unspecified. Thus we arrive at the characteristic sound of, say, a Bach orchestra, in which the continuo underlies the other instruments.

of the continuo. This was a method of providing a firm bass line and a solid harmony. Two instruments were necessary: one to play the continuous bass line (say, a bass viol, a cello or a basson), and one to provide the harmony (a harpsichord, a lute, or a small organ – anything that could play chords). The harmonies themselves were shown by figures underneath the notes of the bass line – a form of musical shorthand.

All early orchestras made use of continuo instruments. The various keyboard and plucked instruments listed for Monteverdi's *Orfeo* all supply harmonic support, just as the cellos, bass viols, and double-bass viols supply the firm continuous bass line. The practice continued until well past the middle of the 18th century, even though it would have been perfectly possible to supply the full harmony using other instruments to fill the missing parts.

Public accessibility

One final aspect of the early orchestral scene remains to be considered: the gradual rise of public concert-giving. On the Continent this seems to have come about in two ways: either through the courtesy of the princes and nobility who made certain of their private concerts available to a slightly wider, though still carefully selected audience; or through the spread of various societies devoted to artistic pursuits. In Italy, and to some extent France, there was the *Accademia,* and in Germany the *Collegium Musicum.* The members of such societies were wealthy, educated, and often aristocratic. Something of the flavor of their meetings can be seen in the late 18th century account given by Dr Charles Burney, quoted opposite.

The earliest approximation to the modern public concert came, perhaps not surprisingly, from England – the most democratic and middle-class of European countries, where court and aristocracy had been put in their place by the events of the Civil War (1642-45). On December 30th 1672, John Banister, a member of the King's Band of 24 Violins, placed the following advertisement in the *London Gazette*:
"These are to give notice, that at Mr John Banister's house (now called the music school) over against the George Tavern, in White Friars, near the back of the Temple, this Monday, will be music performed by excellent masters,

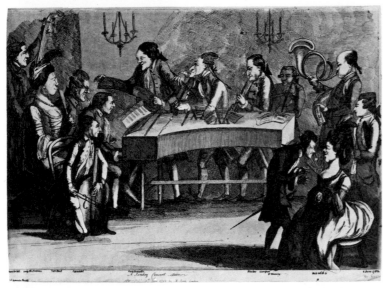

Orchestral music in the Baroque age might be heard at gatherings of amateurs. Burney (**right**) described an Italian *accademia* thus: '*Il padrone* played the first violin, and had a very powerful hand; there were twelve or fourteen performers: several good violins; two German flutes, a violoncello, and a small double bass; they executed reasonably well several of our (JC) Bach's symphonies . . . ' Burney himself (inattentive in the gathering, **above**) was not immune from caricature. **Top:** a German Collegium Musicum. The accent was on pleasure, but these societies were often directed by a professional Cantor.

beginning precisely at 4 of the clock in the afternoon, and every afternoon in the future, precisely at the same hour.''

The event was what we would now call a chamber concert, and was not unlike the kind of spontaneous 'concerts' that took place in ale-houses. Banister's audience sat at small tables and, for a shilling, were entitled to as much ale and tobacco as they pleased. The music, however, was rather more select than an ale-house would offer. But to protect his musicians from the possibility of being mistaken for mere tavern serenaders, Banister made them perform on a raised platform behind drawn curtains.

The idea caught on, and in later years he offered similar entertainments in Chando Street, Lincoln's Inn Fields, and Essex Street off the Strand. In 1676 the composer and theorist Thomas Mace put forward the idea of a concert hall, to be built at public expense. Although the scheme came to nothing, by 1689 a building with a specially designed music-room capable of holding about two hundred people had been erected. It is probably this music-room, York Buildings, that deserves the title of the first public concert hall in Europe.

The Classical Orchestra

ALTHOUGH BY THE TIME of Bach and Handel it was generally agreed that an orchestra should consist of strings (violins, violas, cellos, and basses), a harpsichord continuo, with woodwind (flutes or oboes, and bassoons) as probable extras, and brass (trumpets and horns) as less frequent additions, there could be no guarantee that orchestras even in different parts of the same country would resemble each other in anything but the most general outline.

Nor did it particularly matter. For this was a time when travel was still restricted, and arduous when undertaken. If a composer moved from one country to another as Handel did (first to Italy and then to England), he stayed a long time and adapted such scores as he brought with him to the orchestral conditions of his new berth. More often he would simply write new works on the spot, tailoring them to the conditions as he found them. Music was written for immediate consumption. Nobody wrote with an eye to posterity – or even the next country.

And if travel was a problem, communications in general were equally uncertain. Unless a composer actually visited another area, he would have little chance of knowing what its music was like. Although the individual orchestral parts of symphonies and concertos were sometimes printed (increasingly after about 1760), only operas and oratorios were printed in full score. The first symphonies to be published in this way were a handful by Haydn, printed by the Paris firm of

Leduc in 1801. Before that time a few manuscript copies might be in circulation, but they were more likely to be jealously guarded by their composers, since there were no laws to protect their copyright in those days. Information about the latest developments in music was therefore difficult to come by, and there was little incentive to conform to a generally accepted standard of practice.

A comparison of the actual constitution of various European orchestras (see opposite) shows how variable conditions were.

As the century wore on and com-

Some major musical centers of Europe (**below**): Bach worked in Leipzig from 1723 to 1750. Earlier in his career, he walked the 200 miles from Arnstadt to Lübeck to hear Buxtehude. During Mozart's tour of Italy he was made a member of the *accademia* of Bologna. In Salzburg, in his role as Court Organist, he was of equal rank with the valets. Haydn was better appreciated by the Esterhazy princes, but was moved from Eisenstadt to the isolation of Esterhaza, in Southern Hungary.

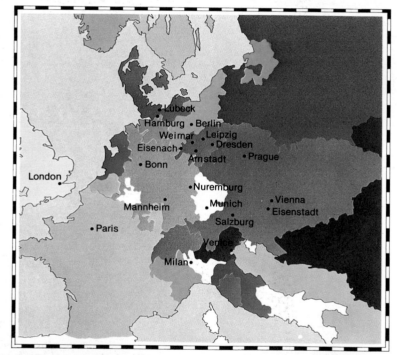

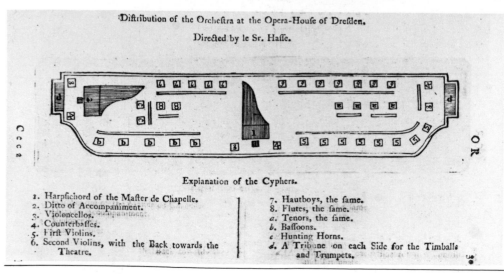

Distribution of the Orchestra at the Opera-House of Dresden.

Directed by le Sr. Hasse.

Explanation of the Cyphers.

1. Harpsichord of the Master de Chapelle.
2. Ditto of Accompaniment.
3. Violoncellos.
4. Counterbasses.
5. First Violins.
6. Second Violins, with the Back towards the Theatre.
7. Hautboys, the same.
8. Flutes, the same.
a. Tenors, the same.
b. Bassoons.
c. Hunting Horns.
d. A Tribune on each Side for the Timballs and Trumpets.

Hasse's arrival at the court of Elector Augustus II (**above**) marked the beginning of a rise to European fame of the orchestra of the Dresden Opera (**left**). Hasse was centrally situated at the harpsichord with the players around him.

A growing uniformity

In the early eighteenth century there was no universally accepted model for an orchestra. The three earlier ensembles on the left differ quite significantly.

By the end of the century orchestras had not only grown in size, but settled into a more uniform pattern. Frederick the Great's orchestra, when completed by theorbo,

harp trumpets and drums was capable of playing most scores of the time. That provided by Salomon for Haydn's visit in 1792 was even more complete. By the end of

the century the 'classical orchestra' of the older Haydn or Mozart, or earlier Beethoven, could be discerned. The continuo, too, was finally recognized as redundant.

	Frederick William I of Prussia (1712)	Paris Opera (1713)	King of Poland at Dresden (1719)	Frederick the Great (1782)	Salomon, for Haydn (1792)	The 'classical' orchestra
Violins						
Violas						
Cellos						
Basses						
Flutes						
Oboes						
Clarinets						
Bassoons						
Trumpets						
Horns						
Timpani						
Harpsichord						
Theorbos Pantaleon						

munications improved, the work of individual outstanding composers became more generally known and sought after, and the qualities of the better organized orchestras began to be appreciated. Thus it became more and more evident exactly what an 'orchestra' ought to be, and by the end of the century what we now think of as the 'classical orchestra' – the kind enjoyed by Haydn and Mozart at the end of their lives, and by Beethoven in his prime – was an accomplished fact.

The Court at Mannheim
In achieving this end certain orchestras inevitably set the pace. The most interesting and influential was to be found in Mannheim at the court of Duke Carl Theodor, the Elector Palatine. Its history began in 1742 when the duke engaged the Czech violinist Johann Stamitz (1717-57) to be Kapellmeister of his court music. Stamitz was a brilliant virtuoso player and was encouraged to seek out fine musicians from all over Europe – rather as the manager of a football team buys in new players

nowadays. Carl Theodor, himself a trained musician, wanted nothing but the best, and this is exactly what he got. In his book *The Present State of Music in Germany, the Netherlands, and United Provinces,* published in 1773, Dr Charles Burney recalled the visit he paid to the Elector's court in August 1772:

"I found it (the orchestra) to be indeed all that its fame had made me expect: power will naturally arise from a great number of hands; but the judicious use of this power, on all occasions, must be the consequence of good discipline; indeed there are more solo players, and good composers in this, than perhaps in any other orchestra in Europe; it is an army of generals, equally fit to plan a battle, as to fight it."

Stamitz was succeeded by another fine musician, Christian Cannabich (1731-98); and Stamitz's own talented sons, Philipp and Anton served in the orchestra, besides a number of other equally gifted instrumentalists – most of whom were also competent composers. With this galaxy of talent at its

When Frederick the Great (**above**); became King in 1740 he clearly intended to indulge his musical proclivities at least as far as his father had indulged his own military ones. The opera house he built in Berlin in 1742 was possessed of a startling gamut of props and effects. And he employed as many first-rate composers and players as he could in the 60-strong orchestra which served the opera and his palace. He dictated musical taste, however, and preferred the style of J S Bach and Handel to that of up-and-coming 'modernists' such as CPE Bach, who he employed but hardly encouraged. He was an accomplished composer and flautist, and employed a full-time composer, Joachim Quantz, to write for the flute. Quantz wrote 299 concertos, No. 300 being completed by Frederick after Quantz died writing it. Frederick's repertoire seems to have consisted entirely of these.

The Mannheim Orchestra

The court orchestra of Mannheim under the Bohemian musician Johann Stamitz deserves the title of the first great virtuoso orchestra. Its outstanding musicians believed that music should display the quality and capability of an orchestra and its instruments. Stamitz composed symphonies and sonatas in the new style using contrasting keys and themes. The bass line played by cellos and basses, and doubled by bassoon, was, however, retained. Even this orchestra seems to have had limitations: Burney found their flutes and oboes imperfect.

Public concerts were to be found in London from 1672, and in the eighteenth century pleasure grounds such as Vauxhall (**above,** with its central pavilion known as the 'orchestra') Marylebone (**left**) and Ranelagh (**right,** the 'Rotunda') reached the height of their popularity. The style of London-based composers such as J C Bach — graceful, unextravagent — was perhaps partly echoed in the gardens.

RANELAGH HOUSE.
ON Monday next will be performed a Concert of
Vocal and Instrumental MUSIC.
Horns, Clarinets, &c. before and between the Acts.
The Doors to be opened at Half past Six.
The Horns, &c, to begin at Seven, and the Band a Half past Seven.
Admittance 2s. 6d. each Person,
Coffee and Tea included.
To be continued Mondays, Wednesdays and Fridays.
Ladies and Gentlemen may walk in the Rotunda, Gardens, &c. every Day (Sunday excepted) at 1s. each.
1775

Public concerts in Vienna at the time of Mozart (**above**) often took place in the Mehlgrube (on the right of the picture, **left**) or the Augarten (**top**). Mozart is shown meeting Emperor Joseph II and his mother Maria Theresa. He outlived Joseph by about a year — perhaps just long enough to see that his reforms would not survive him. The acclaim of the powerful did not save Mozart from a pauper's grave.

disposal, it is not surprising that the orchestra flourished.

But its importance rests not merely on excellent performances. Because so many of the players were also composers (in the 18th century the two skills usually went hand in hand), great strides were made in the development of the kind of music orchestras played. The Mannheim composers not only helped to bring the symphony into existence as a musical form, but also invented a whole armory of ways of playing such music. They thought out phrasing with great care. They introduced the notion of uniform bowing for each string section. And the idea of a controlled *crescendo* and *diminuendo* – the music gradually growing louder, and then dying away – was theirs.

Discovering how they played

Despite the reports of such commentators as Dr Burney it is impossible to tell exactly how well or badly the 18th century orchestras actually played. But some idea can be gained by a study of the music written for them.

In the first half of the century composers tended to set down their music without any particular regard for the different tonal colors of the instruments. The strings did most of the work. Violins were likely to be doubled by oboes or flutes, and cellos by double basses and bassoons. Sometimes the strings played a passage by themselves which would be repeated by the woodwind alone. There was little about the music that made it impractical for one group or the other – save for the few occasions when the strings went beyond the range of the woodwind. The parts for woodwind and strings look exactly alike: there is very little in them that says "these notes can *only* be played by strings," or "these can *only* be played by woodwind." In other words, from a purely orchestral point of view the music was conceived in very general terms.

When trumpets and horns were used a certain individuality crept in, simply because at this date neither instrument could command a full set of notes. Each was limited to its 'open' notes – that is to say, the notes of the harmonic series of the particular length of tubing being used at the time. At the lower end of the compass the available notes were few and far between.

Only in music written for the opera house did composers deliberately search out effects of orchestral 'color'. A woodland scene might encourage flutes to twitter and warble like birds, while a visit to celestial regions would almost certainly bring harps into play. Throughout orchestral history many of the most interesting experiments come directly from opera.

One further 18th century musical type deserves mention as a pointer to the way in which orchestral colors were to be explored, and that is the *concerto grosso*. Developed from the idea of contrasting different groups of instruments or voices, to be found in the music of 16th century composers such as Giovanni Gabrieli, the *concerto grosso* depended both for its formal structure and its musical effect on the idea of contrast between a small group of soloists and a complete orchestra. Sometimes, as in the music of Corelli and Handel, the two groups were both strings. The contrast then was simply that of weight: solo strings against massed strings. But the solo instruments might also be woodwind or brass, or a mixture of both – as they often are in the *concerti grossi* of Bach and Vivaldi – and then the contrast would be one of color also.

It is from sources such as these that the idea of 'orchestration' derives. Gradually composers began to find out how to use the color qualities of each instrument – rather as an artist uses paints on his canvas: sometimes mixing and blending them, sometimes contrasting them boldly. Little by little they began to explore the special characteristics of each instrument and write music that would bring out the best in its personality.

A comparison between an orchestral score of, say, Bach and Mozart will illustrate exactly how far this art developed during the 18th century. In a Bach score it is not really essential that notes allotted to the flute should be played only by that instrument – an oboe would do as well, or even a high trumpet. But a flute phrase in a late Mozart symphony is designed only for the flute, and though it might physically be played by an oboe or a clarinet, something would be lost in the exchange. The music has been conceived, right from the start, in its special orchestral dress.

The orchestra's growing importance

Along with these developments, changes of a more general nature were

At the end of the eighteenth century, the church's role as the house of music as well as the House of God was in decline. The Handel Commemmoration still took place in Westminster Abbey (**right**, 1785) but the opera house, especially in Italy (**above**) had won popular allegiance.

Corelli

Vivaldi

Massed strings

Solo strings

Massed strings

Woodwind and brass

Handel   Bach

taking place that eventually brought orchestras and the music they played into the forefront of musical activity. At the end of the 17th century music for the church mattered a very great deal, opera was important, and orchestral music was in its infancy. By the end of the 18th century orchestral music vied with opera for pride of place, and church music scarcely came into the picture.

In assuming such importance the orchestra brought into existence its own special forms of music. The earliest recognizable type is the suite: a collection of movements which contrast with each other in key, speed, rhythm and mood. From this simple idea grew all the major orchestral forms of the 18th century.

One of these was the operatic *overture*: really a little suite of contrasted movements, arranged fast-slow-fast, or slow-fast-slow according to taste. Such pieces were also found useful in the concert hall. In Italy, however, they were often called *sinfonias* (*sinfonia* being a general word for any passage of purely orchestral music in an opera). During the middle of the century the

sinfonias began to develop – each section acquiring a character and shape of its own, until at last the symphony was born.

Once safely launched, the symphony and the symphonic style dominated every aspect of orchestral music. So thoroughly did it become the staple diet of every orchestra that, sometime during the 19th century, the two words became almost synonymous. Today we talk quite happily of the 'symphony orchestra' – quite forgetting that it can give a perfectly satisfactory concert without playing a single symphony!

The varied musical centers
Alongside the development of characteristic orchestral forms went the gradual democratization of the orchestral concert. In Germany, as we have seen, the most significant musical activity centered on the courts that dotted a land made up of autonomous states of various sizes and importance. Their influence lasted throughout the 18th century, depending for effectiveness entirely on the wealth and musical enthusiasm of the local prince or duke. When the portents were favorable, as

they were at the palaces of Eisenstadt and Esterház during the lifetimes of Prince Paul and Prince Nicholas Esterházy, then a composer of Haydn's stature might be content to live out the greater part of his life as *Kapellmeister*: a paid, liveried servant, but with every opportunity and encouragement to write operas, church music, symphonies, concertos, songs and chamber music for instant performance – and, what is more, instant and informed appreciation.

In less happy courts, such as that of Archbishop Colloredo at Salzburg, Mozart chafed for a while under an arrogant and musically insensitive yoke and then left, to try his luck as a free-lance composer in Vienna. Here he would gladly have accepted a suitable court appointment, but when one did come (in 1787) it proved to be little more than honorary. The small salary it carried was, in Mozart's words, "Too much for what I do, too little for what I could do!" He was thus forced to depend on free-lance opportunities: writing operas to commission, teaching, and giving 'academies' – that is to say, sponsoring concerts of his own music and trusting that the wealthy music-loving families of Vienna would subscribe in sufficient numbers to make the venture profitable.

Concerts of this kind took place in a theater, or in the music-rooms of aristocratic town houses – or sometimes, as Mozart's letter to his father dated May 8th 1782 makes clear, in the famous Augarten pleasure ground on the banks of the Danube:

"This summer there is to be a concert every Sunday in the Augarten. A certain (Philipp) Martin organized last winter a series of amateur concerts, which took place every Friday in the Mehlgrube.* You know that there are a great many amateurs in Vienna, some very good ones too, both men and women. But so far these concerts have not been properly managed. Well, this Martin has now got permission from the Emperor under charter (with the promise too of his gracious patronage) to give twelve concerts in the Augarten and four grand serenades in the finest open places of the city. The subscription for the whole summer is two ducats. So you can imagine we shall have plenty of subscribers, the more so

---

* A large old building with public rooms. Now the Hotel Kranz.

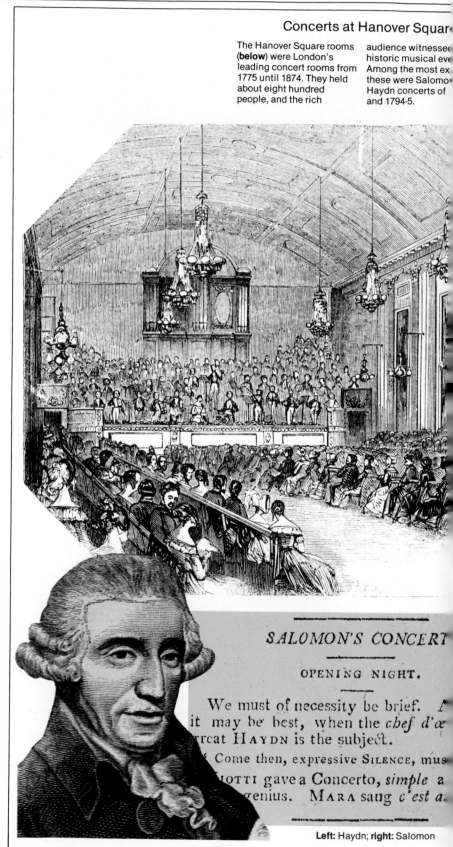

Concerts at Hanover Square

The Hanover Square rooms **(below)** were London's leading concert rooms from 1775 until 1874. They held about eight hundred people, and the rich audience witnessed historic musical eve Among the most ex these were Salomo Haydn concerts of and 1794-5.

SALOMON'S CONCERT

OPENING NIGHT.

We must of necessity be brief. it may be best, when the *chef d'œ* reat HAYDN is the subject.

Come then, expressive SILENCE, mus IOTTI gave a Concerto, *simple a* genius. MARA sang *c'est a.*

Left: Haydn; **right:** Salomon

One of the oldest existing Music Rooms is the Holywell Music Room in Oxford, England (**left**). It was opened in 1748 and, following restoration, is used today for its original purpose.

as I am taking an interest in it and am associated with it. Assuming that we get only a hundred subscribers, then each of us will have a profit of three hundred gulden (even if the costs amount to two hundred gulden, which is most unlikely). The Baron van Swieten and Countess Thun are very much interested in it. The orchestra consists entirely of amateurs, with the exception of the bassoon-players, the trumpeters and drummers."

The first concert was given on May 26th and went, according to Mozart 'tolerably well'.

In countries such as England, where there was only one court and an aristocracy more at home on the hunting field than in the music-room, concert life necessarily flourished in a more public and democratic way. Public pleasure gardens were opened at Marylebone (in about 1659), Vauxhall (1730), and Ranelagh (1742). They provided a particularly pleasant setting:

"(The) orchestra is among a number of trees situated as in a little wood, and is an extremely handsome one. As you enter the gardens you immediately hear the sound of vocal and instrumental music. There are several female singers constantly hired here to sing in public. On each side of the orchestra are small boxes, with tables and benches in which you sup. The walks before them, as well as in every other part of the gardens, are crowded with people of all ranks."

Note that the writer, the German traveller Pastor Moritz, visiting Vauxhall in 1771, uses the word 'orchestra' to describe the little pavilion in which the performers sat – a practice that continued until the end of the century.

Besides the native English compos-

ers, visiting continental masters such as Bach's son Johann Christoph were happy to write music for the 'pleasure gardens' – songs, short operas, and orchestral music of all kinds. Virtuosi were eager to perform there – as did the eight year old Mozart in 1764. Though the accent was on pleasure, quality was not forgotten.

Rather more formal were the subscription concerts organized by individual musicians. J C Bach, who arrived in England in 1763, joined forces with another German composer, Karl Friedrich Abel, to give several such series: first at Carlisle House, then at Almack's Rooms; and then, after 1775, in the Hanover Square Rooms, of which they were part-owners. It was here that the violinist and impresario Johann Peter Salomon presented Haydn to an eager British public in 1791 and 92, and again in 1794 and 95, and here that London first heard the "Twelve Grand Symphonies" which he had written as part of his engagement.

By modern standards such music-rooms were not large. The main hall of the Hanover Square Rooms measured 95ft by 35ft (29m x 10m) and was famous for its excellent acoustic (it remained in use until 1874). Similar buildings existed in the larger provincial cities. The Holywell Music Room in Oxford is an example: opened in 1748 and therefore one of the oldest existing buildings of its kind, it is now restored to its original appearance and is still used for concerts.

Concerts in Italy seem to have been less widespread – that country having given itself wholeheartedly to opera. But in Venice several charitable institutions set up for the care of illegitimate and orphaned girls became famous for their music. From 1704 to 1740 Antonio Vivaldi himself was in charge of music at one hospital, the *Pietà*, and during his tenure no visit to Venice was complete without attending one of its concerts:

"They sing like angels, and play violin, flute, organ, hautboy, violoncello, bassoon; in short there is no instrument so large as to frighten them . . ."

So wrote an enthusiastic Charles de Brosses in 1743. Forty years later (1780) the Englishman William Beckford was a little less starry-eyed:

"The sight of the orchestra still makes me smile. You know, I suppose, it is entirely of the female gender, and that nothing is more common than to see a delicate white hand journeying across an enormous double-bass, or a pair of roseate cheeks puffing at a French Horn. Some that are grown old and Amazonious . . . take vigorously to the kettledrum; and one poor limping lady, who had been crossed in love, now makes an admirable figure with a bassoon."

In France concert-giving centered mainly on Paris and was often dependent on royalty for its existence and

encouragement. For example, the famous series of *Concerts Spirituels*, given annually from 1725 to 1791, arose out of the fact that the Académie Royale de Musique (the official title of the Opéra), which had been established by royal letters-patent in 1669, closed its doors during the main religious festivals. It was therefore decided that the musicians normally engaged in performing operas might reasonably give concerts at these times without offending religious susceptibilities. The first 'concert spirituel' took place on March 25th 1725, the Sunday of Passion Week.

It was most successful. There were never more than twenty-four performances in any one year, but the standard was very high and the scheme was much admired in other countries. It was for one of these concerts that Mozart wrote his 'Paris' symphony (K 297) in 1778.

From 1770 many of the best Paris musicians were to be found in the orchestra of the *Concert des Amateurs* (renamed in 1780 the *Concert de la Loge Olympique*). It was for this association that Haydn wrote the six so-called 'Paris' symphonies.

Most orchestral music in eighteenth century Italy was put to the service of opera, but Vivaldi (**above left**) made his *Pietà* hospital concerts an essential port of call for the many tourists of the day. The female orchestra seems to have aroused much interest at the time, and a good deal of surprised respect. It is clear from the illustration (**right**) from *Punch*, 1875, that women orchestras were still worthy of comment one hundred years later.

All in all it can be seen that the business of giving public concerts of one sort or another increased by leaps and bounds during the 18th century. Societies for the encouragement and further exploration of music sprang up everywhere, from Bergen, whose still-surviving Musical Society (the *Harmonien*) was founded in 1765, to Boston, which opened its own concert hall in 1754. And perhaps the most remarkable and encouraging feature of all this activity was the extent to which the best amateurs played alongside the professionals. In an age of rigid class distinction, music-making was able to leap the social barriers. The patron might be a vastly wealthy prince, or merely Thomas Britton, London's "musical small-coal man." The performer might rise unexpectedly from the humblest of backgrounds, or, Bach-like, from a long line of professional musicians. The composer could be Haydn, whose parents were obscure peasants; or Mozart, whose father was an eminent musician; or Frederick the Great himself. Music was the rising art, and in the 19th century it was to take precedence over all others.

Left: perhaps the greatest musical family, at home. All Bach's sons were thoroughly trained composers and musicians, but neither of the two greatest, Carl Philipp Emanuel nor Johann Christian, followed his style of composition. Thomas Britton (**right**) enjoyed no such background, but still made his mark on musical history.

The Romantic Orchestra

The growth of Romanticism

The increase in size of the symphony orchestra which took place over the nineteenth century can be readily appreciated from a glance at the table below, which shows the instruments required for a performance of Beethoven's First Symphony (1800) and Strauss's *Ein Heldenleben* (1898). For Beethoven, the structure and development of his musical thought took priority over any exploration of the personalities of the instruments at his disposal. But already, in his First Symphony, commentators have detected additional moments where he would have included, say, trumpets in his score, had the instruments at his disposal received the benefit of the greater range that was to be available to them later. These gaps are often filled in modern performances. Beethoven was later to find reasons why woodwind and brass should be extended by the addition of piccolo, double bassoon and trombone. But it was not only the inner demands of musical logic or the improvement of

	1st Violins 2nd Violins	Violas	Cellos	Double Basses	Piccolo	Flutes	Oboes	Cor Anglais
Beethoven Orchestra for the performance of *The 1st Symphony*	6 + 6	4	4	2		2	2	
Richard Strauss Orchestra for the performance of *Ein Heldenleben*	8, 8, 4 + 8, 8, 4	4, 4, 4, 4	4, 4, 4	3, 3, 3, 1	1	3	3	1 (doubling 4th oboe)

ROM THE PLAYER'S point of view everything in the 19th century orchestra grew bigger and better. The comparison above between the orchestras required by Beethoven for his First Symphony (1800) and Richard Strauss for the Symphonic Poem *Ein Heldenleben* (1898) makes the extent of this growth dramatically clear.

Whereas Beethoven was thinking in terms of an orchestra of about 35 players, Strauss had one of more than 100 in mind!

Of the many factors that brought about this astonishing growth perhaps the most important are: the improvement in the mechanism of woodwind and brass instruments, which enabled them to become as flexible, agile, and dependable as the strings; the change of artistic temper which demanded that music should become increasingly *expressive* – thus prompting composers to find out new harmonies and new orchestral colors; and the vast increase in the demand for public concerts, and the consequent increase in the number of orchestras themselves.

The Improvement of Instruments
In the 18th century only the strings could be said to be truly flexible, agile, possessed of a wide range of notes and dependable. Such 'mechanism' as they may be said to have had lay almost wholly in the player's fingers. Bowing and fingering techniques improved, through the example of virtuoso soloists who began to make an impact at the beginning of the century. But the basic construction of the instruments remained almost unchanged since the work of the great violin makers of the 16th and 17th centuries.

Although flutes, oboes, and bassoons had formed part of the orchestra almost from its beginnings, each had certain limitations which only mechanical invention could cure. There are two main difficulties in any instrument that depends on a player's fingers covering and uncovering holes cut along the length of a pipe: how to provide a sufficient number of holes for all the

Composers, like other artists, having come to understand their materials, are not always satisfied by them. Not infrequently, they have written music which was beyond the capacities of contemporary instruments and instrumentalists. And, if a particularly adept player arises, they typically seize the opportunity of extended freedom in composition he provides. This tendency, along with theories of harmony and balance which dictated that certain sections of the orchestra should extend their range of 'confidence', and the frustration of having to allow players time for technical adjustments, motivated instrument makers into more and more sophistication of design. Not all innovations were accepted without question. In 1862, Wagner stipulated natural horns and crooks (**right**) for *Tristan*. And in 1865 Brahms wrote a Horn Trio for a natural, not a valved horn.

instruments that forced an expansion in the size of the orchestra. Berlioz' concern to use instruments in the registers in which they were most at home was part of his belief that color was part and parcel both of	expressiveness and of the development of musical thought processes. Wagner aimed to blend color with a slightly different purpose: to achieve a richness of sound, of orchestral	texture, which combined overwhelming sensuousness with visionary power. Both of these composers found that an orchestra of massively increased capacity was essential to		their purposes. Strauss saw himself as the spiritual heir of Wagner, and aimed for a richness greater even than Wagner's. He built his music on a massive string sound, adding unusual instruments, or many more		of the conventional ones, to achieve the expressive or evocative power, or the sheer all-embracing splendor that he and others had discovered the symphony orchestra to be capable of.					
Clarinets	Bass Clarinets	Bassoons	Double Bassoon	Horns	Trumpets	Trombones	Tubas	Timpani (1 player)	Percussion (4 players)	Harps	

notes you need, and yet make it possible for the player to service them with the fingers of his two hands; and how to arrange that the holes are cut in the acoustically appropriate place, and yet remain within the player's reach.

With simple instruments like the recorder the answer is one of compromise and limitation. The holes are cut in as near the right place as can be reached by the fingers, and it is accepted that only a certain number of notes are available for use.

With more complex instruments the sound holes do not fall into line quite so readily. What was needed, and what was supplied during the 19th century, was a mechanism that could reach what the fingers could not reach: in fact a system of pivoted keys and levers, such as will be described in later chapters.

For horns and trumpets the problem was slightly different. Both derived their notes from the actual length of tubing the player was blowing down. Each length could produce its own fixed series of notes. But these notes

did not form a complete scale over the whole range. This could only be obtained by using different lengths of tubing, so that if one could not provide the required note another could.

The first solution was to use several different instruments, each with a different length of tube. Later, mainly in the case of the horns, it was arranged that different lengths of tube (crooks) could be added to or subtracted from the basic instrument by hand, thus changing its total length. But either way was cumbersome. The player had to stop playing and take up a new instrument, or insert a new length of tube. What was needed was a mechanism that could bring the new lengths into action automatically. This the 19th century supplied in the shape of valves which, when pressed with the finger, would open up or seal off new lengths of tubing coiled up alongside the body of the instrument, thus making available the entire range of notes from top to bottom of the instrument's capabilities.

Strangely enough, the one instru-

ment that had always been able to change its length at will – the trombone – did not become an accepted part of the orchestra until the beginning of the 19th century. Built with its tubes working on a telescopic-slide principle, it enjoyed a full range of notes from the very beginning. But the trombone was traditionally a church instrument, and it was only employed orchestrally for solemn moments in operas and oratorios. The principle of the telescopic slide was applied to the trumpet during the 17th century, but it never found favor amongst the players.

The size and nature of the orchestra

The achievement of the 19th century was to provide an orchestra in which the woodwind and brass sections could be as self-contained as the strings, and cover a comparably wide range of notes. To this end, alongside the mechanical improvements already mentioned, new instruments were introduced that enabled each section to provide the four- and five-part harmonic texture already available to the strings.

Clarinets therefore became an integral feature of the woodwind section. They had been available since the beginning of the 18th century, but it was not until about 1780 that compos-

ers began to insist on their presence. Of Mozart's 41 symphonies only the *Paris* (K297), the *Haffner* (K385), and the first of the three miraculous symphonies of 1788 (the E flat, K543) had clarinets – though they were added to the G minor Symphony (K550) after 1788. And in all Haydn's 104 symphonies it is only the last six (the second series written for Salomon's London concerts) that employ clarinets – partly because London was willing to supply them, and partly because he was fired by Mozart's example.

With the addition of clarinets the woodwind section was now a complete and multi-colored unit, needing only to be extended in its upper and lower registers. The piccolo, a miniature, higher-sounding version of the flute, was introduced in Beethoven's Fifth Symphony (1808) and used by him again in the Sixth, Seventh, and Ninth symphonies. A double bassoon, which took the bassoon notes down a further octave, appeared in Beethoven's Ninth Symphony (1823), but was not in general use until the 1880s brought improvements in its mechanism.

Flutes, oboes, and clarinets also acquired deeper-sounding versions of themselves. An alto flute (often wrongly called the bass flute) was perfected in the 1850s, but only occasion-

Extending the range of the orchestra

In the nineteenth century woodwind, brass and percussion received improvements or additions that enabled them to accompany the strings to whatever heights or depths the composer chose to send them. Woodwind instruments were improved by the addition of keys and the section was extended in its upper and lower reaches by piccolo and double bassoon. In the brass section valves finally replaced crooks on horns and trumpets, and by 1860 tubas were frequent members of the section. Trombones were also wrested from their ecclesiastical and royal duties, and the percussion section began an expansion in the name of power color and expressiveness that was to be extended well into the next century, this time in the name of rhythm.

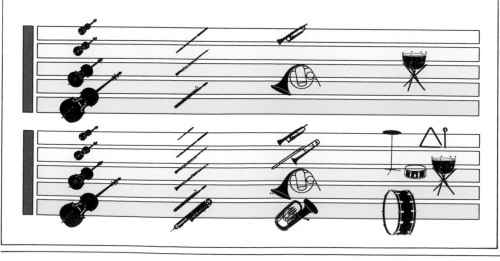

ally used in symphonic works. An efficient version of the true bass flute, pitched a whole octave below the ordinary flute, did not appear until 1910 and was not perfected until the 1930s.

The cor anglais, the tenor version of the oboe, came into existence in the 18th century, but was not mechanically efficient until about 1850. Even so, Berlioz made use of it in the overture *Le Carnaval Romain* (1844), though not in his symphonies. Two further large oboes, the *oboe d'amore* and the baritone oboe were widely used in the 18th century, but had fallen out of favor by the 19th.

The only lower-voiced clarinet to maintain an orchestral footing was the bass clarinet, pitched an octave below the ordinary clarinets. Meyerbeer used one in his opera *Les Huguenots* (1832), anticipating its more general use by about forty years. The alto clarinet, usually called the basset-horn, was very popular in Mozart's day (particularly in music for wind bands) but fell out of orchestral use in the 19th century and was only revived by composers like Richard Strauss.

To the trumpet and horns were also added appropriate bass instruments. First the tenor and bass trombones, which appeared symphonically for the first time in the last movement of Beethoven's Fifth Symphony (1808); and then the tuba, borrowed from the German military bands of the 1820s and entering the orchestra in the 1840s.

Additions to the percussion department had already begun in the 18th century. To the kettledrums (timpani) were added the side drum, again an instrument borrowed from military bands, and then a group of more exotic instruments brought in as the result of a sudden craze for 'Turkish' percussion – first heard in Western Europe in the 1720s when Augustus II of Poland received a full Turkish Janissary Band as a gift from the Sultan. Soon European military bands felt obliged to add similar instruments, often recruiting genuine Turks or negroes to play them. Bass drum, triangle, cymbals, and glockenspiel all came to the orchestra from this source, though their use remained somewhat restricted until the second half of the 19th century.

The 19th century orchestra also found a regular place for the harp. Berlioz's *Symphonie fantastique* (1830) is perhaps the first important orchestral work to make use of it. But, even so, it

The instruments which had found their first real home in Turkish Janissary Bands (**left**) were, not surprisingly, seized upon when they reached Europe to suggest a Turkish — or perhaps simply an exotic — atmosphere. Mozart used bass drum, cymbals and triangle to this effect in the Janissaries' Chorus from *Die Entfuhrung aus dem Serail* (1782) and Haydn brought them into play in his *Military Symphony* (1794). Beethoven, too, used them for simple evocative effect in his *The Ruins of Athens* (an overture and incidental music, including a Turkish March, written for a play by Kotzebue produced in Pest in 1812). However, in the Ninth Symphony (1824) it is no longer used as an 'effect' but to suggest — in the tenor solo of the Finale — something of rather more universal significance.

The nineteenth century view of the musician, whether he be soloist, composer or conductor, was often extremely romantic. Here (**right**) the conductor directing a performance of Beethoven's Fifth Symphony is depicted as part devil, part magician. Other ages, including our own, have taken a rather more sober view of the role.

is remarkable how few actual symphonies call for a harp before the days of Mahler and Richard Strauss. It makes a regular appearance in symphonic poems and the more obviously 'light' and colorful orchestral pieces, but composers of symphonies seem to have regarded it with some suspicion – as being, perhaps, too sensuous and frivolous for their sober thoughts.

Whereas the overall size of the 19th century orchestra can range from the modest 35 players required for Beethoven's First Symphony to the forces of 100 or more demanded by Strauss and Mahler, an orchestra capable of tackling most symphonic works written before about 1880 will consist of between 50 and 60 players increasing to 75 for certain heavier scores.

The Romantic vocabulary

Except in the field of opera, where the need to depict a dramatic situation often prompted them to be more daring, 18th century composers were not particularly interested in exploiting the different color combinations available from the instruments of their modest orchestras. It is really only in the later symphonies of Mozart that a genuine feeling for orchestral color can be discerned. The exploration of orchestral color as a thing in itself is decidedly a 19th century pre-occupation.

What stimulated the search was the change of artistic attitude which led from the 'classicism' of the 18th century to the 'romanticism' of the 19th. Though the classical artist was perfectly well able to portray intense emotion, his principal concern was with a sense of form, balance, and logical argument. Though the romantic artist was equally the master of form and logic, he was fascinated by the expressive possibilities of his art, and wished above all to convey emotion and move the senses. It is no accident that the symphonic poem and the program symphony were inventions of the 19th century: both seek to tell a story (the subjective story of an emotion, often) in addition to their function as purely musical forms. The romanticist elevated music into the supreme art: logical of form, irresistible of emotion – the total experience, in fact.

An important aspect of music's new expressive power is to be found in the way in which the orchestra came to be used. Instruments, it was found, had distinct personalities that would affect the music they played. A tune played on the flute might have quite a different impact on the clarinet or oboe. A chord played by two flutes and two clarinets would sound quite different if played by two oboes and two bassoons. Composers began, therefore, to con-

The Father of Orchestration

'Instrumentation' to Berlioz was the study of individual instruments and their attributes. 'Orchestration' was the art of combining these instruments in an effective score. The study informed the art, and Berlioz was able to make demands which no earlier composer would have considered. Dvořák (**top right**), and Debussy (**next to top**) both benefited from his explorations. Schubert (**third from top**) was a fellow pioneer and Strauss (**bottom**) explored further than even Berlioz dared imagine.

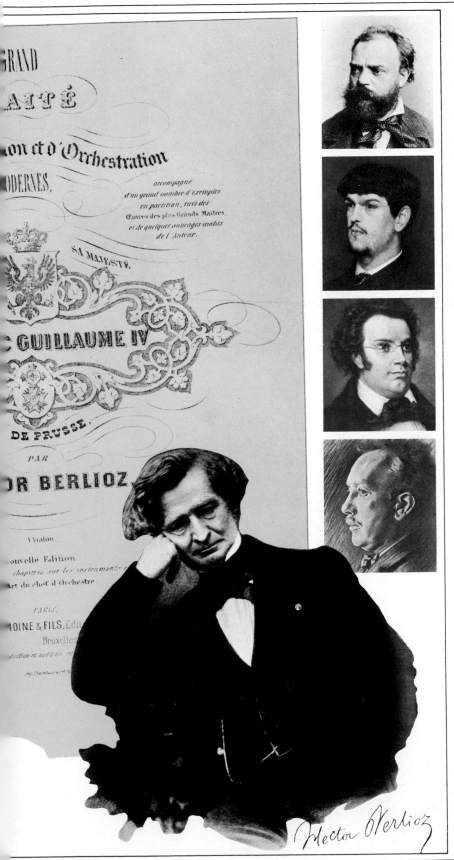

ceive their music in terms of specific instruments, and it was no longer acceptable to play the notes on any other. The typical 19th century composer would not write, as Mozart had written on September 30th 1786: "Should His Highness not have any clarinets at his court, a competent copyist might transpose the parts into suitable keys, in which case the first part should be played by a violin and the second by a viola." The art of orchestration was being born, and the score was now holy writ.

Certain composers stand out as pioneers in these explorations. Schubert and Weber, for example, and later Meyerbeer and Wagner. But the most remarkable and imaginative was Hector Berlioz (1803-69). Through the example of his own works and the great orchestral text book he wrote in 1843 (*Traité de l'Instrumentation et d'Orchestration Modernes*) he fully deserves the title 'father of orchestration'.

With the territory mapped out in great detail it was a relatively simple matter for other composers to follow the Berlioz example. Dvořák, Tchaikovsky and Rimsky-Korsakov, Mahler, Elgar and Debussy, and above all Richard Strauss, were all masters of the special art of orchestration. Through their efforts music became possessed of a vocabulary of great power and variety. By the end of the century it could express almost anything. Strauss, it was said, could have made his music describe a knife and fork, had he so wished!

The Conductor

Once orchestras had reached a certain size, and once the art of orchestration called for a certain subtlety in balancing the weight of sound made by the different instruments, it became absolutely essential to have one man clearly and visibly in charge of an orchestral performance. This man was the conductor. We now take his presence for granted, but it was not until the beginning of the 19th century that he came into existence in the form we know today.

In the 18th century there were three ways of controlling a musical performance. Operas were under the dual control of a *Kapellmeister*, who sat at the continuo keyboard, and a *Konzertmeister* who led the first violins. The *Konzertmeister* was in charge of the orchestra,

In Mozart's day a keyboard player or first violin could readily keep control of the tempo of a piece. Such control works best in small groups. Modern jazz players (**above**) typically convey such information to each other whilst playing. And contemporary musicians who attempt to play early scores in authentic fashion, such as Christopher Hogwood (**top**) find 'dual control' of their relatively small ensembles most successful. For larger assemblies, however, maintaining balance and co-ordination by these means is more difficult. The lead violinist first tried to resolve these difficulties with his bow (**center**).

and the *Kapellmeister* was in charge of the performance as a whole, but directed much of his attention to the stage (using the keyboard not only as a continuo, but as a means of cueing in the singers). Only at the Paris Opéra were things done differently. Here the time was marked firmly and loudly by beating the floor with the tip of a long, elegant pole. (Lully is said to have died as the result of an abcess caused when he inadvertently stabbed his own foot during an opera!)

Orchestral performances were frequently under the same dual control: from the keyboard continuo and the first violin. But generally speaking it was the first violin that took overall charge.

Choral music was traditionally directed by a time-beater, who marked time visibly. This was because performances often took place in church where the singers could not be close together. The time-beater was much nearer the present-day conductor – except that instead of a baton he was likely to use a roll of manuscript paper.

Though it may seem odd that a performance should in any way be directed by a man whom one would suppose to be fully occupied in playing his instrument, it is really not so impossible – *provided that the orchestra is small*. In the case of the keyboard player, he can either stop playing for a moment and make gestures with his hands, or play with one hand and gesture with the other. He can move his head in such a way as to indicate the time, and bring singers in with a

glance and a well-timed nod. Even the first violin can momentarily stop playing and gesture with his bow. But more often the movement of the bow itself, or a movement of the left arm and shoulder and the instrument, or the merest change of facial expression can be sufficient indication of the way a performance should go. Everything depends upon the orchestra being small and the players in close contact with each other. A string quartet still regulates its performances in this way – usually through eye-contact and the minute physical gestures that pass unnoticed by the audience. So too will many jazz combinations. If the group is small enough, a rapport can be established quite easily and effectively.

With the larger 18th century orchestras the method must have had its disadvantages, however. In theory the keyboard director set the pace, handed it on to the first violin (and the leading cello, who played in harness with the keyboard as an essential part of the continuo), who in turn passed the good news to the other performers. The odds are that by the time the information affected the orchestra's outer reaches the performance had become pretty ragged!

As orchestras grew the continuo was no longer needed to supply a complete harmony. By the 1780s both string and wind sections were self-contained and horns and trumpets accustomed to supplying vital sustaining notes. The later symphonies of Haydn and Mozart need no continuo support. Inevitably, then, the direction of a performance tended to pass to the first violin, and he, more and more, began to use his bow as a baton.

The baton makes its debut

The use of an actual baton, wielded by a conductor who stood in front of the orchestra (just as the time-beater had stood in front of his choir) seems to have come in very gradually – starting in Berlin in the 1790s and becoming widespread by the 1820s. The composer Louis Spohr, invited to 'lead' the orchestra at a Philharmonic Society concert in London in 1820, described the sensation he caused by 'conducting' them instead:

"I . . . took my stand with the score at a separate music desk in front of the orchestra, drew my conducting stick from my pocket and gave the signal to begin. Quite alarmed at such a novel

The composers wield the baton

As leader of the orchestra at the Theater an der Wien Spohr had had occasion to witness Beethoven's conducting of his own work, and noted his rather extravagent manner, which cearly had nothing to do with keeping a steady beat. Six years later, in London, he was to conduct a concert for the first time ever —so he was to claim later — in the modern way with his 'conducting stick'. Many other composers have followed his example. Mendelssohn seems to have aimed at fluency and elegance in his conducting. Berlioz and Wagner typify two opposed attitudes to conducting. Berlioz saw the score as law, and felt there was little need for 'interpretation'. Wagner felt that there was always room for interpretation because everything could simply not be written down: 'allegro' meant a different thing in the scores of different composers. Mahler, although a great interpreter of other men's music, regarded conducting with mixed feelings, for it was a distraction from his main purpose in life-composition. Some baton instructions are shown (**right**): **A**, 2 in a bar; **B**, 3 in a bar; **C**, 4 in a bar; **D**, 5 in a bar.

HECTOR BERLIOZ

GUSTAV MAHLER

FELIX MENDELSSOHN

RICHARD WAGNER

procedure, some of the directors would have protested against it; but when I besought them to grant me at least one trial, they became pacified. The symphonies and overtures that were to be rehearsed were well known to me, and in Germany I had already directed their performance. I could therefore not only give the *tempi* in a very decisive manner, but also indicate to the wind instruments and horns all their entries, which ensured to them a confidence such as hitherto they had not known there. I also took the liberty when the execution did not satisfy me, to stop, and in a very polite but earnest manner to remark upon the manner of execution, which remarks Mr Ries (the first violin) at my request interpreted to the orchestra. Incited thereby to more than usual attention, and conducted with certainty by the visible means of giving the time, they played with a spirit and correctness such as till then they had never been heard to play with. Surprised and inspired by this result the orchestra, immediately after the first part of the symphony, expressed aloud its collective assent to the new mode of conducting, and thereby over-ruled all further opposition on the part of the directors."

Doubtless similar scenes took place at

Early orchestral scores include few detailed instructions as to the precise manner in which the music is to be played. In the example (**above left**) from Bach's Second Brandenburg Concerto even the speed (allegro) and the dynamics (f) are modern editorial additions and are therefore printed in brackets. This, of course, does not mean to say that such works were originally played without any kind of interpretive nuance, but merely that these matters were left to the good sense and artistic judgement of the performers. By Debussy's time (see the page from *La Mer*, **above right,** 1905) composers were much more exacting in the way they specified the detail of interpretation. Scarcely a note appears without some instruction as to the manner in which it is to be played.

many rehearsals. Very often it was the composers who led the way – Spohr himself, Mendelssohn, Berlioz, Liszt, and Wagner were all outstanding conductors, as keen to direct performances of other men's music as their own.

By the middle of the 19th century the conductor was an established part of orchestral life. The first violinist – the 'leader' of the orchestra – still retained a considerable importance and would be expected to give advice about bowing and phrasing, control orchestral discipline, and generally act as spokesman for the other players. That is why, to this day, he makes a separate entrance immediately before the conductor, and gets his own private round of applause.

But it was the conductor who was now in overall charge. As the demands that composers made increased in complexity it became necessary for someone to make detailed decisions about such matters as the exact 'weight' of sound each instrument should contribute to the general picture . The conductor now became the essential midwife between the written score and the actual performance. He was no longer a time-beater, but an *interpreter*.

A glance at a 19th century orchestral score will make clear how essential

Though different in detail the pattern of concerts, concert halls and audiences established during the nineteenth century clearly foreshadows present-day practice. Modern audiences, however, might not appreciate the rather overcrowded conditions of the Monday 'popular' concert at St James' Hall (**top,** 1872), or the hard seats of Munich's Odeon Concert Hall (**above,** 1825). The mixed vocal and orchestral program (**right:** Vienna, 1842) is typical of the period.

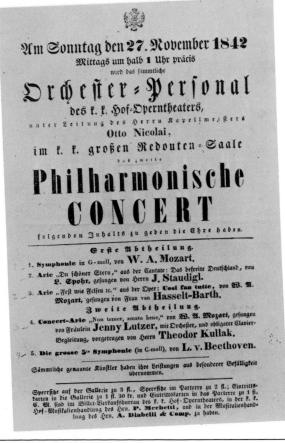

'interpretation' had become. Whereas a Bach score simply sets down the notes and gives a few indications that certain passages are to be loud and others soft, a Strauss score is covered with minute directions as to the manner of playing and the weight of sound required. A Bach movement will progress throughout at the same basic speed. But a Strauss work will fluctuate in the most subtle way – a little faster here, a little slower there, a sudden pause. All these are matters which only a conductor can control.

The Concert Scene

Such was the proliferation and democratization of concert-giving during the 19th century, it is not possible to give a detailed picture of the process. Examples of what happened in certain cities may, however, give a general idea of what was happening all over Europe. Though the route to public concerts as we know them today may have been different in different countries, and different even in the various cities of the same country, the effect was the same: concerts ceased to be the exclusive property of the wealthy. By the end of the century it was no longer the rich individual who paid the bill and called the tune, but the general public paying for a ticket at the box office.

For example, in Munich towards the end of the 18th century the court orchestra obtained permission to give a series of twelve subscription concerts in the *Redoutensaal* (Assembly Hall) of the royal palace. Calling itself the *Musikalische Akademie* for the occasion, the orchestra divided the profits between its members. So long as the concerts did not interfere with their normal court duties, the King of Bavaria was pleased to let the venture continue. And because it was so successful the Bavarian government built a special concert hall in the city itself (1825), thus bringing the concerts a step nearer the general public.

In Vienna the process was somewhat different. In 1813 a 'Society of the Friends of Music' *(Gesellschaft der Musikfreunde)* was formed by professional and well-to-do amateur instrumentalists, who then proceeded to give regular concerts. In 1817 the Society helped to found the Vienna Conservatoire, and later a music library and a museum. In 1858 it founded a Choral Society, and in 1860 its own professional orchestra. Vienna's first wholly

Queen's Hall (**left**) and St James's Hall (**above**), two famous and much-loved concert halls, are no longer part of the London musical scene, but the Royal Albert hall (**right**) plays as important a part as ever. The photograph of St James's Hall shows the audience at the last concert in 1905. The Albert Hall is depicted in 1868.

professional orchestra came into existence in 1842, when the orchestra of the Court Opera House (now the Vienna State Opera) was given permission to perform a public concert in the *Redoutensaal* of the Hofburg. Out of that occasion grew the Vienna Philharmonic Orchestra (the word philharmonic means simply *music lovers'*), which is still entirely recruited from members of the State Opera Orchestra.

Similar patterns of development occurred throughout Europe and America. In 1842, for example, a Philharmonic Society was established in New York, and its orchestra (the third oldest permanent professional body) gave a season of three very successful concerts.

Wherever an enterprise of this kind began to flourish it stimulated competition. It is no exaggeration to say that the kind of rivalry that prompted 18th century dukes and princes into taxing their subjects for money to support their court orchestras and opera houses now affected the guardian authorities of the larger cities of Western Europe and America. If London could have orchestras and public concerts, then so too could Manchester, Liverpool, and Birmingham. If New York could boast an orchestra, then why not Boston and Philadelphia? The public demonstra-

tion of cultural enlightenment had become a matter of civic pride. Orchestras were founded, concerts given and concert halls magnificently planted in each city center.

Music for a metropolis

Perhaps because it had always been in the forefront of public concert giving and never beholden to the influence and exclusive patronage of a king and court, the musical life of London was particularly lively during this period. London, the heart of a growing empire and mainspring of the most industrially advanced nation of the age, was rich and could afford to demonstrate the fact in ever larger public buildings – some of which were concert halls, or could at least be used for concerts.

The Crystal Palace (1851), showpiece of the Great Exhibition, became an ideal home for large-scale choral and orchestral concerts, such as those given by the German-born conductor August Manns from 1854 onwards. National pride, coupled with a desire to commemorate the life and work of the Prince Consort (a great enthusiast for music) led to the construction of the mammoth Royal Albert Hall, opened in 1871 and able to seat nearly 10,000 people. It soon became a home for choral and orchestral concerts – as it is

London's music owes much to the courage and persistence of one man, Sir Henry Wood (**above**), in founding the famous promenade concerts which now take place each summer at the Royal Albert Hall (**left**) and elsewhere. The People's Palace (**top right**) was opened by Queen Victoria in 1887 to serve the needs of London's East End. The 'Grand Opening Concert' at Queen's Hall in 1893 is shown (**right**). The work chosen for the occasion was Mendelssohn's *Hymn of Praise.*

The resplendent and eccentric Jullien (**below**) helped popularize serious music at his 'Promenade Concerts' (**left**). Equally part of the rather extravagent Victorian musical scene were the mammoth Handel Festivals at the Crystal Palace (**above**).

to this day. Even publishers were willing to speculate: it was Messrs Beale & Chappell & Co who built the St James's Hall in Piccadilly in 1858, and then established it as the home of a whole series of 'popular' concerts, which only came to an end in 1898. Private enterprise also added Queen's Hall to Regent Street in 1893, and the much smaller Wigmore Hall (originally the Bechstein Hall, after the piano manufacturers who built it) in 1901. Even London's East End was considered worthy of cultural attention and an appropriately named 'People's Palace' erected for the purpose.

Concerts given in these and the already existing music-rooms and theaters were almost as varied as the halls themselves. At the upper end of the social scale were those sponsored by the Philharmonic Society (founded in 1813), which charged a guinea a concert, or four guineas for a series of eight.

At the other end were the rival series of 'Promenade' Concerts (so called because part of the audience was allowed to stand and 'promenade' at will) that entertained London from the 1840s. Here the price of admission started at one shilling, and the music played could be anything from a Beethoven symphony (complete or truncated) to a set of quadrilles on popular tunes of the day. The most remarkable and successful were those given by the Frenchman Louis Jullien (1812-60) at Drury Lane and Covent Garden theaters. Jullien amazed and entertained his audiences with gigantic orchestras, massed choirs, military bands, virtuoso soloists, and his own rather eccentric brand of conductor's showmanship. He even managed to educate them into listening to good music.

Equally 'educational', though much more serious, were the concerts sponsored by the publishing firm of Novello & Co in the 1870s. Pioneers of inexpensive printed music (particularly choral), their 1875 concerts at the Albert Hall remarkably anticipate the series of Promenade Concerts established by Sir Henry Wood in 1895, which still flourish to this day. There was a scheme of special nights throughout the season: Monday for 'Ballads', Tuesday for 'English music', Wednesday for 'Classical', Thursday for 'Oratorio', Friday for 'Wagner', and Saturday for 'Popular music'.

Between these extremes could be found almost every other type of musical entertainment a discerning public could desire – for truly in the 19th century the age of mass entertainment had begun.

The Modern Orchestra

HE 19TH CENTURY began prematurely in the events of the French Revolution and lingered on well into the 20th – to be swept away only by the First World War. Until that cataclysm forced society to change its ways, it seemed as if its artistic assumptions might never be called into question.

Composers active just before 1914 certainly behaved as if they believed that orchestras would continue to grow in size. Quadruple woodwind, eight horns, four trumpets, four trombones, two harps, endless percussion, and strings to match were almost the order of the day. The young and somewhat optimistic Schoenberg thought it perfectly reasonable to ask for 8 flutes, 5 oboes, 7 clarinets, 10 horns, 6 trumpets, 1 bass trumpet, 6 trombones, 4 harps, a large battery of percussion (including heavy iron chains), and a vast assembly of strings to accompany the speaker, 7 soloists, 3 male choruses, and a mixed double choir (8 parts) for the two-hour *Gurrelieder* which he began in 1900. The orchestration was not finally completed until 1911, and in that very year Richard Strauss began work on the *Alpine Symphony*, which he scored for 20 horns, 6 trumpets, and 6 trombones, though modestly restricting himself to quadruple woodwind!

Inflation on this scale could not last. First an artistic reaction against excessive romanticism set in. And then the sheer reality of economics began to tell. Composers never again (or hardly ever) thought to ask for such enormous forces. Instead they began to explore the possibilities, and the challenge, of small-scale ensembles. Sometimes they deliberately returned to Baroque and Classical proportions – as Prokofiev did in his *Classical Symphony* (1917). Sometimes they ordered the traditional orchestra in a different way. Stravinsky accompanied the chorus of his *Symphony of Psalms* (1930) with an orchestra that has no violins or violas. In short, the typical 20th century composer took a pragmatic view of the orchestra and scored his works as he pleased and not in accordance with any preconceived notion of what an orchestra should or should not be. The situation had become curiously similar to that enjoyed by the first opera composers of the 17th century.

New instruments were, of course,

The early music of Arnold Schoenberg (**left**) was cast in the high-romantic mould, employing vast orchestras and a lavish harmonic palette. Later works explored a more rigorously intellectual style, though the grand romantic gesture still peeps through from time to time.

Yesterday's cacophony is often today's sweetness and light. Few would now object to the most astringent harmonies of Richard Strauss (**above left**) or to his skilful manipulation of gigantic orchestral forces, but contemporary audiences were often scandalized by his 'modernism'. The drawings (**left**) show the reactions of two cartoonists of the day to his innovations. As a typical page (**above**) from *Ein Heldenleben* (1898) shows he could handle the largest orchestra with ease, and proved himself over and over again one of the most original and inventive orchestrators of all time.

THE AUGURS OF SPRING
DANCES OF THE YOUNG GIRLS
LES AUGURES PRINTANIERS
DANSES DES ADOLESCENTES

added to the orchestra. In particular the percussion department grew both in size and importance. Exotic percussion instruments, tuned and untuned, came in from Latin America, Africa, and the East. Traditional Western percussion was itself considerably improved. For example, the timpanist no longer had to tune his drums laboriously by hand, for he could now do so automatically with speed and total reliability. An increasing interest in complex rhythms on the part of such composers as Bartók and Stravinsky meant that the use of more and more percussion instruments became one of the chief characteristics of 20th century music.

In the other departments comparatively few new instruments made an appearance – though certain old ones, like the harpsichord, were given a new lease of life. Perhaps the most important additions were the members of the saxophone family. These had been invented in about 1840 and eventually found their most congenial home in the jazz world. A few 20th century symphonic composers have made effective use of them – for example Aaron Copland in the *Concerto for Piano and Orchestra* (1926), Vaughan Williams in the Sixth Symphony (1947) and Britten in the *Sinfonia da Requiem* (1941) – but most have felt their jazz connotation is a little too strong for comfort.

In terms of instruments and size, the orchestra has remained what it was at the end of the 19th century. The standard orchestra has to be large enough to tackle the major classics of the 18th and 19th centuries as a matter of course – for these form the staple diet of an ever-increasing musical public. For mammoth works extra players must be called in – though as costs grow heavier, they appear less regularly in concert programs.

The mood of the times

At the same time many varieties of specialist orchestras have come into existence. Sometimes, as with the purely string orchestra, they operate on a full-time basis. Sometimes they are formed for the occasion from members of a standard orchestra. In recent years there has been a strong move towards playing the music of the past in as authentic a manner as possible:

The irregular rhythms and barbaric harmonies of Stravinsky's ballet *The Rite of Spring* shocked many listeners in 1913. In the dance quoted (**above**) the strings hammer out a single chord, each stroke a down-bow (⊓). Stravinsky places strong accents (>) on different beats of the bar, thus upsetting the regular 2/4 pulse. The chord itself is harsh:

The concert (**right**) took place at the Royal Albert Hall, London, in 1944 Members of the Red Army were guests of honour.

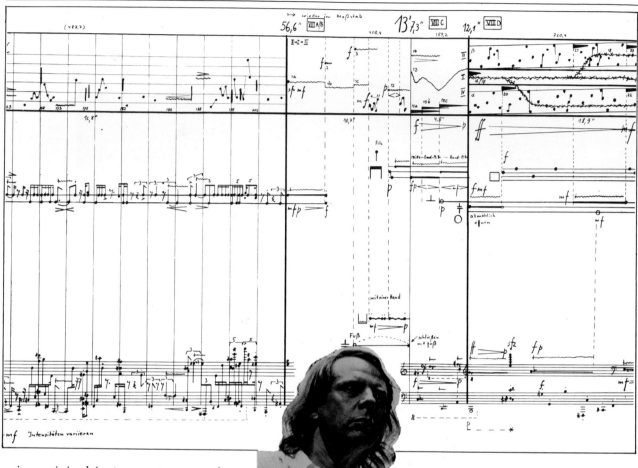

using original instruments, or modern copies. It would now be quite unthinkable to perform Handel with a choir and orchestra of 4,000, as was regularly done at London's Crystal Palace in Victorian times.

But if orchestras have acquired a sense of proportion and moderation, conductors have not. They have now grown to be all-powerful figures, often commanding vast fees and immense public adulation. Probably the rise of the gramophone record has helped to bring this about. For it is now possible to collect and compare different men's interpretations of the classics. We cheerfully speak of "So-and-so's Beethoven", quite forgetting (as do some conductors!) that it is "Beethoven's Beethoven" that should concern us.

Among certain avant-garde composers there has been a tendency to partially by-pass the conductor by forcing each member of the orchestra to make creative decisions for himself. Scores are written in special notations that leave all manner of decisions to the player – exactly what note to play, how long to hold it, how loud or soft to

Although the international jet-setting 'star' conductor such as Karajan or Solti (**top** and **bottom right**) is literally the dictator of an orchestral performance, often imposing his own 'interpretation' on the hapless composer, many modern scores, such as Stockhausen's *Kontakte* (**above**), call for detailed interpretive decisions by the performers themselves. These decisions inevitably vary from performance to performance and players thus share in the creative process more equally with the composer and conductor.

make it. But these experiments, together with the exploration of sounds and performing techniques that run contrary to the natural genius of the instruments, are not enjoyed by the average orchestra – or by the average audience.

Patronage finance and sponsorship

The manner in which 20th century orchestras are financed depends largely on their historical origins and the musical history of the country. Where earlier orchestras were attached to a court and paid for by a prince out of the taxes he imposed, the State now tends to step in and shoulder the burden. The public also pays at the box office, but the players are on an agreed salary, with pensions, paid holidays, and sickness benefits. This is the system adopted by most European orchestras. In America, big business has been successfully tapped to make up the difference between a reasonable price for the tickets and the soaring costs of day-to-day administration.

In Great Britain the amount of government subsidy is still very small and

Open-air concerts like those at Kenwood (**above** and **right**) provide an opportunity for a special sort of musical appreciation. Acoustics may vary, but the effect can often be magical.

International Business Machines Corporati

The Kennedy Center presents:

Visit of The Vienna State Opera

dates only from the foundation of the *Arts Council* in 1946 (a body which grew out of CEMA, the Council for the Encouragement of Music and the Arts, set up in 1939 to boost civilian morale during the war). In the last few years industrial sponsorship has increased somewhat, since it is now accepted as a legitimate and effective form of advertising which can be set against taxes. Certain provincial orchestras enjoy a measure of financial support from the local authorities. But for much of their income, most British orchestras have to fend for themselves, exactly as in the 19th century. Only the BBC Symphony Orchestra is engaged on a regular basis on continental lines.

Private patronage, in the old 19th century sense, played a part in funding orchestras at the beginning of this century, but is now very rare indeed. Gone are the days when a music-loving financier like Henry Lee Higginson could use his fortune to found and maintain the Boston Symphony Orchestra (1881). Gone are the days when Sir Thomas Beecham could use his father's business empire to subsidize his own orchestral activities. The only patron nowadays is likely to be the State.

Consumer demand

And yet, despite the problems of balancing the books, it is clear that orchestras and orchestral concerts are wanted as never before. Neither the rise of the gramophone record industry, nor of broadcasting and television have done anything to diminish the taste for live concerts. If anything, they have increased it. Since Artur Nikisch and the Berlin Philharmonic recorded the first complete symphony in 1913 (Beethoven's Fifth, cut on eight single sides at 78rpm by The Gramophone Company, now HMV) the flood of recorded classics has become a torrent. And over the radio good music can be heard at any time of the day or night. Music from every period and every country is available in vast quantity. Even the most casual listener now hears more music in a month than Bach or Mozart heard in a lifetime.

Yet paradoxically the very range of present-day taste and music experience has led to its own limitation of vision. Earlier orchestras played the music of their own day and very little else. We play music of every period, and consequently have less time for contemporary composers. Indeed, the primary occupation of the orchestra has become the presentation of a *museum* repertoire.

What precisely the future of the orchestra may be is hard to guess. Will it continue merely as a vehicle for reviewing the past, while contemporary composers turn more and more to electronic ways of realizing their dreams? Will conductors continue to inflate their egos in a dizzying star-system reminiscent of the worst excesses of Hollywood? Will the tottering economies of the Western world be able to support as many orchestras as we now enjoy? In short: is the history of the orchestra at an end?

Only one thing is certain. There will be music in the future, and it will be the music the future wants. And if it is not the orchestra as we know it today that helps to supply the need, then whatever takes its place may well be just as remarkable.

Armonk, New York 10504
914/765—1900

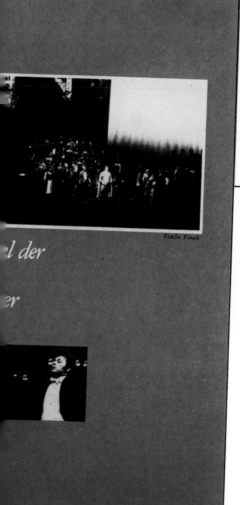

Fidelio, Finale

Der erste Besuch der Wiener Staatsoper in den Vereinigten Staaten geht auf eine Initiative des Kennedy Centers zurück und wurde durch Förderungsmittel der Österreichischen Bundesregierung ermöglicht. In den USA wurde das Gastspiel von der Morris und Gwendolyn Cafritz Foundation und von IBM finanziell unterstützt.

Sidney Harth, concertmaster of the Los Angeles Philharmonic, one of the 7 major orchestras that comprise the Bell System's "American Orchestras on Tour" program, conducts a master class in violin at Vassar College.

Laureate Conductor Leonard Bernstein tours with the New York Philharmonic, one of the 7 major orchestras that comprise the Bell System's "American Orchestras on Tour" program.

At Lincoln Center's Avery Fisher Hall, Zubin Mehta conducts the New York Philharmonic, one of the major orchestras that comprise the Bell System's "American Orchestras on Tour" program.

Maestro Carlo Maria Giulini is the Music Director of the Los Angeles Philharmonic, one of the 7 major orchestras that comprise the Bell System's "American Orchestras on Tour" program.

Bell System American Orchestras on Tour

BOSTON SYMPHONY ORCHESTRA

CHICAGO SYMPHONY ORCHESTRA

CLEVELAND ORCHESTRA

LOS ANGELES PHILHARMONIC

NEW YORK PHILHARMONIC

PHILADELPHIA ORCHESTRA

PITTSBURGH SYMPHONY ORCHESTRA

There has almost always been a gap between the amount a public, no matter how music-loving, was willing to pay for the pleasure of musical entertainment, and the cost of producing such entertainment to the highest standards. Music of quality survives through two main forms of assistance. Those who have received a disproportionate amount of the world's wealth may feel inclined to return some of it to society. The Emperor Maximilian (**below**) was no doubt better loved for his patronage of music . . .

. . . and the same probably goes for the many corporations (**left**) who now sponsor orchestral work. Alternatively the public purse, by common albeit indirect consent, can lift musical organizations into the black. In England the value of state patronage was first revealed during the war (see **below**). The days of private patronage, when the likes of Beecham (**left**, in his dapper phase) could draw on the profits of a paternal pill business are probably over.

MUSIC THE MOSAIC OF THE AIR

The Instruments

Besides its group history as
a member of the orchestra, each
orchestral instrument has a history
of its own, commencing, more often
than not, long before concerts and
concert halls were thought of.
This section outlines the basic
instruments of the modern
orchestra, their origins, function
and development.

Left: Kyung-Wha Chung

Introducing Sound

VERY MUSICAL instrument that was or ever will be is a device for creating the minute pressure changes that pass through the air and are interpreted by our ears as *sound*.

When these pressure changes form an irregular pattern, the sound we hear is mere noise. When the pattern is regular, the sound is a note of definite pitch. All but the simplest musical instruments (some of the percussion, for example) are concerned with sounds of this kind.

When the rate of change is rapid, the note we hear has a high pitch. When the rate is slowed down, the pitch of the note falls. We call this rate of change the 'frequency' of a note.

Instruments set up pressure changes by making something vibrate. It can be a tightly stretched string, or a flexible reed, or the player's lips acting as a reed, or even the entire body of an instrument – such as a block of wood or a piece of metal. But these vibrations are usually very small and are apt to die away rapidly. Most instruments, therefore, have the additional power to *sustain* vibrations and *amplify* them.

For example: the violin's initial vibrations come from its four strings, which are stretched tight and set in motion by being plucked with the fingers or by the hairs of a bow being drawn across them. The body of the violin responds sympathetically to these vibrations, controls them by its bulk, increases their strength, and then passes them on in the form of pressure changes. The whole art of the instrument maker revolves around the delicate balance between these systems. If the response between them is not totally sympathetic, the sound will be unsatisfactory.

Changing the pitch

There are two main ways in which an instrument can be made to produce notes of different pitch. The first and, in a sense, the most clumsy way is to have a series of individual vibrators of different sizes – one for each new note. This is how the harp, or the piano, or the xylophone works: each note has a different length of string, or a different-sized block of wood. Such instruments inevitably tend to be rather large.

The more elegant solution is to have a limited number of vibrators and make

The shorter column of air in the piccolo (**top**) produces a rapidly changing vibration and a high pitch. The longer column in the tuba (**above**) produces slower changes and a lower pitch.

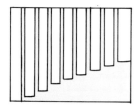

Most instruments must be capable of consistently producing notes of differing pitches. There are two main ways in which they are designed to make this possible. They can be constructed with a whole series of vibrators of different lengths built into them, or the vibrators can be altered in length during the course of playing. The tubular bells (**top**) provide a simple instance of the first sort of design. The pitch increases as the length of tube decreases. A plucked string, however (**above**), produces a note according to its length, and this can be readily altered by 'stopping' it in a given position. Other factors affecting the pitch of a string are tension and thickness. If a player tightens a string its pitch will be raised. if he uses a thicker rather than a thinner string, he will obtain a lower pitch.

changes to them while actually playing. Thus the violinist changes the length of his string by 'stopping' it with the fingers of his left hand, while the oboist changes the length of the air column inside his instrument by opening and closing holes cut along its side. Each change produces a different note.

A third method involves the way in which the player tightens or slackens his lips and facial muscles and the force with which he blows into his instrument. This enables him to change the pattern (the 'mode') of vibration and therefore the pitch of the note. This method can produce only a limited number of note changes, and makes use of the fact that musical sounds are not as simple and straightforward as they may seem. Each note, in fact, contains within itself many different notes which we hear as 'harmonics'.

Making use of harmonics

Take for example a stretched string. When it vibrates it does not simply move backwards and forwards in one great swing, but in a swing that includes a whole series of lesser movements. These lesser vibrations occur in both halves of the string, each third, each quarter, in each fifth, and so on. Each lesser vibration also produces a note. But these notes are not heard clearly in their own right – instead they give color and body to the fundamental note which comes from the *main* vibration. We call them 'harmonics', 'overtones', or 'partials'.

Harmonics always follow the same mathematical progression, arising from the whole, the half, the third, the quarter, the fifth and so on. And the notes they correspond to are equally predictable.

Instrument makers use this acoustic fact to give each type of instrument its characteristic voice. A clarinet, for example, emphasizes different notes of the harmonic series from those that an oboe picks out. Each therefore speaks with a different voice – the clarinet's is warm and rounded, whereas the oboe's has a sharp edge. The shape and size of the mouthpiece, the dimensions of the reed, the bore within the instrument, the very materials from which it is made – all these influence the way in which the harmonics behave.

Players can also use the phenomenon and deliberately highlight a harmonic. Thus a brass player can blow more

Unlike string players, brass and woodwind players depend not only on the agility of their fingers, but also upon breath control and the manipulation of facial and lip muscles (**left**). Even a dental mishap can affect the way a wind player performs. Good intonation and tone quality arise from a subtle interplay of all these factors.

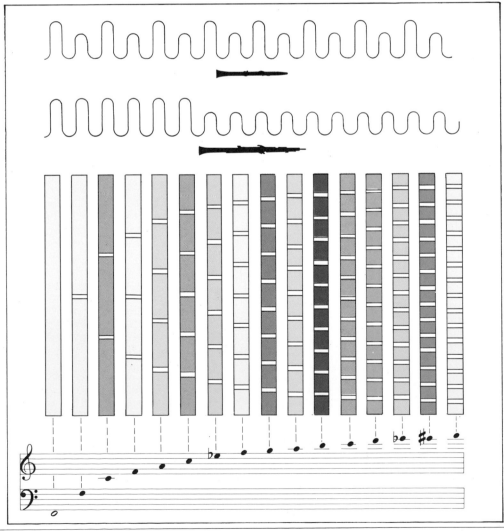

The pitch produced by a vibrating string or column of air is called the 'fundamental' note. The reason for this is that a string or column of air vibrates in sections as well as along its whole length. And each of these smaller vibrations produces a note that is not heard separately, but does add to the quality of the main note. These secondary notes are called harmonics. They rise in a mathematical progression. The second harmonic is always an octave above the first, the third a fifth above this, and so on, until the distance between the notes becomes negligible. The harmonic series of the note F is shown (**below left**). As the fractions to which the partial notes correspond decrease (**centre left**), so the frequency increases. Different harmonics can be emphasized by altering the intensity of an air stream. This intensity in turn can be determined by the particular shape of a tube or bore. In this way different instruments are given different tone colors (**top left**). For example, when the lowest pitch of the clarinet is played (**top**) the odd-numbered harmonics are emphasized by its cylindrical bore. The conical oboe bore, on the other hand (beneath) emphasizes the lower harmonics.

fiercely ('overblow') and force a particular harmonic to become prominent and overpower the fundamental note of whatever vibrating length he is using at the time.

Transposition

Certain members of the woodwind and brass families are said to be 'transposing instruments' – that is to say, their music is written at a different pitch from the notes as they actually sound. The reason for this goes back to the days when they could not be constructed in a way that would enable them to achieve every note satisfactorily. It was necessary then to make them in different sizes, each with a range of notes arising out of the harmonic series appropriate to its size. Thus in the clarinet family a clarinet in C (size: 22¾in, 57.8cm) was only on really safe ground in the keys of C and F, while a clarinet in B flat (26¼in, 66.7cm) could cope more happily with the keys of B flat and E flat, and a clarinet in A (27½in, 69.8cm) with the keys of A and D. If the music required the player to change instruments, it would clearly be confusing if he had to adopt a completely different system of fingering for each clarinet. Therefore his life was made easier by writing the music out as if it were always in C so far as the instrument was concerned. Music for a B flat clarinet was written a tone higher than it sounds, because the instrument's size meant that B flat was its natural equivalent of C. To get the note C on the B flat clarinet you have to *write* D.

Transposition affects only the clarinets, the cor anglais, the trumpet and the horns nowadays. In each case the transposing difference is the distance between the key of the instrument and C. Although modern playing techniques and methods of construction

On the relatively less sophisticated instruments that woodwind and brass players once had to be content with, it was sometimes necessary to change from smaller to bigger instruments, or vice versa, during a performance, so that required notes could fall comfortably within an instrument's capabilities. This could have led to a confusing alteration of the fingering patterns which were used to play given notes: if two instruments of different lengths use the same finger pattern for a note at a particular position on the stave, they will obviously sound notes of different pitches. It therefore became conventional to alter the position of the notes on the stave, and play the instruments as if they were all in the same key. When writing the part, the difference between the key of the instrument in question and C always had to be taken into account. Thus (**above**) the part for the A clarinet (center) is written a semitone higher than that for the B♭ clarinet (top), which in turn is a tone higher than what the listener actually hears (bottom).

make the use of transposing instruments unnecessary, they have survived partly out of tradition, and partly because the different sizes sound better than their counterparts in C.

The double bass and piccolo are transposing instruments in a slightly different sense. Their music is written an octave lower and an octave higher respectively, simply because to do otherwise would take the notation too far below and above the printed stave and so make it very difficult to read.

Classification of instruments

Instruments are scientifically classified according to the way in which they produce their sounds. The simplest are the *idiophones* – instruments such as bells, gongs, rattles, cymbals, jingles: anything, in fact, which produces its sound from its entire body vibrating as a whole.

Next come the *membranophones* – all the different types of drum which have a skin stretched tightly over a hollow vessel. The skin sets up the vibrations when struck. The hollow vessel beneath responds and amplifies them. Some skins can be tuned to different notes by varying the degree to which they are stretched, others are left as notes of more or less indefinite pitch.

Chordophones work in a similar way, except that the vibrating agent is now a stretched string which is plucked (as in the case of a guitar), or hammered (as on a piano), or bowed (as on a violin).

Last come the *aerophones* – the wind instruments, whose sound depends upon the vibration of a column of air inside a tube. This is set in motion when the player blows through a reed (as in the oboe, clarinet, and bassoon) or across the sharp edge of a hole (as in a flute) or downwards on to the edge of a hole (as in the horn, trumpet, and trombone). The column of air being made to vibrate can be shortened or lengthened by various means and the note changed accordingly.

A fifth category could be introduced for those instruments which now produce their notes by *electronic* means, but since they do not normally find a place in the orchestra they will not be treated separately in this book.

Such then, in simple form, are the acoustic facts behind musical instruments. But their long history concerns the struggle to harness these facts so that music is served in ways that are accurate, pleasant, and predictable.

The classification of instruments.

The method devised by von Horbostel and Sachs for classifying musical instruments now enjoys more or less universal acceptance. Orchestral instruments fall into four of the major categories in this system. Woodwind and brass produce sound through the vibration of a column of air, and are accordingly aerophones. This vibration can be set in motion by a player blowing through a reed, or onto a hole. The hole may be surrounded by a cup mouthpiece. The violin family belongs to the chordophone category of instruments. These produce sound by the vibration of strings. While violin strings are normally bowed, the strings of chordophones may also be plucked or struck. The percussion section contains members of two categories of instruments. Drums produce their sound through the vibration of a stretched skin. This makes them membranophones. Percussion instruments such as bells, gongs and xylophones vibrate with the whole of their body when they are played. Such instruments are idiophones.

Membranophones

Chordophones

Idiophones

Aerophones

The String Section

The string section, consisting of violins, violas, cellos and bases, comprises the main part of the orchestra, and sits flanking the percussion, woodwind and brass sections in the orchestra (**above**). **Right:** an Italian violinmaker follows in the footsteps of fellow countrymen such as Antonio Stradivari, Andrea Amati and Giovanni Maggini.

HE STRING SECTION of the modern orchestra are all members of the Violin Family and consist of the following instruments: violin; viola; cello (short for violoncello); bass (short for double bass or contrabass).

All that can be safely said about the origins of this family is that it emerged during the 16th century and took many of its characteristics from various bowed string instruments of earlier times. These include the rebec (a small three-stringed instrument popular during the Middle Ages, and descended from an 11th century Arab instrument), the fiddle (really a generic name for a number of stringed instruments of different shapes and sizes played by European folk musicians in medieval times), the *lira da braccio* (a 15th century refinement of the common fiddle), and the *viola da gamba* (the viol; played in a vertical position held upright on the knee – hence *da gamba*, as opposed to *da braccio*, that is 'on the arm'). Any attempt to trace a clear line of descent from all or any of these instruments is bedevilled by the fact that the word 'violin' was applied, in the early days, to a variety of different instruments in a very haphazard way, and it was not until the end of the 16th century that any kind of agreement began to appear.

The members of the violin family are bowed instruments, each with four strings tuned a fifth apart (except the double bass, which is tuned in fourths). The soprano and alto members, the violin and viola, are held against the shoulder, with the player's chin resting on the edge of the instrument. The bass members (cello and double bass) are so large that they have to rest on the floor: the cello held between the player's widespread legs as he sits on a chair, and the bass in front of the player as he sits on a stool, or stands.

The construction of the instrument

In all cases the sound is produced when a bow is drawn across a tightly stretched string, thereby setting it in vibration. These vibrations are communicated to the body of the instrument, which is in effect a hollow wooden box. This responds in sympathy, controls and amplifies the vibrations and passes them on as sound waves.

The upper end of the instrument terminates in a slender neck which carries a peg box and a fingerboard, and is finished off in an ornamental scroll. The strings are attached to pegs set laterally in the peg box, and then run down over the fingerboard, across a bridge (which lifts them clear of the body) to a tailpiece. This is held in a floating position by a piece of gut looped round an endpin set in the base of the instrument.

The body itself consists of a front plate (the 'table' or 'belly') carved from one or two pieces of softwood (usually straight-grained pine or spruce), and a back plate of hardwood (sycamore, maple, or fruitwood). Both plates are convex and rise to their highest point just below center. They are held apart by shallow hardwood ribs, beyond which they project very slightly all round. This overhang is usually inlaid with 'purfling': a narrow lamination of different woods, which adds strength and elegance. The plates are made from solid wood, both internal and external surfaces being carved. The precise thickness and contours of the final convex shape have a critical bearing on the quality of sound of the completed instrument.

Inside the body there are two important items which not only strengthen the instrument, but help to distribute the vibration of the strings evenly. These are the soundpost – a short wooden rod sprung between the front and back plates on the left hand side of the instrument, just below the left foot of the bridge; and the bassbar

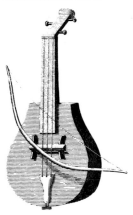

Two ancestors of the violin. **Top:** the *goudok* was a Russian three-stringed version of the medieval rebek. It was played with a curved bow. **Below:** the *lire da braccio* was a fiddle which was played on the arm. It had a similar body to the violin, with seven strings — five on the finger board and two drones.

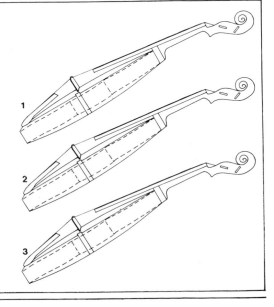

The violin, like every musical instrument, is an example of functional elegance. Every part of its structure, apart perhaps from its ornamental scroll, is involved in producing and distributing sound. The unseen details, too play their part: (1) the string transmits the vibration to the bridge; (2 & 3) soundpost and bass bar help spread the sound through the body fo the instrument.

Some of the greatest instrument makers have been Italian. Antonio Stradivari was born in Cremona, Italy in 1644, and became one of the most famous craftsmen the world has even known. He was taught to make stringed instruments by Andrea Amati, himself a great craftsman. **Above:** a violin made by Stradivari, now exhibited at the museum at Cremona.
Right: it is thought possible that Stradivari calculated the dimensions and tone values of his instruments using the Pythagoras Construction.

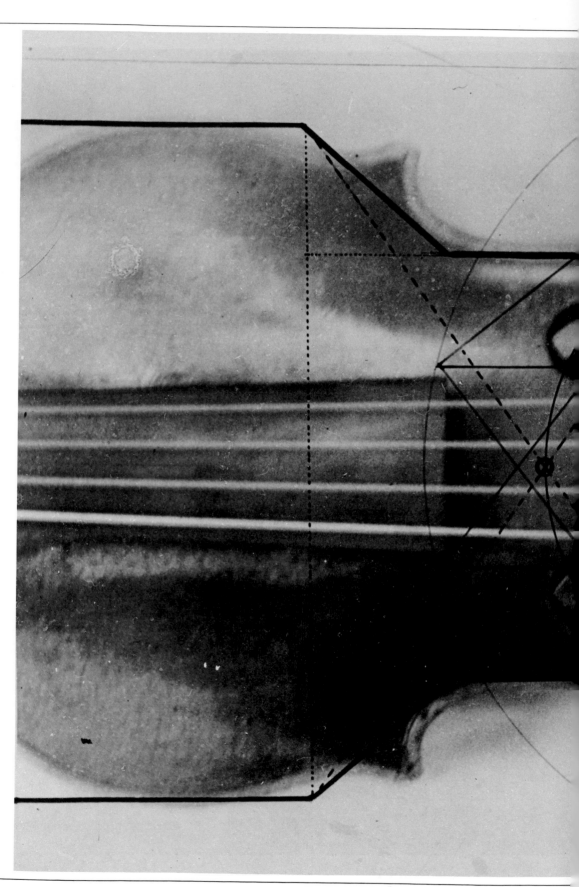

– a strip of wood glued to the underside of the belly, parallel to the strings from just beneath the right foot of the bridge. Besides spreading the vibrations, both help to spread the pressure created by the strings as they press down on the bridge.

The external aspect

Two soundholes are cut in the belly of the instrument on either side of the bridge. They are shaped like an italic 'F' (they are often called F-holes) and they allow the belly to vibrate freely. The outline of the instrument, with its characteristic waist, does not actually influence the sound, but it does allow the bow a complete clearance when playing on the outside strings. The swelling curves and elegant corners are there more for aesthetic reasons than anything else, and indeed for sheer beauty the shape would be hard to beat. The shoulders of the double bass slope more than those of the other members of the family.

The body of the instrument is varnished – largely as a protection against sweat and dust. There is no 'magic' ingredient in the varnish that will ensure a fine tone, but it must be carefully chosen so as to be flexible enough not to impair the natural response of the wood.

The bridge over which the strings pass is not fixed to the belly of the instrument, but is held in place by the downward pressure of the strings. It is made of hardwood and arched in such a way as to spread the strings on slightly different levels, so that they can be bowed one at a time.

The sounding length of each string is measured from the bridge to the point where it passes over the raised edge (the 'nut') of the pegbox. The fingerboard beneath the strings is quite smooth and, unlike that of the viol, carries no raised frets to guide the player's fingers. It is usually made of ebony. Looked at sideways on, the neck and fingerboard slope downwards so as to keep the strings level as they rise to pass over the bridge.

Most violin and viola players use a chin-rest – a wooden platform, shaped to receive the player's chin, and clamped to the upper edge of the instrument alongside the tailpiece. This helps the player to grip the body of the instrument in a way that is less fatiguing. For the same reason a large shoulder pad is sometimes used beneath the

The Violin and Viola

The violin is probably the best-known of all Western orchestral instruments, and forms the nucleus of the modern symphony orchestra and string quartet. It was developed in the 1500s, and was used in the 17th century in Italian opera orchestras. In 1626 Louis XIII established *Les vingt-quatre violons du Roy* at his court. They became very famous later in the century under Lully. Originally, the violin strings were thick and produced a rather quiet, dull tone. However, during the 18th and 19th centuries thinner strings and a higher string tension were produced, because violinist-composers like Tartini and Vivaldi demanded a better sound from the instruments for which they were writing new music. The internal structure of the violin and the finger board were altered to take the strain imposed by the new tension of the strings. Also around this time the practice of holding the violin under the chin instead of against the chest was developed. The bow was also altered to produce a richer sound from the violin. Today, the violin measures just over 23½ inches (59.7 cm) overall. The body is 14 inches (35.6 cm) long and the sounding length of the string (from nut to bridge) is just over 12¾ inches (32.4 cm). It is tuned in fifths to G, D, A and E. The bow is 29 inches (73.6 cm) long. The viola (**below**) is slightly larger, measuring about 27¼ inches (69.2 cm) overall. The body is about 16½ inches (41.9 cm) long and the sounding length of the strings 15¼ inches (38.73 cm). The bow is a little thicker than the violin bow and rather heavier. The strings are tuned in fifths to C, G, D and A. The viola uses the alto clef mainly, and sometimes the treble. The viola personified the Romantic poet in Berlioz's *Harold in Italy* (1834), where it is used to express melancholy thought. Berlioz and Mozart, in his Sinfonia Concertante, were, perhaps, the only early composers to find the right type of expression for the viola.

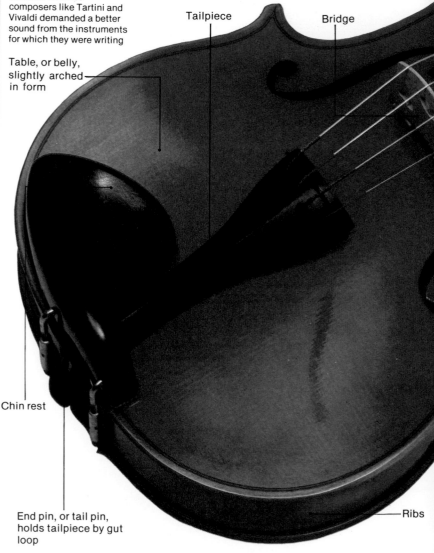

Tailpiece

Bridge

Table, or belly, slightly arched in form

Chin rest

End pin, or tail pin, holds tailpiece by gut loop

Ribs

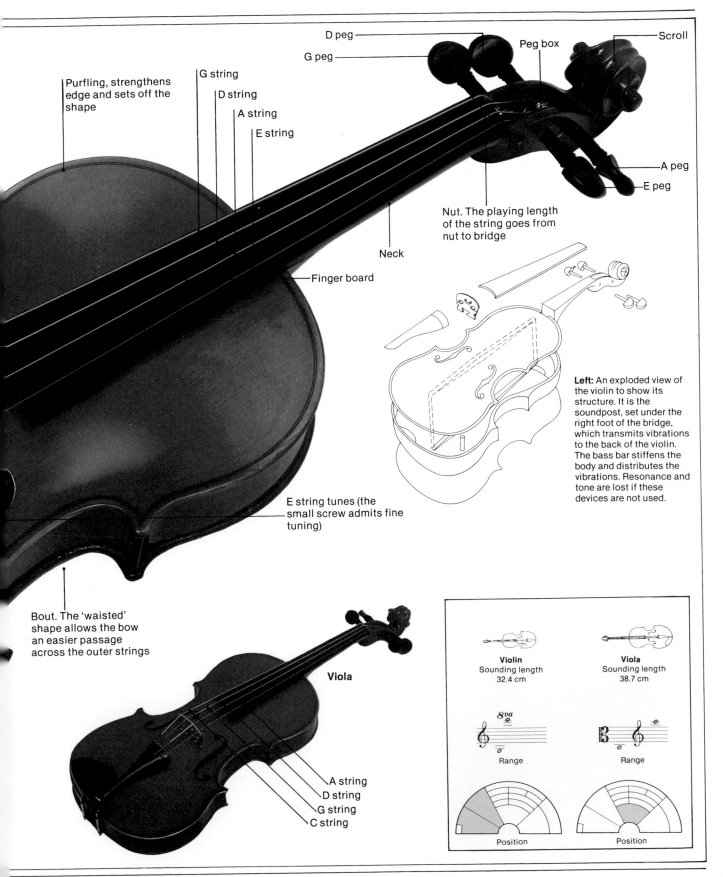

D peg

G peg

Peg box

Scroll

Purfling, strengthens edge and sets off the shape

G string

D string

A string

E string

A peg

E peg

Nut. The playing length of the string goes from nut to bridge

Neck

Finger board

E string tunes (the small screw admits fine tuning)

Left: An exploded view of the violin to show its structure. It is the soundpost, set under the right foot of the bridge, which transmits vibrations to the back of the violin. The bass bar stiffens the body and distributes the vibrations. Resonance and tone are lost if these devices are not used.

Bout. The 'waisted' shape allows the bow an easier passage across the outer strings

Viola

A string

D string

G string

C string

Violin
Sounding length
32.4 cm

Viola
Sounding length
38.7 cm

Range

Range

Position

Position

The Cello

The cello, more properly called the violoncello, is the bass member of the violin family. It was developed in the 1500s, but its importance began in the early 17th century when it began to be used as a continuo instrument in both orchestras and chamber groups, playing the bass line in conjunction with a harpsichord or organ. In spite of its size, it is one of the most expressive and adaptable instruments. Its large body ensures good resonance, and it is equally versatile as either a solo or an accompanying instrument. Its overall measurement is about 4 ft (122 cm). The body measures about 30 inches (76.2 cm), the neck 11 inches (28 cm), and the strings are about 27 inches (68.6 cm). When it is held in the playing position it is supported by a metal peg which slides out of the body just below the tailpiece. The strings are tuned in fifths to C, G, D and A. At 28¼ inches (71.8 cm) the cello bow is shorter and thicker than that of the violin and viola, and it is also less springy.

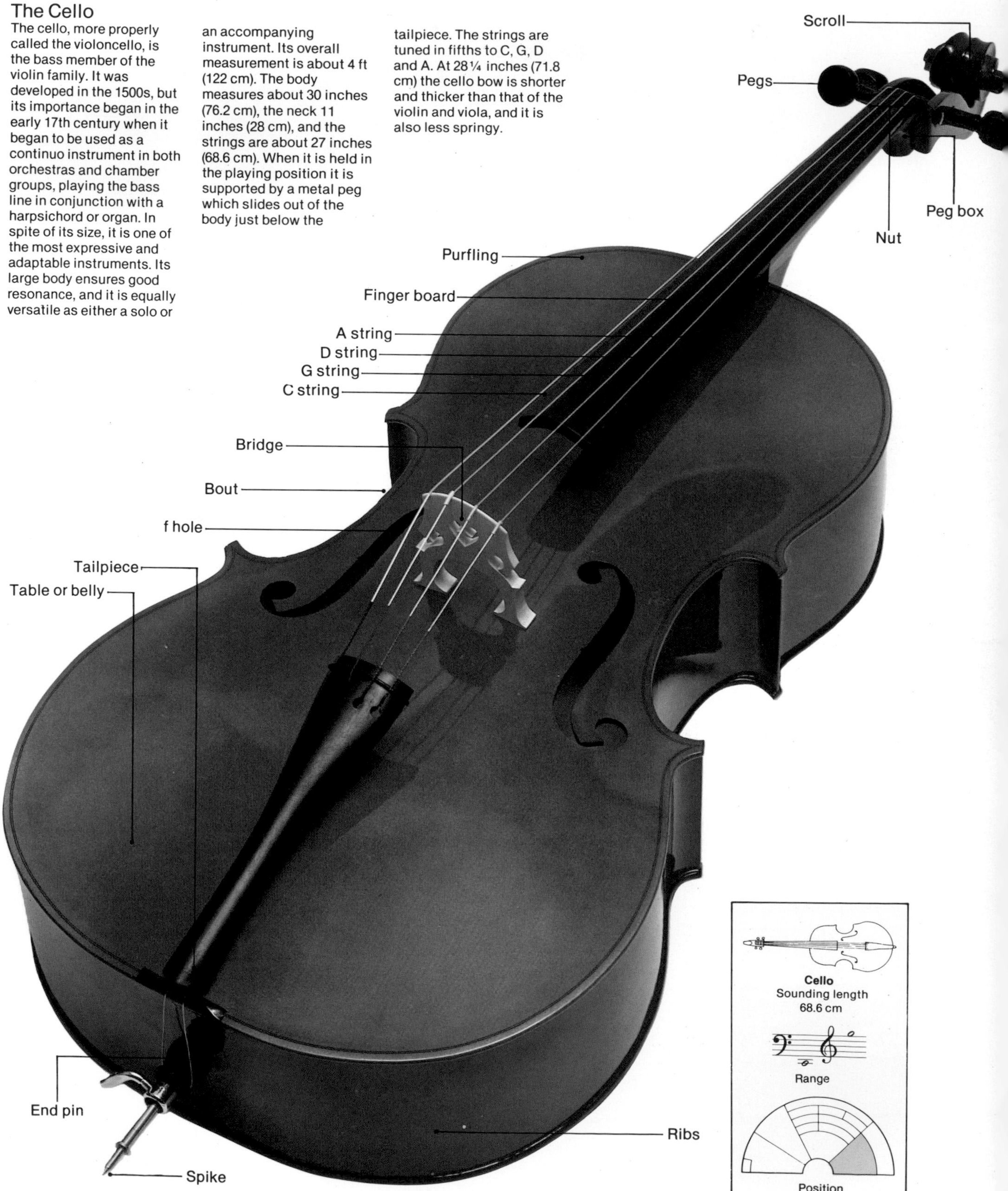

Scroll

Pegs

Peg box

Nut

Purfling

Finger board

A string

D string

G string

C string

Bridge

Bout

f hole

Tailpiece

Table or belly

End pin

Spike

Ribs

Cello
Sounding length
68.6 cm

Range

Position

...telier, one of the most celebrated cellists of modern times. He is also a conductor and composer.

instrument: this can be literally a cloth 'pad', or a wood and metal support fixed to the tail end of the back plate.

The fan-shaped tailpiece to which the strings are attached is made of ebony. Nowadays most players equip it with small screw devices which help with the fine tuning of the strings.

Violin strings were originally made from catgut – the specially prepared intestines of sheep. The lowest, thickest string (G on the violin itself) seems always to have been loaded with a fine wire covering, spun from copper or silver in a tight corkscrew. Until gut

Flat wound steel cello strings. Cellos used to be strung with catgut.

was replaced by steel wire, towards the end of the 19th century, the thinnest string (E on the violin) was always a problem to keep in tune. In more recent years there have been experiments with alternative materials, including all-metal strings (with steel cores and aluminum coverings), nylon rod and similar plastics, and the so-called 'rope core', a type of fine, stranded, steel rope covered with a ribbon of aluminum or silver.

The bow

The bow that sets the strings vibrating is almost as complex as the violin itself, and just as important. Originating probably in the Middle East, it consists of a long stick which holds at tension a hank of horsehair. The relationship between this and the archer's bow is obvious. Viewed under a microscope, the horsehair can be seen to have a serrated edge. It is these teeth that delicately grip the violin strings and cause them to vibrate.

The modern bow is a slender, tapered stick about 28¾in (73cm) long. It is made of pernambuca wood which has been bent in a dry heat into a gently inward curve. The horsehair is fixed as a flat ribbon in a small hatchet-shaped head at the upper end of the bow and in a movable 'frog' at the

The construction of the bows which are used to play the instruments of the violin family is complex and crucial. If it is not correct, the instrument will not be played to its best advantage, and many subtleties will be lost. Bows originally curved outwards, but this design was changed towards the end of the 18th century when the Frenchman François Tourte produced the shape known today. He was following in the footsteps of many bow makers such as Cramer, Tartini, Corelli and Viotti. The bows of Cramer have recently been re-examined and have been shown to blend early 18th century

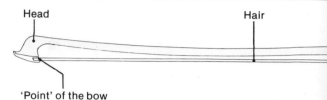

Head
Hair
'Point' of the bow

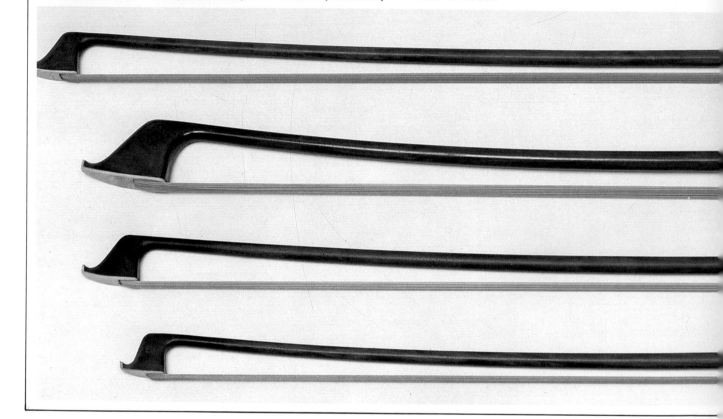

lower, thicker end. It is this lower end, called the 'butt', that is held between the player's thumb and fingers. The frog is held in place by an adjustable screw and can be wound sideways, thus tightening the horsehair. If the bow has been correctly designed it preserves its shape under every playing condition, despite the tension. This gives the player a very sensitive control over the kind of tone he produces. The present shape of the bow dates from the end of the 18th century, when it was perfected by the Frenchman François Tourte. Before that date bows usually curved outwards, away from the horsehair, which in practice meant that the player could not exert as great a pressure and generate as decisive and passionate a tone.

The relationship between the various parts of a violin and its bow is an extremely subtle one. Each has a bear-

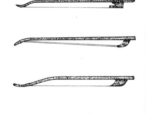

Many experiments have gone into the development of the modern bow, as can be seen from the different shapes illustrated above. Some of these experiments are associated with famous composer-violinists such as Corelli (top) and Tartini (third from top).

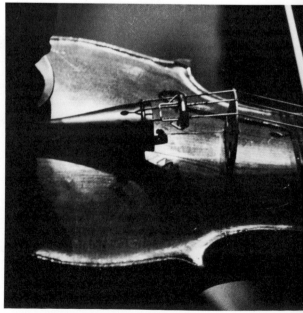

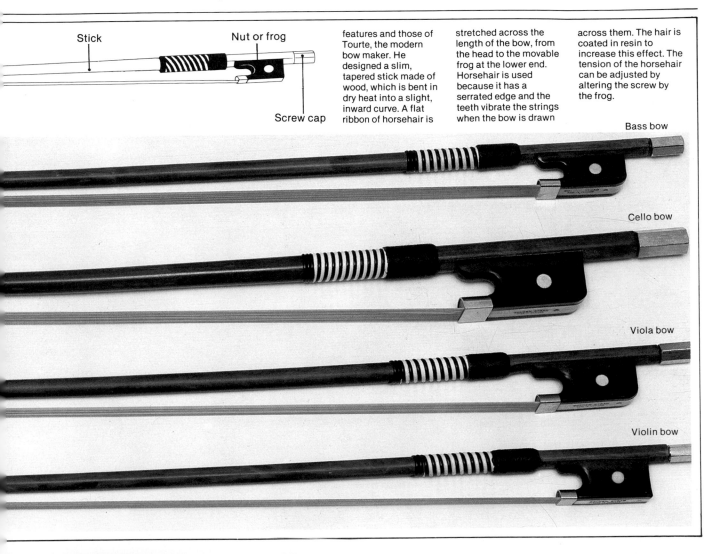

Stick | Nut or frog

Screw cap

features and those of Tourte, the modern bow maker. He designed a slim, tapered stick made of wood, which is bent in dry heat into a slight, inward curve. A flat ribbon of horsehair is stretched across the length of the bow, from the head to the movable frog at the lower end. Horsehair is used because it has a serrated edge and the teeth vibrate the strings when the bow is drawn across them. The hair is coated in resin to increase this effect. The tension of the horsehair can be adjusted by altering the screw by the frog.

Bass bow

Cello bow

Viola bow

Violin bow

The bows used today for the violin family are designed to be very flexible and versatile, enabling the player to extract as much feeling and tone as possible from the instrument (**left**). They also allow each string to be individually bowed.

ing on the others, and developments in one sphere can have striking repercussions on the way the rest behave. The modern bow and violin, though superficially much the same as their 16th century counterparts, are in fact as different as the music they were each designed to play. Indeed, very few early instruments have survived in their original condition – for to be playable they have had to be modified to suit the new kinds of stress that changing conditions have put upon them. To get back to the original sound it is necessary not only to make instruments and bows to the original patterns, but also to play them in a way that uses original techniques.

The first true violins date from the beginning of the 16th century and come largely from Italy. Among the great classical makers of this period are Gaspara da Salò (1540-1600) and Giov-

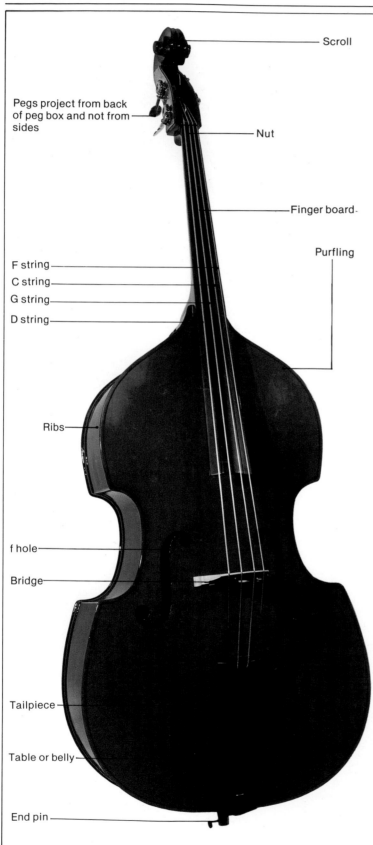

Scroll

Pegs project from back of peg box and not from sides

Nut

Finger board

Purfling

F string

C string

G string

D string

Ribs

f hole

Bridge

Tailpiece

Table or belly

End pin

The bass players of the Chicago Symphony Orchestra

The double bass was developed from the double bass viol, the violone, in the 1500s, and owes much of its construction to this instrument. It measures about 74 inches (188 cm) overall, with a body length of 44 inches (111.8 cm) and sounding strings of 42½ inches (108.6 cm). The bow is thick and heavy and between 26 and 27 inches (66 and 69 cm) long. The strings are tuned in fourths to E, A, D and G. In recent times the double bass has been given an optional extension which takes the E string down to C, thus giving the instrument a complete lower octave covering of the cello range. The E string is extended upwards at the top by a mechanism that can be flicked in and out of action by a thumb switch. The advantage of this is that it throws no extra pressure on the instrument and involves no special adjustment to the arching of the bridge and the spacing of the string.

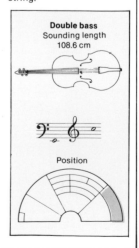

Double bass
Sounding length
108.6 cm

Position

anni Maggini (1580-1623), both of Brescia; Andrea Amati (?1520-78) his sons and grandsons, and his pupil Antonio Stradivari (1644-1737); Carlo Bergonzi (1683-1747), and Stradivari's pupil Giuseppi Guarneri (1698-1744) and his family – all of Cremona. Their surviving instruments, which include violas and cellos, are greatly prized, jealously guarded, and priced accordingly.

Alfredo Campoli (**left**) has enjoyed a long career as a virtuoso soloist.

How the strings are played

Though stringed instruments can be plucked with the fingers (*pizzicato*) they are usually played with a bow, which is held in the right hand and passed smoothly up and down over the required string either in short or full-length strokes, according to the duration of the note. At the same time the fingers of the player's left hand 'stop' the string at the appropriate length for whatever note is required. For example, halving the length of the string raises the note a full octave above that of its sounding length. Halving it again (ie. placing the finger three quarters of the way along) raises it another octave. The length of string involved in passing from one note to another therefore diminishes as the hand moves towards the bridge. And the distances involved are proportional to the overall length of the string. Thus to move from G to A on the lowest string (G) of a violin involves a shift of about 1¼in (3.2cm), whereas the same interval on the G string of a cello requires a jump of more than twice the distance.

When the fingers are held over the open strings ready to stop the first four degrees of the scale the hand is said to be in 'first position'. It is then moved in a series of four-note stages into second, third, fourth, and fifth positions, and so on.

Whatever the position, the hand can always reach all four strings.

It is also possible to play two or more notes simultaneously, provided that they can be produced on adjacent strings. According to the number of notes involved this is called double, triple, and quadruple stopping. Two notes can be played quite smoothly, because the adjacent strings will always lie on more or less the same plane. But triple and quadruple stopping involves three and four strings and thus forces the player to arch his bow over the curve that the bridge gives to the strings.The sound therefore has something of a 'scrape' about it, which may

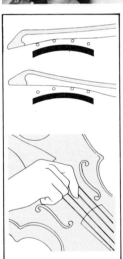

Strings can be played in two main ways: they can be plucked (**above**) or bowed (**top**). The strings of a violin are all situated in slightly different planes, so that each one can be played cleanly. The planes are close enough together, however, to allow for the simultaneous playing of two adjacent strings (double stopping). Three strings can be played together, but the resulting sound is not smooth.

only be desirable for special effects. Only two notes can be played with equal smoothness at any one time.

Notes can be played smoothly (*legato*) or in a clipped manner (*staccato*), or with various degrees of emphasis in between these two extremes. In *legato* playing the change of direction as the bow sweeps up and down cannot be heard as such, even though the down-bow is naturally inclined to be more forceful than the up-bow. Several notes can, of course be played with one stroke of the bow.

Various effects of color are also possible. Thus, playing with a mute (*con sordino*) produces a gentle, silvery tone. The mute is a small metal clamp that is placed on the bridge and serves to damp down the vibrations. Playing with the bow much nearer the bridge than usual (*sul ponticello*) produces a glassy, metallic effect. Playing over the fingerboard (*sul tasto*) gives a soft, floating quality to the sound. The strings may even be struck with the wooden part of the bow (*col legno*) to produce a dry, rattling sort of effect. And finally it is possible to pick out many of the individual harmonics that are present whenever a note is sounded. The string is bowed and stopped in the normal way, but lightly touched a little higher up at the same time, thus inducing the harmonic to sound forth as a clear, thin, bell-like note.

Of all the orchestral instruments the strings are the most versatile and tireless. Unlike the wind and brass the players do not have to pause for breath! The ear is apparently able to take in the string sound almost indefinitely without becoming bored, and in any case they can produce a great variety of sounds. By far the greatest share of the work in any average orchestral piece is undertaken by the strings – they are truly the basis of the orchestra and its music.

On their own, as a self-contained string orchestra, they can be extremely effective – as witness such masterpieces as Elgar's *Introduction and Allegro* (1905), Vaughan Williams's *Fantasia on a Theme of Thomas Tallis* (1910), Britten's *Variations on a Theme of Frank Bridge* (1937), and Tippett's *Concerto for Double String Orchestra* (1939).

As solo instruments, either in small groups such as the string quartet, or as virtuoso soloists, they are equally impressive. Together with the piano, the violin dominates the solo concerto as the only instrument able to compete with a full orchestra on equal terms. Among the great violin concertos are those of Beethoven, Mendelssohn, Tchaikovsky, Brahms, Elgar, Sibelius, Berg, Stravinsky, Prokofiev, and many more. Viola concertos are less plentiful, since its voice is less dominating, but Berlioz's symphony *Harold in Italy* (1834) is really a viola concerto, and Walton's Viola Concerto of 1929 shows what a 20th century composer can do. As a concerto instrument the cello has been well catered for by Dvořák, Elgar, Delius, Finzi, Walton, and Britten (*Cello Symphony*, 1963). The double bass has attracted less interest, though concertos by Dittersdorf (a contemporary of Mozart) and the modern German composer Hans Werner Henze (1966) are worth a hearing.

The Harp

The simple, basic harp consists of a hollow body which acts as a resonator, and a neck which projects out of one end of it at an angle. Between the two are stretched a number of strings which, when plucked, produce a series of notes according to their different lengths. A more sophisticated type has a pillar at the open end, between the body and the neck. This, as its name implies, takes the strain that the strings impose on the other two. In this form the instrument is known as the 'frame harp', and it is this type that developed into the modern orchestral instrument. Both forms, however, are of great antiquity.

The main problem in the development of the harp has been to provide a sufficient number of strings to cover a wide range of notes, without making it difficult for the fingers to pick out which string they wish to pluck. The more strings there are the closer they need to be together if the instrument is not to be too large for comfort – but they thus become more difficult to finger.

The solution, still embodied in the modern harp, dates from 1792 when Sébastien Erard of Paris patented an

In order to provide enough strings for the harpist to play without making the harp too large, Sébastien Erard devised a system of pedals and disks.
The first position shortens the string and raises its pitch. The second position raises the sound a further semitone.

'improved' single-action instrument, and 1810 when he extended the principle to a double-action mechanism. These improvements were made to a type of harp-action invented in the 1720s which neatly got round the problem of having too many strings by arranging to change the pitch of the strings while actually playing.

The Erard single-action attached each string to a rotating brass disk fixed to the neck of the instrument. This disk, in turn, was linked to a rod which passed down the inside of the pillar. At the foot of the pillar the rod was connected to a pedal. When the pedal was moved, the disk turned and caused two pins to catch the string and 'hitch it up' a little. The string thus became tighter and so raised in pitch.

As each string of the same name was attached to linked disks, only seven pedals were needed – one for all the C strings, one for all the D strings, and so on through the seven notes of the diatonic scale.

On the modern double-action harp each pedal moves two disks, set one above the other. The first lifts the pitch by a semitone, and the second lifts it by a further semitone. Because of this the entire harp is tuned to the unlikely key of C flat. This means that each string can be lifted from its flat version,

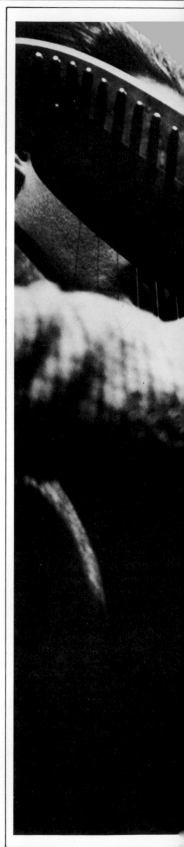

Left: the arrangement of the harp strings, showing part of the disk mechanism, which is operated by the pedals at the base of the harp. **Above:** the harpists sit at the back of the right-hand side of the orchestra, with the first violins. **Top:** Sidonie Goossens began her career playing the harp in London musicals, and then became a member of the Queen's Hall, London Philharmonic and London Symphony Orchestra, before joining the BBC Symphony Orchestra as principal harp in 1930.

up a semitone to its natural pitch, and up a further semitone to its sharp pitch. Thus C flat can become C natural and then C sharp, D flat can become D natural and D sharp, and so on.

A moment's thought will show that this ingenious device has an unexpected advantage in that any two adjacent strings can be made to sound the same note if the pedals are set correctly. Thus if the C string is raised to C sharp and the D string left as D flat, the sound will be the same – for, as you can check at the piano, C sharp equals D flat. This is why it is possible for harpists to sweep their hands effortlessly over the strings and not sound any unwanted notes – each extraneous string having been, so to speak, tidied away into an appropriate pitch.

Playing the harp
The harp is played with both hands, using the thumb and first three fingers. The strings are plucked near their midpoint with the finger tips and the outer edge of the thumb. They are tuned by means of a key which fits into pins on the righthand side of the neck. The upper strings are usually made of nylon and the lower ones of gut – the last eleven being wound with wire to give them extra weight (so that they need not be even longer). All C strings are colored red, and all F strings blue, as a guide to the player. The pedals work in a series of notches. When the pedal is in the upper notch the strings are in their 'flat' position, the middle notch produces the 'natural' pitch, and the lower notch the 'sharp' version. Pedal changes can be made swiftly and noiselessly.

Fine examples of orchestral writing can be heard in the second movement of Berlioz's *Symphonie Fantastique* (1830) and in Debussy's three symphonic sketches *La Mer* (1905). There are several harp concertos, that by the Argentinian composer Alberto Ginastera being one of the most interesting and effective.

The harp's voice, however, is not strong, and in the orchestra it is only of limited use as a melodist. But its capacity to bind an orchestral texture together is unrivalled. Equally, a few notes well placed can make a very impressive contribution. *Glissandos*, repeated chords, delicate figuration, and *arpeggios* are all part of its customary vocabulary. Delicate, ethereal harmonics are also very effective.

The Woodwind Section

The position of the woodwind section in the orchestra is indicated (**above**). A forest of clarinets at the Buffet-Crampon factory in France (**right**) waits for the wind. Clarinets are part of the reed family of instruments, which came from the East and spread through Europe and Africa.

*T*HE BASIC WOODWIND section of the modern orchestra consists of the following instruments: flute, oboe, clarinet, bassoon. To these are usually added the piccolo, cor anglais, and double bassoon, and sometimes also the alto flute and bass clarinet.

All wind instruments produce their notes when a column of air enclosed inside a tube is made to vibrate. These vibrations are set up in the first instance by the player's breath, which either agitates a reed-system (as in oboes, clarinets and bassoons) or impinges against the sharp edge of a mouthpiece (as in flutes). The longer the tube and its column of air, the lower the note that is produced. The deep-sounding bassoon is thus a much larger instrument than the high-sounding flute. To produce different notes, holes are cut in the walls of the tube. When all of these are sealed off, either by the player's fingers or some mechanical means, the tube vibrates along its full length and produces its lowest note. As the different holes are uncovered, different lengths of tube vibrate and so produce different notes. For example, if a hole cut exactly half way along the tube is uncovered, a note

exactly an octave higher than that given out by the full length of tube will be sounded.

Players can also obtain different notes by varying the degree of pressure they use when blowing into their instruments, and by varying the tension in their lip and facial muscles. Changes of this sort are used mainly to correct the intonation.

Wind instrument makers have been faced with three main problems in their search for perfection. First, how to provide a sufficient number of holes for all twelve notes of the chromatic scale, and yet take account of the fact that a player will have only a limited number of fingers to cover them. Then, how to arrange for the holes to be cut in the acoustically perfect place, and yet keep them within reach of the player's fingers. And finally, how to make the holes large enough to produce a good quality of sound and intonation, and yet small enough to be sealed off by the average size of finger.

The answer to all of these problems came with the invention of 'keys'. These are virtually artificial fingers. The earliest consisted of a small metal see-saw, fitted at one end with a leather-padded plate and at the other with a lever, and suitably pivoted in the middle. By pressing the lever the player could raise and lower the padded plate and thus open and close the hole beneath it. In other words, the key could reach where the fingers could not, and also, if necessary, deal effectively with holes of a larger size.

A further refinement came with the introduction of 'ring keys', invented in 1808 by an English clergyman, Frederick Nolan, and applied first to the flute in 1832 by Theobald Boehm (1794-1881), a German flute player. Boehm dispensed with the lever shaped like a metal tongue. Instead a metal ring was fitted round an existing finger hole which had been provided with a raised lip for the purpose. The ring was joined to a rod which ran lengthwise down the instrument and was in turn connected to the padded key. Thus by means of rods, springs and axles the player could open and close a hole some distance away and at the same time use his finger to open and close the hole around which the ring lay. This method, coupled with the new kinds of fingering it made possible, became known as the Boehm System. It is still used today.

When the central hole is uncovered, the note produced is an octave higher than if the full length of the tube is sounded.

The bassoon provides the natural bass to the woodwind.

THE FLUTE

This is an instrument of great antiquity. It has been known in various forms since prehistoric times and to almost all peoples of the world.

There are two main types:
The end-blown flute, which the player holds vertically and blows down one end through a mouthpiece.
The side-blown flute, which is held horizontally, with the player blowing across a hole cut in its side.
The end-blown flute was probably the first on the scene (we have it still in the Recorder family), but it is the side-blown flute (more properly called the 'transverse flute') that forms the basis of the modern orchestral instrument.

In the 16th century transverse flutes were usually made from a single piece of boxwood, bored throughout with a cylindrical hole. They came in three main sizes and were provided with six finger holes. They were, however, somewhat limited and not very easy to control. Improvements began to take place during the 17th and early 18th centuries. These included making the instrument in three sections: a head-joint, a middle-joint, and a foot-joint, which fitted neatly together on the tenon and socket principle. It was now

The flute is an extremely old instrument, found in most primitive or ancient cultures. The ceramic figure of the flautist (**right**) is from the T'ang dynasty of China (618-907 AD).

easier to drill the bore accurately, and the player was able to make minute adjustments of length and so bring any number of instruments into tune with each other. Keys were also introduced, so that players could operate extra sound holes and enjoy a more complete range of notes. And finally changes were made in the bore of the instrument: the middle and foot joints were given a slightly conical shape, tapering towards the open end of the instrument. The French family Hotteterre, who flourished in Paris from about 1640 to 1760, were responsible for many of these developments.

In 1832 the flute acquired Boehm's system of ring keys. Fifteen years later Boehm designed flutes which returned to the old cylindrical bore, but had a parabolic head-joint whose bore had a slightly tapering convex shape. Since then there have been few changes, other than minute adjustments in the size of the bore.

The modern flute, however, is usually made of metal – silver, most frequently, but sometimes gold or even platinum. Wooden flutes are still used, though they are not always made of boxwood, which sometimes warps. Cocus, rosewood, grenadilla, or African blackwood are alternatives. Some makers have tried to combine the bright, clear tones of the silver flute with the softer, mellow qualities of the wooden instrument by adding a silver-lined head joint to an otherwise wooden body.

The flute is 26⅓in (67cm) long and is made in three sections, with a total of 13 sound holes. Its range is just over three octaves, starting at middle C.

It is an extremely agile instrument, able to move at great speed and leap about with absolute assurance. Rapid scales, repeated notes, and brilliant arpeggios are all part of its bread and butter. But it can also be tender and lyrical – especially when dealing with melodies of a pastoral nature. The first six or seven notes of its range are very soft and velvety, but they are easily obscured by other instruments. The higher the flute climbs, the more brilliant and penetrating its notes become.

Examples of flute writing can be heard in almost any orchestral work. The opening of Debussy's *Prélude à l'après-midi d'un faune* (1894) is a particularly fine example. His *Syrinx* (1912) gives a very comprehensive idea of what can be done with an unaccom-

James Galway, one of the most popular

The Flute

Flutes are divided into two types, the end-blown and the side-blown flutes. The side-blown, or transverse, flutes appear in the orchestra. The end-blown flutes are now part of the recorder family. By the 17th century the transverse flute had become a common instrument in the opera or court orchestra. In the late 17th century the French Hotteterre family began to improve the design of the instrument. The German Theobald Boehm developed the modern flute from 1832 onwards, changing the position of the holes, making them larger and developing a system of keys and pads.

Flute

Flute Length 67 cm

Range

Alto flute 87 cm

Range

Piccolo 32 cm

Range

Position

Head joint

Body joint

Lip plate

Keys. 16 in all, which, by means of axles and springs, enable the player to close the sound holes.

Foot joint

Embouchure, or blowhole

Alto flute

Piccolo

panied flute, and there are a number of concertos – three by Mozart – to show it in action as a solo instrument.

THE ALTO FLUTE

Often wrongly called the Bass Flute, this is a larger version of the ordinary flute.

Its length is 34¼in (87cm) and it is a transposing instrument – the notes are written a perfect fourth higher than they sound. The mechanism, similar to that of the flute, was perfected in about 1854 by Boehm. The 18th century version of this instrument was called the *flute d'amour* – a name which admirably suggests its gentle, seductive tone.

The true Bass Flute is a comparative rarity in orchestras. It was not perfected until the 1930s, and is pitched an octave below the normal flute.

THE PICCOLO

A small octave flute that came into existence towards the end of the 18th century. It measures 12½-13in (32-33cm). Its notes are written an octave lower than they sound.

The piccolo has a brilliant, piercing voice and is wonderfully effective when adding highlights to an orchestral tutti. *Piccolo* is the Italian adjective 'little' and is thus meaningless by itself. The Italians call the instrument by its full name *flauto piccolo*, but it is unlikely that others will ever change their ways.

THE OBOE

The word *hautbois* (variously translated as loud or high wood) first occurs in music in France during the 15th century when it was used to describe certain members of the shawm family. It is from them that the modern oboe is descended.

Like the shawm, the oboe is a reed instrument. That is to say, its initial vibrations are set up when a player blows gently through a reed fixed in the top end of the instrument. The reed is in effect a double reed, made by folding a piece of thin cane and binding it to a small tube or 'staple' with a piece of thread. The cane is cut to the required length and its free ends are carefully shaved down. The business of preparing the reed requires the greatest delicacy. It must be thin enough to vibrate freely, but not so thin as to

The Oboe

Modern oboes were first made by the Hotteterre family as direct descendants of the shawm group of instruments, and were played at the court of Louis XIV. They were made in three sections, and their bore dimensions and finger hole positions were accurately calculated. Several sizes of oboe were introduced to the orchestra in the 18th century, including the cor anglais, an alto oboe. Key mechanisms were developed by both the French and the German, with varying degrees of intricacy. French oboes were made with quite complicated mechanisms, while German instruments were much simpler.

produce an impoverished tone. If it is too thick it will not react quickly enough, and if it is too stiff the tone will be harsh. Professional oboe players usually make their own reeds, and spend hours tailoring them to their own requirements.

Before playing, the reeds are moistened. They are then held between the lips so that they do not touch the teeth. A considerable variation in pitch can be obtained from the tension of the lips alone.

The modern oboe began to emerge as a refinement of the shawm (essentially an outdoor instrument) in France

The shawm (**below**) is the most important of the early double-reed instruments, and was played in Europe in the 13th century. It was made in different sizes, the largest of which were most suitable for playing outdoors. In the 17th century it was replaced by the oboe, but the outdoor role (**right**) was retained.

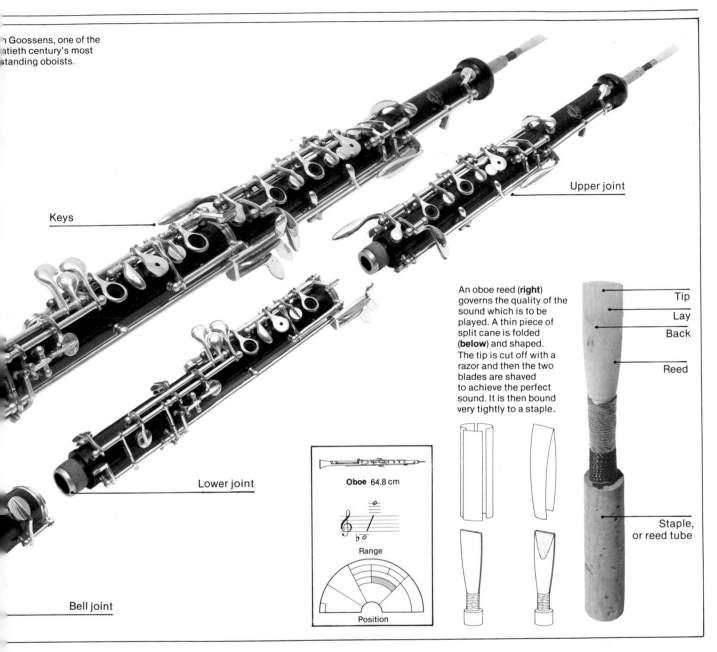

Goossens, one of the
ntieth century's most
standing oboists.

Keys

Upper joint

Lower joint

Bell joint

An oboe reed (**right**)
governs the quality of the
sound which is to be
played. A thin piece of
split cane is folded
(**below**) and shaped.
The tip is cut off with a
razor and then the two
blades are shaved
to achieve the perfect
sound. It is then bound
very tightly to a staple.

Tip
Lay
Back

Reed

Staple,
or reed tube

Oboe 64.8 cm

Range

Position

in the middle of the 17th century. The instrument maker Jean Hotteterre and the composer Michel Philidor may well have been its 'inventors'. The English were in no doubt as to its origins and always referred to it as the 'French Hoboy'. Unlike the shawm, it was made in three separate sections ('joints'), which made it possible to gauge the bore more exactly. By the end of the century the instrument had acquired six finger holes and three keys, and had an overall compass of about two octaves.

Towards the end of the 18th century more keys were added. This gave the instrument a more complete control over the notes of the chromatic scale, but it is during the 19th century that the greatest developments took place. Instrument makers working in Paris, such as Henri Brod and Guillaume Triébert, gradually effected a complete reform. They adjusted the size and position of the note holes, the width of the reed, and the proportions of the bore, taking advantage of the rods, axles, and ring-keys invented by Theobald Boehm.

The modern oboe has a tapering tube, ending in a gently flared bell. It is made in three sections (the upper,

The Cor Anglais

The cor anglais is an alto oboe. It has a tenor range but has a much richer and heavier tone than an oboe. Very early instruments were curved and bound in leather, but later versions were angled and jointed. Today's version is straight, but is distinguishable from the oboe because it has a curved crook for the reed and a globular bell.

Cor anglais
Length 80 cm

Range

lower, and bell joints) and its total length is about 25½in (64.8cm), of which the reed and staple account for about 2½in (6.35cm). The inside bore is conical. Oboes are usually made of wood: grenadilla, rosewood, and cocus wood are very popular. A few are made of ebonite.

Considering its size, the oboe has a powerful voice. The tone has a tangy edge that enables it to be heard quite distinctly, even against quite a full orchestral background. The higher it climbs, however, the thinner the tone becomes and the less 'oboe-like' it begins to sound. Though very agile it is at its best when executing neat, delicately articulated patterns, and singing in long lyrical lines. Its voice can be muted, by stuffing a handkerchief in the bell.

Typical orchestral use of the oboe can be heard at the beginning of Rossini's overture to *The Italian Girl in Algiers* (1813), and indeed throughout the overture. Richard Strauss's *Oboe Concerto* (1946) is a fine example of its capabilities as a solo instrument.

THE COR ANGLAIS

Of the several larger types of oboe that grew up alongside the parent instrument the most widely used is the tenor oboe, or cor anglais. The name appears during the second half of the 18th century; but since the instrument is neither a horn nor English it is very difficult to account for its usage. The cor anglais is a transposing instrument pitched in F. Its notes are therefore written a perfect fifth higher than they sound. Its total length is 31½in (80cm), and it differs from the ordinary oboe in that it has a bulb-shaped bell and its reed is fixed in a bent metal crook.

The deeper, warmer voice of the cor anglais makes it very suitable for solo melodies. A good example can be found at the beginning of Berlioz's overture: *Le Carnaval Romain* (1844).

Among the other types of oboe sometimes found in modern scores is the **Oboe d'amore** – a transposing instrument pitched in A, which is larger than the oboe but smaller than the cor anglais. Its tone is gentler than either. Much used in the 17th and 18th centuries, but out of fashion during the 19th, it now makes an occasional orchestral appearance.

Equally rare is the **Heckelphone**, invented in 1904 by Wilhelm Heckel as a bass to the oboe family. Like the cor anglais and the oboe d'amore it has a bulb-shaped bell, but this is perforated in the front. The notes are written an octave higher than they sound.

THE CLARINET

The clarinet is one of the few orchestral instruments whose inventor can be named: Johann Christoph Denner (1655-1707), an instrument maker of Nuremberg. The precise history of his invention is, however, somewhat confused, and it seems likely that what he did was to improve an already existing instrument, the chalumeau, by adding extra sound holes and two keys.

The clarinet has a cylindrical bore and its tube ends in a flared bell that is similar to the oboe's, but slightly larger. Its vibrations are initiated by a single reed which is bound to the open side of a mouthpiece by means of a metal ligature and adjustable thumb-screws. This mouthpiece is often called a 'beak', which admirably describes its shape.

The development of the clarinet follows that of all woodwind instruments. The earliest versions were made in three sections: a mouthpiece, which was also long enough to carry two keys (one at the back and one at the front), a body joint with six finger-holes in front and a thumb-hole at the back, and a short foot-joint pierced with two small holes side by side, as in many recorders. This foot-joint was later extended and given a key and its characteristic flared bell.

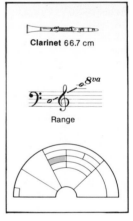

Clarinet 66.7 cm

Range

Clarinet

The Clarinet

The clarinet was developed by Johann Cristoph Denner from the chalumeau in about 1700. He gave the instrument a separate mouthpiece, more sound holes, a bell and extra keys to produce higher notes. At first the clarinet had a poor sound, and it was only towards the end of the eighteenth century, after Mozart had featured it in his music, that the instrument became better accepted. Mozart discovered it in Mannheim in 1778, and his recognition of its character and special contribution to orchestral texture, combined with his friendship with the leading clarinettist Anton Stadler, led him to compose the Clarinet Quintet and Clarinet Concerto. Rameau, too, must take credit for discerning the orchestral potential of the instrument.

Mouthpiece

Barrel joint

The bass clarinet's mouthpiece is mounted on a curved tube, or crook.

Upper joint

Keys

Lower joint

Bell joint

The bass clarinet has an upward-curving bell

Bass clarinet

The mouthpiece of the clarinet is constructed from a single reed. It is bound to the open side of the mouthpiece with a metal ligature. The reeds are usually made of natural cane, but can be made of plastic or fiberglass. The mouthpieces are usually made of wood or ebonite.

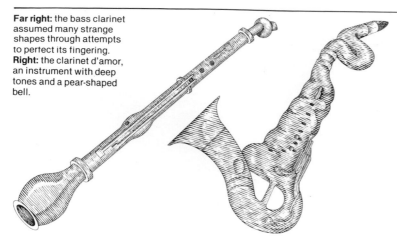

H.E. Klose (**below**) made the Boehm system clarinet known to the world. The basset-horn (angled version, **bottom**) was invented in 1771 and popular in Mozart's day. Mozart used it in his *Serenade for wind instruments* (1781).

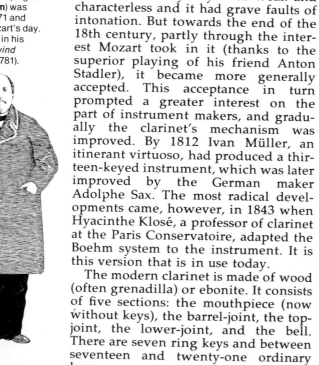

The clarinet only gradually established itself among composers, for its tone in the early days was weak and characterless and it had grave faults of intonation. But towards the end of the 18th century, partly through the interest Mozart took in it (thanks to the superior playing of his friend Anton Stadler), it became more generally accepted. This acceptance in turn prompted a greater interest on the part of instrument makers, and gradually the clarinet's mechanism was improved. By 1812 Ivan Müller, an itinerant virtuoso, had produced a thirteen-keyed instrument, which was later improved by the German maker Adolphe Sax. The most radical developments came, however, in 1843 when Hyacinthe Klosé, a professor of clarinet at the Paris Conservatoire, adapted the Boehm system to the instrument. It is this version that is in use today.

The modern clarinet is made of wood (often grenadilla) or ebonite. It consists of five sections: the mouthpiece (now without keys), the barrel-joint, the top-joint, the lower-joint, and the bell. There are seven ring keys and between seventeen and twenty-one ordinary keys.

The clarinet, as has been said, operates from a single reed bound to a mouthpiece. The player lays the reed on his lower lip, which is curled back over his bottom teeth. The upper teeth rest on the curved surface of the mouthpiece. Tone quality and volume can be adjusted by varying the amount of reed carried in the mouth and the pressure of the lower lip on it. Separate notes are articulated by letting the tongue touch the tip of the reed at each note.

The history of the clarinet has led to it being a transposing instrument (see p52). The player reads his part as if it were for the clarinet in C, and the instrument itself transposes the music according to its size. The most widely used instruments are pitched in B flat and A – transposing a tone and a tone and a half respectively. Military bands use a clarinet in E flat.

The clarinet has an extremely wide range, and its different registers have characteristic tonal qualities. From the lowest note to about F sharp its voice is rich and dark and rather oily. This is the *chalumeau* register – so called after the clarinet's early ancestor. Next comes the short range of 'throat tones'. These are somewhat less vibrant than the instrument's other registers. The *clarino* register which follows is bright, warm, and very expressive. It is not unlike the 'clarino' style of trumpet playing developed during the baroque period. Thereafter come the high and extreme registers, where the clarinet's voice becomes extremely penetrating and finally very shrill.

The clarinet is the orchestra's most versatile woodwind instrument. It is capable of a very wide range of dynamic variation, and is as at home with brilliant, rapid passage work as it is with long expressive melodies. It blends well with other instruments. Examples of its use in the orchestra abound – the 'trio' section of the third movement of Mozart's Symphony No 39 in E flat (K543) is very typical, and shows both the *chalumeau* and the *clarino* registers contrasting with each other. Mozart's Clarinet Concerto (K 622), written in 1791, and Aaron Copland's Clarinet Concerto (1948) with an orchestra of strings and harp show its virtuosity.

THE BASS CLARINET

Usually an instrument in B flat (though examples in A also exist), it is pitched an octave below the B flat clarinet.

Two systems of notation are used: the so-called French system, which employs the treble clef and places the notes a major ninth higher than they sound, and the German system, which uses the bass clef and places the notes a major second higher than they sound. The French system is more logical so far as fingering is concerned (since it is the same as for the B flat instrument), but the German method shows the notes nearer to their actual sound.

Among the less frequently used

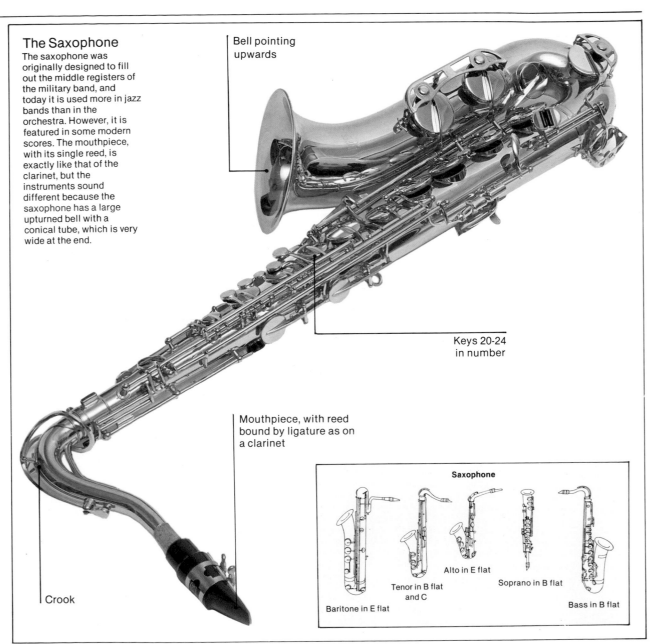

The Saxophone

The saxophone was originally designed to fill out the middle registers of the military band, and today it is used more in jazz bands than in the orchestra. However, it is featured in some modern scores. The mouthpiece, with its single reed, is exactly like that of the clarinet, but the instruments sound different because the saxophone has a large upturned bell with a conical tube, which is very wide at the end.

Bell pointing upwards

Keys 20-24 in number

Mouthpiece, with reed bound by ligature as on a clarinet

Crook

Saxophone

Baritone in E flat

Tenor in B flat and C

Alto in E flat

Soprano in B flat

Bass in B flat

larger members of the clarinet family is the **Basset Horn** – a great favorite in Mozart's day, but ignored during the 19th century and only occasionally used today. It is pitched in F. Its voice is very rich and dark and satisfying, and it is surprising that more composers do not make use of it.

There exists also a **Contrabass Clarinet**, sounding an octave below the bass clarinet. It is made of metal and is folded in upon itself like a bassoon. It has to be, since there are 8ft 10in (2.70m) of tubing to contend with. From the average orchestra's point of view it is a rarity.

THE SAXOPHONE

Although made of brass, the Saxophone is classified as a woodwind instrument because its notes are produced by means of a mouthpiece and a single reed, exactly like the clarinet. Indeed, since its fingering is also the same as the clarinet's it is often played by the same performer without any further training. It was invented in 1846 by the Belgian instrument maker Antoine Joseph Sax (usually known as Adolphe Sax). His intention seems to have been to make an instrument that would help out the middle registers of

Adolphe Sax gave his name to his invention. He also invented bugles called saxhorns.

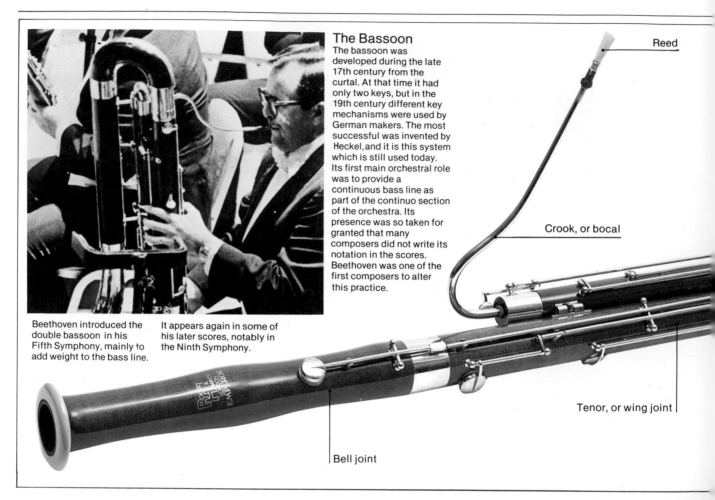

The Bassoon

The bassoon was developed during the late 17th century from the curtal. At that time it had only two keys, but in the 19th century different key mechanisms were used by German makers. The most successful was invented by Heckel, and it is this system which is still used today. Its first main orchestral role was to provide a continuous bass line as part of the continuo section of the orchestra. Its presence was so taken for granted that many composers did not write its notation in the scores. Beethoven was one of the first composers to alter this practice.

Reed

Crook, or bocal

Tenor, or wing joint

Bell joint

Beethoven introduced the double bassoon in his Fifth Symphony, mainly to add weight to the bass line. It appears again in some of his later scores, notably in the Ninth Symphony.

the military band, and he clearly had in mind a whole family of instruments. It was for this reason that he used metal even for the smaller members – since a bass saxophone in wood would have been far too cumbersome.

The saxophone family contains:
Soprano in B flat
Alto in E flat
Tenor in B flat and C
Baritone in E flat
Bass in B flat
A Sopranino in F was devised but is no longer used.

The saxophone has a large upturned bell, and its tube is conical and finally very wide. Its sound is therefore quite different from the clarinet, which has a cylindrical bore. Although it is capable of a pure, steady, and very expressive tone, the style adopted by sax players in jazz and dance bands is so distinctive and 'unclassical' that it is now very difficult to find players who can blend in with the symphony orchestra. Nevertheless a number of important modern works make use of

it – for example, Britten's *Sinfonia da Requiem* (1940) and Vaughan Williams's Sixth Symphony (1948).

THE BASSOON

The ancestor of the bassoon is the Curtal, a bass instrument that made its first appearance in about 1450. Curtals were carved from a single block of wood, through which were bored two parallel conical channels linked at the bottom in a U-shape. This meant that a sounding length of anything from 6 to 8 feet (180-250cm) could still be reasonably portable. The instrument was played with a double reed (like the oboe) mounted on a brass crook. There were seven finger holes in the front of the downward channel, the lowest being served by a key, and three more holes at the back of the upward channel (two being covered by the player's thumbs, and one by a key). Gradually a whole family of curtals came into existence, but it was the largest, called the Double Curtal that provided the

The bassoon (**above**) is rarely used in a solo context in the orchestra, but Mozart and Weber composed pieces for it.

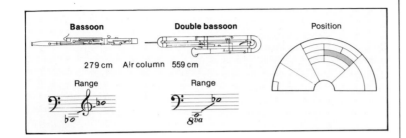

Bassoon	Double bassoon	Position
279 cm	Air column 559 cm	
Range	Range	

Bass, or long joint

Butt

In the 17th century the French invented the butt, which converted the curtal into the bassoon. Instead of boring a U-shaped channel in a single block of wood, they developed a block of wood which had only the hairpin bend of the curve (right), and the upright channels were fitted as separate joints.

Curtals (left) first appeared about 1450. Bassoons evolved from them in the late 1600s.

direct ancestor of the bassoon.

The transformation took place in France during the second half of the 17th century. Rather than risk the problems of boring a U-shaped channel in a single block of wood, the French invented the idea of a 'butt'. This was a block of wood which contained only the hairpin bend of the U-shape, into which could be fitted the upright channels as separate joints. The butt itself carried three sound holes and a key, while the downward joint grew a slightly projecting 'wing', through which the remaining three holes could be bored at an oblique angle. This not only brought the holes closer together for the convenience of the fingers, but also noticeably improved the tone (since the air passages were now longer). Extra keys were added, so that by the beginning of the 18th century the instrument had become a practical addition to the early orchestra.

During the first half of the 19th century considerable work went into redesigning the bassoon, both in France and in Germany. The French Buffet family, and the German Wilhelm Heckel were particularly distinguished for their contributions. There is still a certain disagreement about the relative merits of French and German bassoons, but in the hands of a fine artist the differences scarcely matter.

The modern bassoon has an air column of about 9ft 2in (280cm).

It is not a transposing instrument. It is made of wood, usually maple, in four sections: the bell-joint, the bass-joint, the butt, and the wing-joint. The bore is conical, graduating from ⅛in (0.3cm) to about 1½in (3.8cm) at the bell end. A double reed, ½in (1.3cm) wide, fits into a curved metal crook which in turn fits into the top of the wing joint. The player holds the butt close to his right hip with his right hand, while his left hand grasps the bass and wing joints. The finger holes are therefore pointing away from his body and the thumb holes towards it. A neck-cord attached to the top of the butt helps hold the instrument steady.

The bassoon is an agile instrument – a little heavy in its lowest register (but sonorous and effective), and very expressive in its middle range. The upper register is rather tense and penetrating. Besides forming a perfect bass to the rest of the woodwind the bassoon blends well with certain other instruments, such as the cellos and horns. The opening of the second movement of Bartok's Concerto for Orchestra (1943) is a nice example of its orchestral use, and there are effective concertos by Mozart and Weber.

THE DOUBLE BASSOON

This huge instrument, whose air column is about 18ft 4in (559cm) long, carries the bassoon sound a further octave downwards.

Designed by Wilhelm Heckel in about 1879, it folds into four wooden tubes, connected by a butt and two U-joints. Some models terminate in a brass bell pointing downwards, others in a bell that points upwards. Though, understandably, not an agile instrument, it adds greatly to the sonority of the bass register of an orchestra. The lowest notes require great breath control and cannot therefore be sustained for long. Works such as Ravel's La Valse (1920) and Richard Strauss's symphonic poem Till Eulenspiegel (1895) make excellent use of the double bassoon.

The Brass Section

The brass section of the orchestra, consisting of horns, trumpets, trombones, tubas and sometimes cornets, sits towards the back of the orchestra (**above**). As their name suggests, these instruments are made of metal — brass and silver in particular. **Right:** brass instruments in varying stages of manufacture in the Gautrot factory in France, 1855.

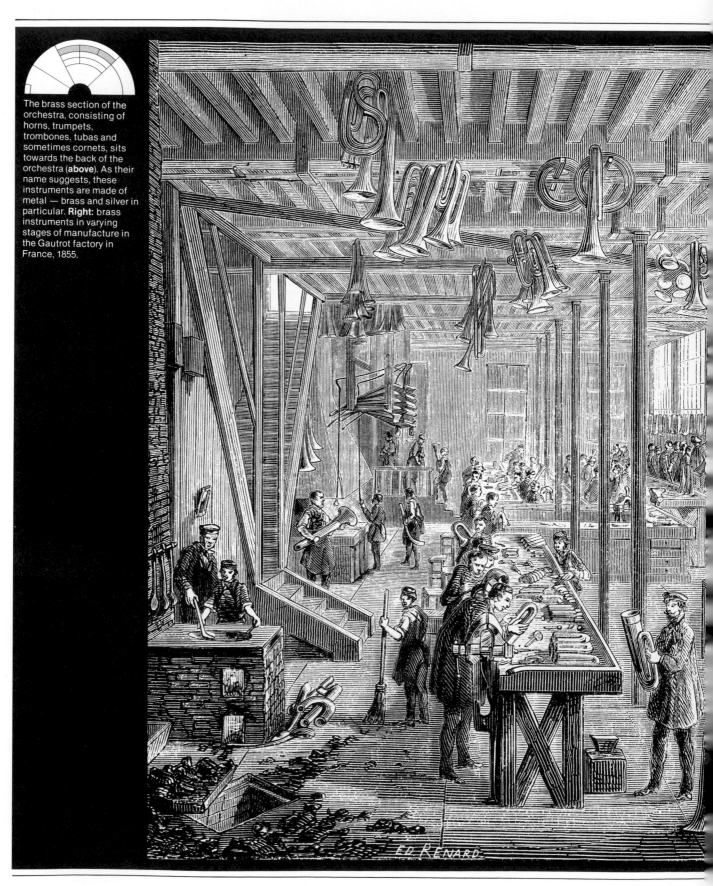

HE BRASS SECTION of the modern orchestra consists of the following instruments: horn, trumpet, trombone (tenor and bass) and tuba. The cornet is also sometimes called for.

Brass instruments produce their notes when the player presses his lips against a cup-shaped mouthpiece, forces air through them, and causes them to vibrate. These vibrations are taken up and modified by the column of air enclosed inside the metal tube that forms the body of the instrument. The player's lips act, in other words, like reeds in woodwind instruments.

Unlike the woodwind, however, the brass do not produce their full range of notes by opening sound holes in the body of the instrument, thus reducing its sounding length. They achieve their different sounding lengths by *adding* extra tubing.

Without the possibility of such additions the brass could only produce the harmonics appropriate to the length of their basic tubes. For example, a tube 8 ft (244cm) long will produce the notes of the harmonic series of an 8ft C.

By varying the pressure of his breath and the tension of his lips, the player can pick out most of these notes with ease. A simple instrument such as the bugle, which cannot change the length of its tube, is played exactly in this

The different notes played on brass instruments are achieved by varying the lengths of tubing through which the player blows. A tube 8 ft (244 cm) long will produce notes of the harmonic series of C, but if an extra 1 ft 2½ inches (36.8 cm) is added, the harmonic series of B flat would be played.

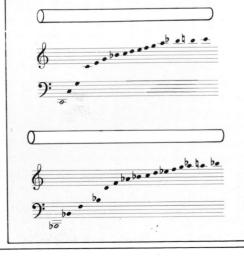

The bugle player has not been deterred by the limited range of his instrument from the invention of ingenious tunes which fall within its capabilities. 'Reveille' (**below**) is one of the most well-known and striking of these.

way. But its tunes are limited to the notes of the harmonic series its length produces. This is why army bugle calls revolve (often very ingeniously) round a few notes.

Although it is relatively easy for the player to pick out the lower harmonics in the series, the upper harmonics are more difficult to pinpoint. Help comes from the shape of the mouthpiece being used. A shallow cup, such as you find in a trumpet mouthpiece, aids the search for upper harmonics. The shape of the cup also influences the quality of the instrument's voice: the shallow trumpet cup invokes a brilliant sound, whereas the gently tapering horn mouthpiece adds warmth and mellowness.

The only way a brass instrument can produce notes outside its basic harmonic series is by adding a new length of tubing and so making available a new harmonic series. For example, if we add a further 1ft 2½in (36.8cm) to the 8ft tube the harmonic series of B flat would emerge.

This gives us notes not in the 8ft (C) series. The whole history of brass instruments has been concerned with ways of changing the tube lengths quickly and efficiently.

THE HORN

Commonly called the French horn, because it was developed from the *trompe de chasse*, a type of hunting horn that came into existence in France during the second half of the 17th century. It consisted of a slender tube which ended in a wide bell and was coiled into a hoop and so carried on the huntsman's shoulder. Early examples

were about 7ft (213cm) long and sounded a trumpet D, but during the 18th century tubes of twice this length became popular. It was this *cor de chasse*, coiled in a double hoop, that entered the orchestra during Bach and Handel's lifetime.

As soon as this happened it became necessary to make horns of different sizes, so that the notes available in their individual harmonic series would fit the key of whatever piece of music was to be played. If the key changed radically during a piece of music (in practice it seldom did), then the composer would either stop writing for the horns at this point, or leave a sufficient number of bars rest for the player to put down one instrument and pick up another. It was scarcely a satisfactory situation.

Moreover, the music these early orchestral horns could play in the lower register was limited to isolated notes, and only approached scale-wise steps at a later stage in the harmonic series. Such smooth melodies as the horn could manage had therefore to be pitched rather high, or be content with fanfare-like shapes.

During the 18th century, however, horn players in Bohemia discovered that they could fill in the gaps in the lower parts of the harmonic series by placing the right hand inside the bell of the instrument. The obstruction changed the wave pattern and lowered the pitch. Eventually a systematic technique was worked out for producing a complete scale in the horn's middle register. The player now placed his clenched fist inside the bell and varied

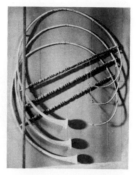

Top: three curved horns which were discovered during the last excavation of Pompeii. **Above:** the French horn was developed from the *trompe de chasse*, used for hunts. Until the 18th century, horns would only play isolated notes in the lower register, but it was then discovered that placing a fist in the bell (**below**) lowered the pitch Moving the fist inside the bell while altering the lips and breath produced notes in middle register.

The Horn

Until the 19th century horn players had to rely on crooks to change the harmonic series. These were removable and were changed whenever necessary during performances. However, they were inconvenient to use, and so valves were introduced to replace them. These enabled the player to switch to a different harmonic series without having to stop playing. This French horn shows the position of the valves which shorten or lengthen the tubing. The mouthpiece of the horn has become more cup-like over the years. Those of traditional instruments are more funnel-shaped. As early as 1639 Cavalli wrote a part for a horn in a hunting scene in one of his operas, and Lully followed his example in 1664.

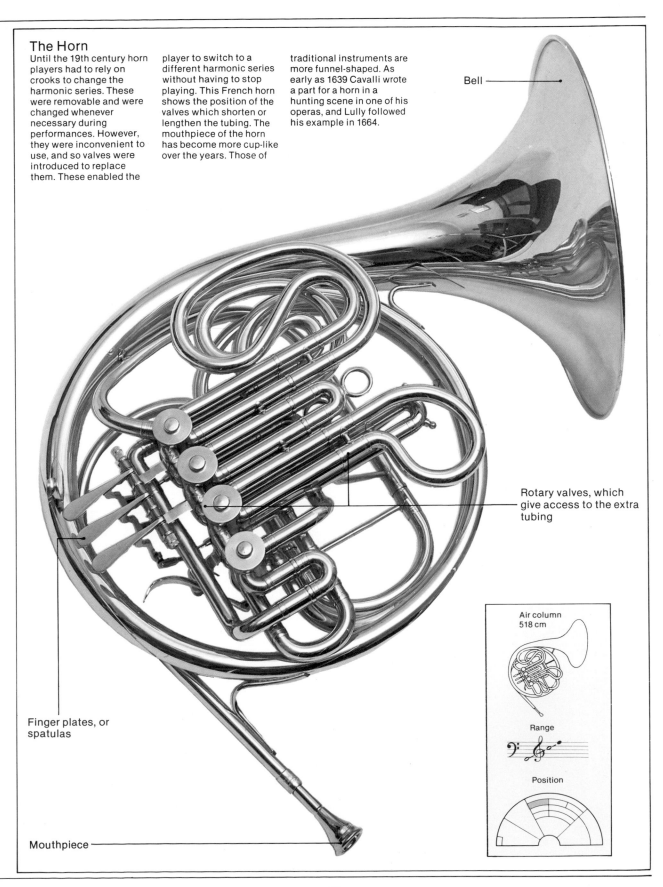

Bell

Rotary valves, which give access to the extra tubing

Finger plates, or spatulas

Mouthpiece

Air column
518 cm

Range

Position

its size by bending his wrist. At the same time he varied also his breath pressure and lip tension, and thus was able to select the notes he needed. The horn, which was originally played with the bell pointing upwards, was now held sideways on to the body – as it is to this day.

Improving the versatility

During the same period attempts were made to produce a single horn with a variable length of tubing. The first solution came with the provision of 'couplers' – pieces of coiled tubing that could be inserted between the body of the instrument and the mouthpiece, so changing the overall length.

The only disadvantage in this method was that the distance between the mouthpiece and the body of the instrument varied according to the number of couplers that had been inserted. This upset the player's technique. Moreover, since the couplers were interchangeable they had to have a cylindrical bore (otherwise they wouldn't fit together). This upset both the tone and intonation, which was based on a tube with a conical bore.

These problems were solved in the middle of the 18th century by the use of couplers that fitted into sockets in the hoop itself – the main tube being cut and specially bent to receive them. The new couplers were called 'crooks'. Separate crooks were made for each new tonality, and each was given the conical bore of the basic instrument. This type of instrument was known as the 'inventionshorn'. It was perfected by the French maker Joseph Raoux in about 1780.

With the use of different crooks for different tonalities it became the custom to treat the horn as a transposing instrument, writing out its part at a pitch that was different from the sound and so leaving each note as a particular harmonic in whatever series had been selected.

The final stages in the improvement of the horn began in about 1820 with the invention of valves. This meant that the player could now switch automatically from one tube-length to another. The crooks were now permanently attached to the instrument, coiled up alongside the main tube, and were brought into play merely by pressing the valve.

The first valves operated like pistons. They are still used today, but most players prefer a later invention, the 'rotary' valve, which is less liable to damage.

Strangely enough, valves were not at first welcomed by horn players, and hand crooks were used well into the 20th century. It is worth noting that players still use their right hands to adjust tone and intonation, just as their forbears did.

The modern horn is a transposing instrument in F (a tube length chosen for its practicality). Its notes are therefore written out a perfect fifth higher than they sound. It has three valves and a total sounding length (including the valves) of about 17ft (518cm), so the available range is considerable.

In recent years a double horn has become common. It combines the F horn and a high B flat horn in one instrument, and has a fourth valve which enables the player to switch from one tube length to the other. The reason for the B flat addition is that this length of tubing has a more brilliant tone and the upper range of harmonics is less tiring to the lips and so easier to produce.

The horn is equally at home providing a warm sustaining harmony in the middle of a score or delivering a lyrical melodic line. It can articulate rapid repeated notes and move about with surprising agility. Its voice is normally warm and soft, but it can produce loud, brassy effects when required. When stopped with the hand (inserted right

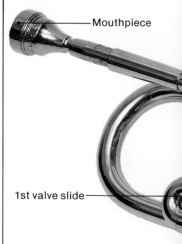

Mouthpiece

1st valve slide

2nd valve slide

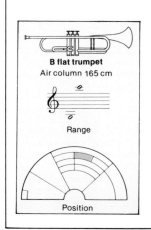

B flat trumpet
Air column 165 cm

Range

Position

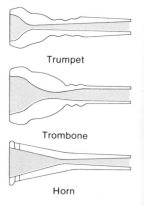

Trumpet

Trombone

Horn

Above: The mouthpieces of the horn, trumpet, and trombone showing their different interior and exterior shapes. The player changes pitch by varying the pressure on the mouthpiece while depressing valves at the same time (**right**).

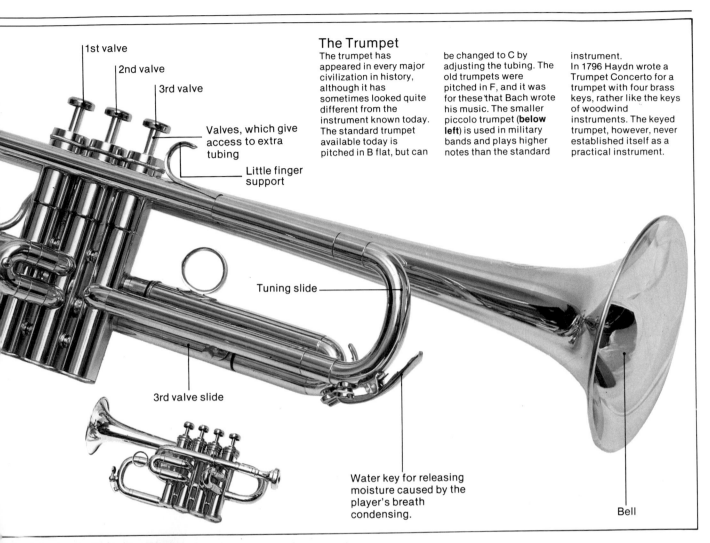

The Trumpet

The trumpet has appeared in every major civilization in history, although it has sometimes looked quite different from the instrument known today. The standard trumpet available today is pitched in B flat, but can be changed to C by adjusting the tubing. The old trumpets were pitched in F, and it was for these that Bach wrote his music. The smaller piccolo trumpet (**below left**) is used in military bands and plays higher notes than the standard instrument.

In 1796 Haydn wrote a Trumpet Concerto for a trumpet with four brass keys, rather like the keys of woodwind instruments. The keyed trumpet, however, never established itself as a practical instrument.

1st valve

2nd valve

3rd valve

Valves, which give access to extra tubing

Little finger support

Tuning slide

3rd valve slide

Water key for releasing moisture caused by the player's breath condensing.

Bell

inside the bell) the sound is vibrant and metallic.

Interesting orchestral horn parts abound, but the works of Richard Strauss, whose father was a horn player, are especially notable – the opening of the symphonic poem *Don Juan* (1888), for example. Mozart's four horn concertos give an excellent idea of what horn playing could be in the 18th century, as Strauss's two concertos (1883 and 1942) do for more recent times.

THE TRUMPET

Although various types of trumpet (made from conch-shells, horn, wood, and even metal) have been used for thousands of years, the instrument as we know it today was developed from the military and ceremonial trumpets of the Renaissance. They were used for sending military signals, and for fanfares to announce the presence of kings and princes – indeed, for a long time the trumpet was regarded as a 'royal' instrument and not to be used for anything so commonplace as the performance of music. In military circles it came to be closely associated with the corps of drums, and when finally it joined the orchestra it tended at first to take an accompanying drum with it.

The Renaissance trumpet consisted of a long cylindrical tube of metal (brass or silver) folded once into a lozenge shape, with a gently-flared bell at the speaking end and a socket for a mouthpiece at the other. The straight tubes were called 'yards', and the joins where the two hair-pin bends began were often concealed by ornamental 'sleeves' or 'garnishes'. The rim of the bell was frequently decorated and signed by the maker. Halfway down the bell there might also be an ornamental boss. By the 17th century the

Until the 19th century trumpets were 'natural' — they had no valves to change keys. They now have three valves (**above**), which lower the pitch of the instrument by two, one or three semitones respectively, and by four, five or six semitones when more than one valve is depressed. The air passes directly through the main tubing when the valves are at rest, but when one is depressed, the air is diverted through an extra piece of tubing, thus lengthening the air column and lowering the pitch.

trumpet normally measured about 7ft (213cm), and therefore produced the harmonic series on D. Though the lowest (fundamental) note of the series was often poor in quality, the other harmonics as far as the sixteenth were brilliant and powerful. The high notes (the so-called *clarino* range) required a special lip position on the mouthpiece which was usually cultivated by specialist players. Orchestral parts in works by Bach and Handel and their contemporaries often feature this style of playing.

Early in the 17th century the trumpet acquired a whole range of crooks (oblong loops of tube) which were inserted between the body of the instrument and the mouthpiece. This enabled it to play in different keys. But, as with the horn crooks, the busi-

ness of changing them by hand was not very convenient.

Towards the end of the 18th century various attempts were made to circumvent this limitation, including, in 1801, the invention of a keyed trumpet. In 17th century England a slide-trumpet (see *Trombone*) was in vogue for a while. But the problem was finally solved with the invention of valves in about 1815, after which date crooks gradually disappeared.

Over the years the preferred pitch of an orchestral trumpet has altered. Today either a transposing instrument in B flat (its notes written a tone higher than they sound) or, more commonly, a non-transposing instrument in C is preferred. The trumpet in C has the more brilliant sound. Not counting the valves, the C trumpet measures 4ft

Mutes (**left**) are fitted into the bells of brass instruments either to reduce the volume or produce an interesting effect. They are made of wood, rubber, metal or plastic. Orchestral mutes have a basic cone shape, but jazz musicians have experimented with more adventurous mutes. Left to right: straight trumpet mute, trumpet and extending tube mute, straight piccolo mute, trombone mute, cup mute and practice mute.

(122cm), and the B flat another 6½in (16.5cm). Many B flat trumpets can be turned into trumpets in A by pulling out a special slide, which adds another 6½in of tube to its sounding length.

Mutes of various kinds have been used with the trumpet since the 17th century. Nowadays they are made in a variety of shapes and materials each producing its own special modification of the trumpet's voice. On the whole, jazz musicians have exploited mutes rather more courageously than orchestral players. Orchestral mutes tend to be the basic hollow cone-shape, which produces a harsh 'squawk' when played loudly, and a soft echo-effect when played quietly.

Though most at ease with fanfare-like passages, the modern trumpet is a versatile instrument capable of anything from lyrical melodic phrases to sharp, stabbing utterances. Chords from three or four trumpets can be especially thrilling. A fine example of orchestral trumpet writing can be found in Janacek's *Sinfonietta* (1926), while Shostakovich's Concerto for Piano, Trumpet and Strings (1933) shows what can be done in the way of effective solo writing.

AUXILIARY TRUMPETS

Small trumpets in D and E flat are now made, both for playing the *clarino* trumpet parts of the early 18th century and for certain modern scores. There is even a B flat sopranino trumpet measuring 2ft 3¼in (69.2cm), but it is used only in military bands.

At the other extreme is the 8ft (244cm) trumpet in C (with crooks in B flat and A) demanded by Wagner for the 'Ring' cycle. This was usually played by a trombonist, using a trombone mouthpiece, and to all intents and purposes it is a valve trombone.

THE CORNET

Really a descendant of the old post horn, this instrument originated in France in about 1825. Usually pitched in B flat, it has a bore that is partly conical and partly cylindrical. It thus shares characteristics of the horn and the trumpet.

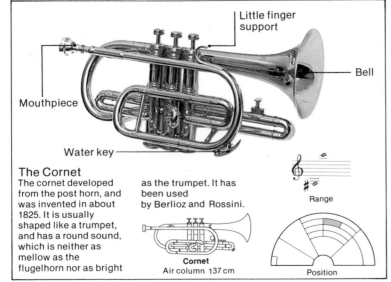

Little finger support

Mouthpiece

Bell

Water key

The Cornet

The cornet developed from the post horn, and was invented in about 1825. It is usually shaped like a trumpet, and has a round sound, which is neither as mellow as the flugelhorn nor as bright as the trumpet. It has been used by Berlioz and Rossini.

Range

Cornet
Air column 137 cm

Position

The Trombone

The trombone derived its name from the Italian for sackbut — *trompone*. The sound is modified by the vibration of the player's lips. Below left: the telescopic slide enables the player to alter the length of the tube, whilst varying his breath pressure, and thereby alter the pitch of the notes he is playing. There are seven playing positions of the slide, and the lowest note is produced when the slide is fully extended. **Below:** an 8 ft (200 cm) tenor trombone. **Right:** a trombone which can play in both B flat and F.

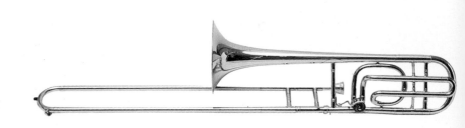

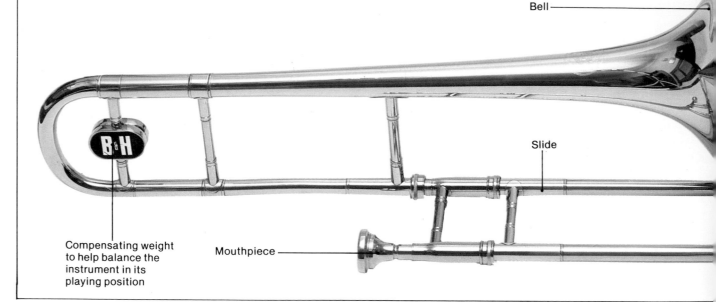

Bell

Slide

Mouthpiece

Compensating weight to help balance the instrument in its playing position

THE TROMBONE

Of all the modern orchestral brass instruments only the trombone arrived on the scene fully equipped to do justice to all the notes of the chromatic scale. It had inherited from its immediate ancestor, the sackbut, the principle of the telescopic slide, which enabled the player to adjust to any length of tube quickly and efficiently. And yet the trombone was not taken into the concert orchestra immediately, simply because its voice had become associated with the solemnity of church music. Apart from an occasional appearance in the theater orchestra, to underline particularly awesome moments in an opera (such as Mozart's *Don Giovanni*), it was not thought to be appropriate for secular music.

The sackbut makes a definite appearance on the musical scene towards the end of the 15th century. The name is probably derived from the French *saquer* (to pull) and *bouter* (to push),

which neatly describes the principle upon which it worked. Two U-shaped tubes were linked at opposite ends to form a flattened 'S'. Where the link took place, one tube slid into the other, and so the overall length of tube could be added to or shortened at will. At the speaking end of the instrument there was a flared bell, and at the playing end a cone-shaped mouthpiece, not unlike that of the modern horn. Such instruments were made in several sizes, and they served as alto, tenor, and bass parts to the shawms. In this way they were used to support the voices in the performance of church music.

With the decline of vocal polyphony the sackbut tended to drop out of favor, serving, for the most part, only in town bands and the like. But at the end of the 18th century its possibilities began to be appreciated by orchestral composers and by the 1820s it was firmly established as a suitable bass for the brass family. The word 'trombone' seems to have been derived from an

Below: a mid-17th century bass sackbut with its characteristic wide bell. Like the horns, the orchestral trombones (**right**) hunt in packs

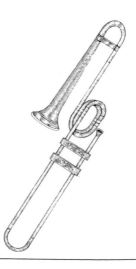

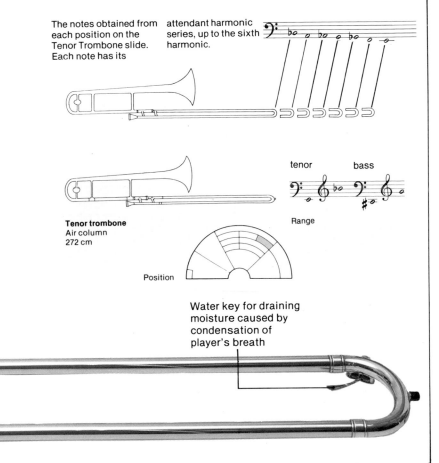

The notes obtained from each position on the Tenor Trombone slide. Each note has its attendant harmonic series, up to the sixth harmonic.

Tenor trombone
Air column
272 cm

tenor   bass

Range

Position

Water key for draining moisture caused by condensation of player's breath

Italian alternative for sackbut: *trompone*. It was adopted when the instrument emerged as a member of the orchestra.

During the 19th century the orchestral trombones existed as a complete family: alto, tenor, and bass. But with the improvement of the trumpet, the alto trombone began to be replaced by a second tenor. Standard practice now designates the trombone section as two tenors (in B flat) and a bass (in F or G). Indeed, the bass trombone may very well be a tenor with an 'F attachment' – that is to say, an extra length of tubing that can be brought into action by means of a valve. The sounding length of the tenor trombone is 8ft 11in (272cms). The player moves his slide through seven positions, each one corresponding to a semitone: B flat, A, A flat, G, F sharp, F natural, and E.

Trombones are made of metal, with a cylindrical tube that becomes conical at the bell end, widening to about 7in (17.8cm) across. The mouthpiece is cup-shaped and about twice as deep as the trumpet's.

Trombones provide a sonorous bass to the brass section, with a tone quality that can range from a soft glow to an intensely dramatic outburst. Mutes add a rather sinister color to the low register. Though they are perfectly well able to play solo melodies, trombones tend to hunt in threes, supplying solid harmonic backgrounds to more fluent

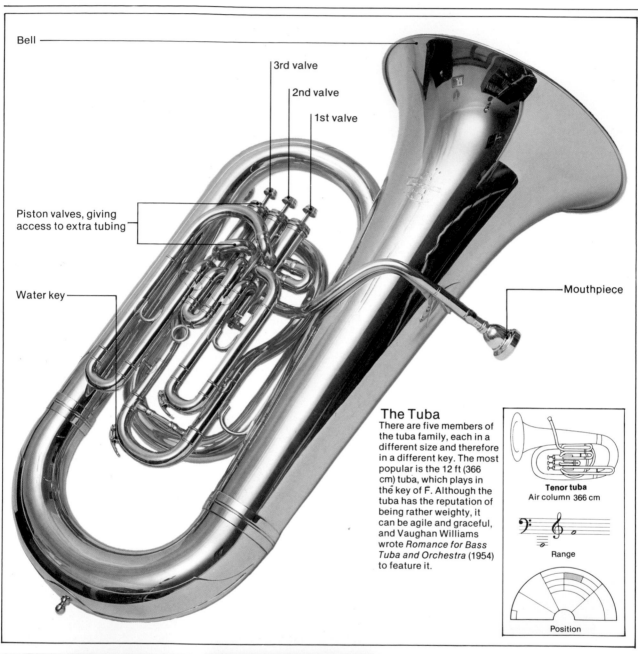

Bell

3rd valve

2nd valve

1st valve

Piston valves, giving access to extra tubing

Water key

Mouthpiece

The Tuba

There are five members of the tuba family, each in a different size and therefore in a different key. The most popular is the 12 ft (366 cm) tuba, which plays in the key of F. Although the tuba has the reputation of being rather weighty, it can be agile and graceful, and Vaughan Williams wrote *Romance for Bass Tuba and Orchestra* (1954) to feature it.

Tenor tuba
Air column 366 cm

Range

Position

Aside from its role in the orchestra, the tuba is often played in military bands (**far left**), where it originated. In essence, it is a large bugle.
Left: a tuba (right of picture) resting on an Austrian grave with other large brass instruments.

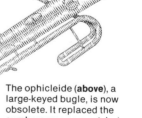

The ophicleide (**above**), a large-keyed bugle, is now obsolete. It replaced the cumbersome serpent, but was itself superseded by the tuba.

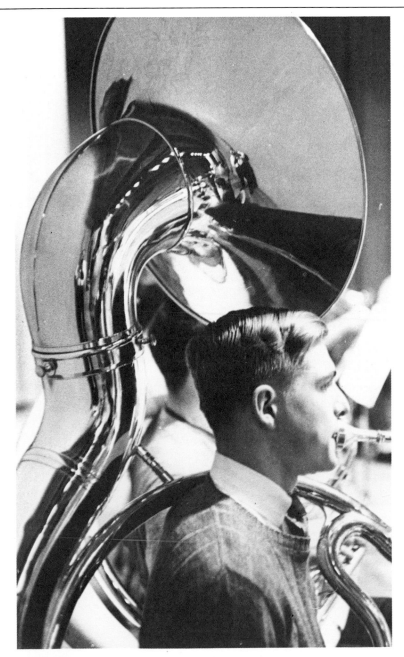

Orchestrally they can be heard to advantage in almost any of the larger 19th and 20th century scores – Strauss's *Alpine Symphony* (1915), or either of Elgar's two symphonies (1908 and 1911) are good examples, as is the chorale in the introduction to the last movement of Brahms' First Symphony.

THE TUBA

Properly speaking, the tuba is not one instrument but a whole family ranging from tenor to contrabass sizes. They first appeared in German military bands in the 1820s, but nobody seems to know who invented them. They are, in effect, large bugles, equipped with valves. They have a wide conical bore, which expands into a large flared bell. They are held with the bell pointing upwards.

Orchestral tubas come in five sizes: the 9ft (274cm) B flat, the 12ft (366cm) F, the 14ft (427cm) E flat, the 16ft (488cm) C, and the 18ft (549cm) B flat. A player selects whichever seems best suited to the music he has to play. The most generally used is the 12ft tuba in F.

Though even less likely as a candidate for concertos than the trombone, the tuba has occasionally been featured as a virtuoso soloist. The only major composer to write what amounts to a concerto for this instrument is Vaughan Williams, whose *Romance for Bass Tuba and Orchestra* was first performed in 1954.

Tubas also go by other names. The 9ft B flat is usually called the Euphonium, and the 12ft F the Bombardon. The 16ft C tuba is the lowest of the so-called Wagner Tubas – a family of two tenors and two basses designed by Wagner for the 'Ring' cycle, but sounding more like horns than the usual tuba. The 18ft B flat tuba is used mainly in military bands, where it is known as the Double B flat Bass.

THE OPHICLEIDE

In the 19th century bass parts were often played by the ophicleide, an instrument which is now obsolete and replaced by the tuba. A whole family existed, from alto to contrabass (called the *ophicleide monstre*). In shape they resembled large metal bassoons, ending with a slightly flared bell and equipped with padded keys to close their rather large note holes.

moving parts elsewhere in the orchestra. They should not be thought of as cumbersome instruments, however. When the need arises they can be as fleet as any. Because of their slide mechanism they are adept at gliding between notes (*glissando*) with a smooth, uninterrupted sound. But this effect can be overdone, and when played loud it has all the vulgarity and nuisance value of a 'raspberry'!

Trombones are not natural concerto soloists, though there is, for example, a very interesting *Ballade for Trombone and Orchestra* by Frank Martin (1940).

The massive sousaphone (**above**), is a form of brass tuba, and is recognizable by its enormous bell. In spite of its size, it is a popular member of marching military bands, and was first made for the American composer and band conductor John Philip Sousa in 1899, after whom it was named. Both bass and contralto sousaphones are still played today.

The Percussion Section

*T*HE PERCUSSION section of the orchestra (known in the trade as the 'kitchen' department) is now so vast that it is probably best to think of it in terms of two main sections, each with its subdivisions. First come the standard percussion. Instruments that are frequently required and therefore *basic* to the percussion section include: timpani, snare drum, bass drum, cymbals, triangle, tambourine, wood block, tamtam, glockenspiel, celesta and xylophone. Standard instruments that are required only occasionally and are therefore *additional* to the basic group include: castanets, tenor drum, bells, antique cymbals, vibraphone and piano.

The second section is known as the auxiliary percussion. Its exotic instruments, often of oriental and Latin-American origin, include: maracas, claves, güiro, bongós, timbales, tomtom and temple blocks. Auxiliary instruments that are really 'sound effects' include: sleigh bells, sandblock, rattle, whip, cowbells, anvil, wind machine and thunder sheet.

The origin of percussion instruments presumably goes back to the moment when primitive man first beat out a rhythm on a hollow tree trunk – either for the sheer pleasure of the noise he made, or as a means of communicating over a greater distance than his voice could reach. Almost all the instruments we shall consider in this chapter enjoyed a long and active existence in music-making before they joined the orchestra. Indeed, the surprising thing is that they had to wait so long before gaining admittance.

The first to be accepted were the timpani, or kettledrums. They joined the orchestra at the beginning of the 18th century, together with the trumpets – both on loan from the army. Trumpets and drums tended to go together because both were the prerogative of the cavalry and, since the king always led the cavalry in battle, they were essentially 'royal' instruments used for fanfares and signals.

Towards the end of the 18th century new percussion instruments made an appearance as the result of a craze for 'Turkish' music. These were cymbals, triangles, bass drum, tambourine, and the forerunners of the glockenspiel, as used by the famous Janissary Bands. They came into the orchestra as exotics,

The percussion section (**above**) usually sits at the back of the orchestra in the center, behind the brass section. Although kettledrums, cymbals, tambourines and triangles were introduced into the orchestra in the 1700s, and some exotic instruments in the 1800s, it was not until the 20th century that the percussion section of the orchestra really came into its own. **Right:** Fibreglass timps being made at the Premier drum factory, Leicester, England.

but opened the way to an understanding of percussion instruments as more than mere noise makers.

A more extensive use of percussion came in the 19th century as composers increasingly explored the possibilities of descriptive, program music. Often it was a matter of adding 'local color' to a score – a piece in Spanish dance rhythm, for example, would naturally call for castanets and tambourines, while an 'oriental' piece would require gongs and bells, and temple blocks. The real breakthrough, however, came in the 20th century when composers began to explore complex rhythms for the first time. In the music of such composers as Bartók and Stravinsky it is the percussive, rhythmic element that is new and exciting, and consequently the percussion department that comes into its own. In many contemporary scores the percussion is all-important and virtually dominates the sound.

THE TIMPANI

Though usually called by their Italian name, these are the kettledrums. They are shaped like large copper cauldrons with a skin stretched tightly over the open top. Never fewer than two are used at a time, so whatever the language their name is in the plural. Initially the two drums were tuned to the tonic and dominant degrees of whatever key the piece was in – that is, the first and fifth notes of the scale (since one or other of them would blend in with most of the harmonies

Kettledrums are a legacy from the army, and joined the orchestra with the trumpet — also from the army. They are played with sticks, which are covered in different materials, such as felt, sponge or wood, according to the sound required.

The Timpani

Today, the kettledrum is tuned with a pedal, which automatically tightens the skin of the drum and therefore increases the pitch. This is an improvement on the old system, where the player had to tune his drum by hand using screws attached to the body of the drum. This meant that he had to stop playing every time he wished to change pitch, and also that composers had to allow for this rest when they wanted a change of tuning. The pitch of each drum is directly related to the diameter of the drum head. Each drum has a range of about five notes. Very small drums are available which can take the pitch up to D, but they lack the resonance and sonority of the characteristic timpani and are not often used.

Drum head

Tuning gauge

Shell

Struts

'Crown'

Pedal

Position

Range

83 cm   78 cm   71 cm   64 cm   57 cm

likely to be used). Nowadays three or four drums are regularly called for, and their pitches are changed frequently during the course of a movement.

The kettledrum is a tuned instrument. Until quite recent times the stretched calfskin which formed the drum 'head' was held in place by a wooden hoop, over which was fitted a metal counter-hoop. This metal hoop could be raised and lowered by means of a set of screws (usually eight) attached to the body or 'shell' of the drum. The screws had T-shaped handles which, when turned, would force the metal hoop over the wooden hoop and stretch the skin more tightly over the open mouth of the drum. The greater the tension this action produced, the higher the pitch.

The same principle is used today, but to save the time taken by having to turn each screw laboriously by hand a mechanism has been introduced which does the job automatically, and accurately, when a pedal is pressed. The player no longer has to put down his drum sticks, but can change the pitch of the instrument even as he plays. And composers no longer have to leave a sufficient number of bars rest when calling for a change of tuning.

The timpani are played with a variety of sticks, depending on the type of sound the composer requires. The handles are wooden, and the heads are covered in various materials – felt, flannel, cotton thread, wood, cork, sponge – and come in a number of different sizes. Hard sticks call forth a louder and more sharply defined sound than soft sticks.

The timps are accustomed to playing single notes and complex groups of notes of different pitches and rhythms, as well as thunderous rolls. The mechanical 'pedal' timps can produce a *glissando* effect – the pitch sliding from one note to another while the instrument is being played. An example of the timps actually playing a 'tune' can be heard in the percussion variation of Britten's *Young Person's Guide to the Orchestra* (1946), while Bartók's *Sonata for Two Pianos and Percussion* (1937) gives a good idea of the very considerable range of sounds these instruments are capable of.

At least two timps are played at one time (**above**), and they can either play single notes or complex groups of notes of different pitches and rhythms. Changing the pitch of the drums while playing them, using the metal pedal, produces a glissando effect. They can be used to generate rhythm, and are very effective when adding emphasis and color to music.

THE BASS DRUM

A large drum with two heads, varying in size from about 24in (60cm) across to 36in (90cm). The most common has a diameter of 30in (75cm). The shell between the two heads is about 16in (40cm) wide, and the instrument is supported on a special stand in an upright position. The player usually strikes it from the right hand side. Although it is not a tuned instrument as such, the two heads have to be 'tuned' in another sense – that is to say, adjusted so as to respond sympathetically to each other and thus produce the best resonance.

The bass drumstick has a wooden handle and a fairly soft head, often made of felt. The stroke produces a very resonant sound which has to be 'stopped' by the player dampening it with his hand if it is not to continue too long. For a very short note, the player has to damp the drum head with his left hand while he strikes it. A roll on the bass drum is effected by using two sticks. When played loud it can be overwhelming. Special effects are obtained by using different kinds of drum stick, including wire brushes. Powerful as the bass drum is, its impact is in inverse proportion to the number of times it is used. A single stroke can be magic – a great many, a bore.

THE SNARE DRUM

Although there are various types and sizes of snare drum they have one feature in common, and it is this that gives them their name. They have two heads. The upper one is used for playing, but across the underside of the lower head is stretched a set of gut strings. These are the 'snares'. They vibrate when the drum is beaten and give a dry rattle to the stroke.

Snare drums are also frequently called 'side drums' – a reference to their military origins, when they were carried at the player's right side.

The snare drum cannot be tuned, but the different sizes that exist all have their characteristic pitch and so, to some extent, can be used for different effects. The basic 'note' of the snare drum is rather high. The snares themselves can be loosened by means of a lever (their normal position when the drum is not in use). This procedure lowers the pitch and produces a hollow sound that is very effective. When this

Standard percussion instruments

These instruments all belong to the standard percussion. The bass drum is supported by a special stand, and is struck from the right. It produces very effective drum rolls and adds to the atmosphere and excitement in an orchestral piece. Snare drums are able to produce either a hollow sound if the snares are loose, or dry rattles, if they are tightened. Cymbals are round plates made of brass alloy which are either clashed together or suspended singly on stands and struck with sticks. Tambourines are really small drums which are either shaken or tapped producing a sense of rhythmic urgency.

Snare drum

Tambourines

Bass drum

Cymbals

is required the composer directs the instruments to play *senza corde* or *scordato* ('without snares').

The most common drum sticks are made of hardwood (hickory, usually), and have oval tips. Sticks with felt tips are sometimes used; and wire brushes, which induce a whispering, shuffling sound. The standard snare drum is about 14–15in (35–38cm) in diameter and about 6in (15cm) deep.

Crisp, rhythmic figures are the bread and butter of snare drums, together with prolonged rolls – starting quietly and growing to a forceful climax. It is, however, a mistake to think of any drum merely as a noisemaker. Played quietly they can be even more effective.

Chinese gong

The Chinese gong is best used when it is struck softly but repeatedly, producing a ripple which builds into a crescendo. Triangles are used economically in the orchestra, but produce a penetrating bell-like note with no definite pitch.

Triangle

Left: Snare drums in use during a recording session. They are usually played with wooden drum sticks, but can also be struck with felt-tipped sticks or wire brushes.

loud, however.

A single cymbal suspended on a special stand may be struck with various types of drum stick, or stroked with a wire brush, or rolled with soft timpani sticks.

Tactfully used, the cymbals can add greatly to the sense of excitement at a climax.

THE TRIANGLE

A thick steel rod bent into the shape of an equilateral triangle, but left open at one corner. The average triangle measures about 6½in (16.5cm) on the side. The triangle is held suspended from a loop of string and struck with a small metal beater in the remaining closed corner. Trills are possible if the beater is moved rapidly back and forth in the angle. The sound is high, clear, and very penetrating, but it has no definite pitch. Since it now sounds rather like a telephone bell, the triangle must be used very sparingly. This is a limitation which 19th century composers (such as Dvořák) were unfortunately unable to anticipate!

THE TAMBOURINE

A small drum, about 10in (25cm) in diameter, with a single calfskin head and a narrow wooden shell. In the shell are a number of slots in which are fixed pairs of thin brass disks called 'jingles'. These tinkle when the tambourine is shaken or struck.

There are four main ways of playing this instrument. First, by holding it by the rim in the left hand and striking it with the right hand knuckles, fingertips, fist, or back of the hand, or tapping it against the knee.

The tambourine can also be shaken in the air. This is called a 'jingle roll'. Then again it may be laid on the player's lap and rolled with fingers or drumsticks – the strokes being made near the rim.

Finally, the tip of the player's thumb may be moistened and run round the rim of the tambourine, causing a delicate trill from both the head and the jingles.

Tambourine effects can add sparkle to an orchestral *tutti* and a bright festive atmosphere to the rhythms. They are by no means limited to music of a Spanish or Italian flavor, though it was largely for this purpose that tambourines entered the orchestra. A very

THE CYMBALS

A pair of round plates made of brass alloy. They are slightly convex, and the center portion of each disk is a raised dome with a hole in the middle, through which passes the leather strap the player holds. The best are usually made in Turkey, and the symphony orchestra carries them in two sizes: 15in (38cm) and 18in (46cm) across. The normal cymbal stroke is a clash – the two plates being brought together in a swinging, brushing movement (and not head on, which merely sounds like a fallen tea tray!). The sound will continue to vibrate unless damped by the player holding the plates to his side. The two-plate stroke need not be effective use of the instrument can be heard in the second movement of Berlioz's *Romeo and Juliet* symphony (1839).

THE WOOD BLOCK

Of Chinese origin (and sometimes called the Chinese block) this is an oblong of wood which has a slot cut in the side to form a resonating cavity. Tapped with a wooden stick or mallet, it gives a hard, high-pitched 'toc toc' sound. Though of indefinite pitch, the sound varies with the size of the block – 6½, 7½, and 8in (16.5, 19 and 20cm) sizes being the most common.

THE TAMTAM

A type of gong. A large disk of bronze alloy, either flat or saucer-shaped, with a shallow rim round the edge. Orchestral tamtams are made in various sizes from about 18in (46cm) across to 36in (91cm) or more. When struck softly in the center, a deep clear sound emerges. When struck forcefully at the rim, the sound is rather harsh and discordant. The larger tamtams give out their best sounds when struck quietly and repeatedly so that a powerful *crescendo* gradually builds up like ripples spreading over a pond.

The true Chinese gong (often wrongly called a tamtam) is made of a much heavier bronze alloy and has a much deeper rim. The center is usually beaten out into a dome. The sound is much more powerful than that of the tamtam.

THE GLOCKENSPIEL

The 'bell play' is, as its German name suggests, a set of thirty oblong steel plates of different sizes, arranged like a piano keyboard and mounted in a case.

The glockenspiel is played with small mallets, with heads of various materials, such as hard and soft rubber, yarn, wood, and metal. The tone is silvery and bell-like. The origin of the glockenspiel goes back to a military instrument called the 'Jingling Johnny' – a set of tuned metal plates carried in an ornamental frame on a pole.

THE XYLOPHONE

Similar to the glockenspiel, except that the bars are made of rosewood.

The notes sound an octave higher

The xylophone

The xylophone probably originated in prehistoric times, when players laid the wooden bars across their legs. Today, it consists of two rows of wooden bars suspended over hollow tube resonators. The most common orchestral versions have a range of 3½ to 4 octaves. They can be struck with sticks of varying hardness.

Range

The Glockenspiel

The glockenspiel consists of two rows of graduated steel bars arranged like the keys of a piano. It has a range of 2½ octaves and is played with fairly hard beaters to produce a bell-like tone. It is available in three sizes, and the notes sound an octave higher than they are written. It was originally a military instrument.

Range

Bells
Tubular bells are made of either brass or steel and are used in the orchestra in the place of real bells. Standard sets of bells have 18 tubes The tubes are struck near the top and dampened if necessary with a mechanism operated by the foot.

Range

BELLS

Since real bells are not very practical in an orchestral setting, substitutes are used in the form of steel tubes of various lengths, hung in a wooden frame and played with a small hammer. The player strikes the tube at a point near the top.

CASTANETS

An instrument from Spain, which consists of two small hardwood shells (ebony or rosewood). They are used in pairs of different sizes. A string passing through holes at the end of the castanets is wound round the player's thumb and second finger and the two shells are clicked together. They are used mainly to suggest a Spanish atmosphere, but they are found in many other parts of the world and are of very ancient origin.

There are also castanets which are hinged to the end of a stick, so that they can be shaken like a rattle.

VIBRAPHONE

Similar to the glockenspiel, but with a resonating tube fixed beneath each steel plate. The tube is tuned to the note of the steel plate. At the top of the tube there is a small disk which is made to revolve by an electric motor. This gives an added *vibrato* to the note and creates a gentle, pulsing sound. Though used mainly in dance bands (it was an American invention of the 1920s) a few modern orchestral works call for it – even though its rather over-sweet tones do not blend very well with ordinary orchestral sounds. A pleasant example of its use can be found in Walton's Cello Concerto (1957).

than they are written. As with the glockenspiel, mallets with round heads of varying degrees of hardness are used. Modern instruments are often furnished with resonators (short hollow tubes, set beneath the wooden bars) which add a hollow clop clop effect. Saint-Saëns' famous *Danse Macabre* (1874) makes effective use of the xylophone's boney voice.

THE CELESTA

A set of small steel bars which are struck by hammers operated from a keyboard and housed in what looks like a small upright piano. It was invented by Auguste Mustel and patented in Paris in 1886. As each steel bar rests on a small resonating box, the celesta's tone is much softer than the glockenspiel's. Tchaikovsky was the first composer to use the sound seriously, in his ballet *Casse Noisette* (1892)

Castanets (**above**) are traditionally held in the hand but can also be attached to a stick and shaken like a rattle. Wood blocks (**below**) have no definite pitch but their sound varies according to the size.

PIANO

Though not generally considered a percussion instrument by those who pride themselves on the poetic, singing qualities of their playing, this in fact is what the piano is: a series of hammers operated from a keyboard which strikes a set of strings arranged in different lengths and sizes according to the chromatic scale. The piano is used in certain 20th century scores purely as an addition to the percussion department – for example, Aaron Copland's *El Salón México* (1937). The effect is very distinc-

The piano is involved with the symphony orchestra almost exclusively as a solo instrument, and the acclaim accorded to piano soloists such as Svyatoslav Richter (**above**) is equalled only by that given to conductors and violinists. Scientifically, the piano remains,however, a percussion instrument, and many 20th century composers have treated it as part of the orchestra. In such cases its role is often percussive.

tive, partly because the tuning of all keyboard instruments is fixed and cannot be adjusted during performance (unlike wind, brass, and strings). The sound therefore stands out very slightly from the general blend of the orchestra.

Apart from the timpanist, who remains solidly with his instruments, the percussion player will generally move from one instrument to another during the course of a piece of music. He must therefore be ready to tackle anything and everything that can be classed as a percussion instrument. This can include many bits and pieces that are extremely exotic, and some that are scarcely instruments at all.

ANTIQUE CYMBALS

Small brass disks of various sizes, rather like miniature cymbals. They are made in pairs and struck gently together. The note is delicate and clear, like a small bell. If two different notes are required in quick succession, two players are needed. Antique cymbals are intended to be replicas of an instrument known to the ancient Greeks.

Incorporating the exotic

A collection of ethnic instruments which are used in the Western orchestra. In addition to the well-known timbales (tom-toms), maracas, claves and bongos are the more unusual instruments such as the güiro, which is a dry gourd from South America, and talking drums from Africa, which are beaten with a curved stick. African cocktail drums are a modern version of the congas.

Cocktail drums

Talking drum

Bongos

Maracas

Claves

Güiro

These instruments are not used in Western orchesatras, but are closely related to ones which are. **1:** Finger cymbals, known as *gerbats*, in the National Folklore Festival of Marrakesh. **2:** Steel drums being played during the Port of Spain Carnival in Trinidad, West Indies. **3:** A Himalayan village band in the Marsyengdi Valley, Nepal. **4:** A Spanish flamenco dancer using hand castanets. **5:** A Gamelan orchestra at a cremation in Bali, Indonesia. **6:** A metallophone being played at a wireless station in Bandoeng, Java.

AUXILIARY PERCUSSION

Maracas
A pair of gourds mounted on stick handles. They contain dry seeds, which rattle when the gourds are shaken. They are of South American origin.

Claves
Two short round hardwood sticks (usually cocabola). One is held in the hollow of the left hand, so that when it is struck with the other it produces a resonant 'toc-toc' sound.

Güiro
A large oval gourd which has notches cut in the surface. When these are scraped with a stick, a dry rasping sound emerges. The güiro comes from South America.

Bongós
A pair of small single-headed drums. Some are conical and some cylindrical in shape. They are fixed together horizontally and either held between the knees or mounted on a special stand. They are beaten with the bare hands, and produce a high and a low note of indefinite pitch. They come from Cuba.

Timbales
Also called tom-toms. A pair of single-headed drums, fixed to a stand and played with drumsticks. They are slightly larger than bongós and have a fairly high pitch. They came into Western music in the 1920s as an imitation of native African drums.

Chinese tom-tom
A small lacquer-shelled drum with upper and lower heads made of pig-skin. It is played with hard and soft drumsticks.

Temple Blocks
A set of five round wooden blocks mounted on a rail. They are usually lacquered red, and have slots cut in the side. When hit with felt-headed mallets they produce a hollow sound, rather like that of a gourd.

Indian tom-tom
Similar to the Chinese tom-tom, but with only one playing head, which is fixed over a wooden bowl.

Sleigh bells
Hollow round metal bells about an inch (2.5cm) in diameter, each with a

loose metal ball inside. They are usually attached to a leather strap in sets of ten different sizes. When shaken they jingle merrily. Special orchestral models exist with the bells fixed to a long steel frame with a wooden handle. With these the player can obtain a more precise rhythm.

Sandblock
Two blocks of wood with strips of sandpaper stretched over them. When rubbed together they produce a dry, shuffling sound.

Rattle
A cog-rattle, like those used by enthusiastic football supporters: a hard resonant blade of wood is fixed in a frame in such a way as to click against the teeth of a cog when revolved.

Whip
Also called the 'slap stick'. Two flat pieces of wood, hinged at one end. When slapped together they imitate the crack of a whip.

Cowbells
Usually authentic cowbells with the clapper removed. They come in various sizes and are hung from a leather strap and played with a snare drum stick. They suggest an alpine atmosphere. Instrument makers produce an 'orchestral' model in which the bells are more triangular in shape and are mounted on a stand in sets of four.

Anvil
A large metal block, usually suspended and struck with a hammer. The 'clunk' varies with the type of hammer head being used. Anvils are sometimes placed on a piece of felt, though this damps the sound somewhat.

Wind Machine
A large wooden cylinder with slats, fixed in a frame. When the cylinder is revolved the slats brush against a sheet of silk and produce a swishing sound which rises to a whistle as the speed increases. Nowadays electronically produced wind-sounds are generally preferred. They are pre-recorded.

Thunder sheet
A large piece of tin which buckles and crumples when shaken and so produces a thunder effect. Richard Strauss uses a 'thunder machine' in his *Alpine Symphony* (1915) which consists of a

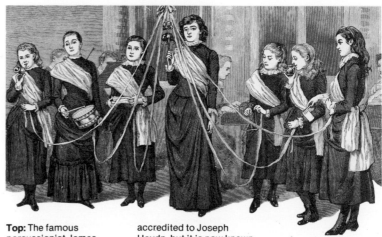

Top: The famous percussionist James Blades with some of the instruments used to play *The Toy Symphony*. This work has been mistakenly accredited to Joseph Haydn, but it is now known to have been written by Leopold Mozart, with the toy instruments probably added by Michael Haydn.

Above: A performance of the symphony by children of the Royal Asylum of St Anne, Redhill (1887).

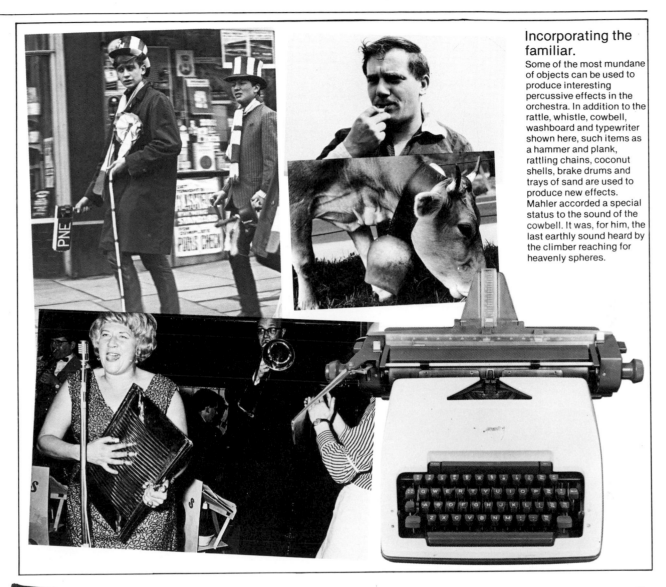

Incorporating the familiar.

Some of the most mundane of objects can be used to produce interesting percussive effects in the orchestra. In addition to the rattle, whistle, cowbell, washboard and typewriter shown here, such items as a hammer and plank, rattling chains, coconut shells, brake drums and trays of sand are used to produce new effects. Mahler accorded a special status to the sound of the cowbell. It was, for him, the last earthly sound heard by the climber reaching for heavenly spheres.

Special sets of sleigh bells (**top**) are made for orchestral use, but authentic cowbells are used.

number of heavy balls inside a revolving drum. As with the wind machine, recordings of thunder can be used instead.

Miscellaneous

Sirens, motor horns, typewriters, whistles, washboards, musical saws, and virtually anything that can produce an unusual sound have been pressed into service by 20th century composers desperate to make a novel, if ephemeral, effect. The development of electronic methods of making strange sounds, however, has left these expedients behind. It is now possible not only to record ordinary sounds and then distort them in various ways (speeding them up, slowing them down, playing them backwards, and so on), but also to create entirely new sounds.

Unfortunately, weird sounds rapidly become clichés – especially when they are taken up by 'space-odyssey' films and radio plays. Unless carefully and imaginatively handled, they can rebound on the serious composer – so that what was initially a delightful surprise rapidly becomes a deadly bore. Moreover, it is hard to make them fit into the living world of orchestral sound without some slight feeling of incongruity.

The great hunting ground for percussion sounds is, of course, among 20th century composers. Some have already been mentioned, but the following works may also be found very interesting: Karlheinz Stockhausen's *Kontakte*, Jean Barraqué's *Chant après Chant*, and Carlos Chávez's *Toccata for Percussion*.

The Orchestral Full Score

HE ORCHESTRAL full score is the composer's blueprint for the correct performance of his work. In it the music that each instrument is to play is laid out in such a way that the relationship between the various parts is clear and unmistakable. The score is a detailed picture of what the sound should be.

Although nowadays there is universal agreement as to what a full score should look like – especially with regard to the order in which the instruments appear on the printed page – it was not always so. The standard score as we know it did not begin to emerge until the middle of the 19th century, when the printing and publishing of orchestral scores finally became common practice.

In the 18th century, when most full scores remained in manuscript, the order in which instruments appeared varied very considerably from country to country, and even from composer to composer. In England and Germany, for example, the tendency was to place brass and drum parts at the top of the page, with oboes and flutes beneath, and then violin and viola parts. Next came parts for voices (if there were any) and finally the string bass part – which, in practice, was also likely to be doubled by bassoons, even if this was not actually stated in the part. In Italy and France, however, the violins and violas came to the top of the page, with flutes and oboes beneath, and brass below them. Vocal parts and bass line came last – the only feature that most scores had in common, doubtless because the keyboard-director would be expected to play his continuo part from the full score, and therefore needed the bass line and vocal parts near together so that he could cue-in the singers more easily.

The major point at issue in organizing the orchestral full score seems to have been whether it was better to keep instruments together in their family groups, or whether all high-sounding instruments should appear at the top of the page and all low-sounding ones at the bottom. In the end it was the family group system that won, and modern scores print the instruments in the order shown in the score example (p.107).

Pairs of instruments, such as first and second flutes, or instruments that play as a body, as do the violins, share a single stave – even if they are playing different notes or are divided. A second stave is only necessary if the parts are so independent and complicated that it would be confusing to try to cram them on one line. Where there are two independent parts on one stave, the 'first' instrument has its notes printed with the tails pointing upwards, and the second' with tails pointing downwards.

The four horns occupy two staves, unless their music is so complicated as to require one stave each. Instruments such as the harp and piano also need two staves. Tuned percussion instruments have their notes at the correct pitch on a stave, but untuned percussion parts may be printed as a rhythm on a single line, or be confined to one particular pitch on a stave.

Information about the manner of playing also appears in the full score. At the very beginning of each movement or section an indication is given of the speed and general mood of the piece. Convention puts this in Italian – though some scores, irritatingly, prefer the national language (which may be all very well if it is English, French, or German, but not so helpful if it happens to be something like Swedish or Hungarian!) Information about the dynamics of each note and its exact nuance is also given.

Major changes of speed or mood that affect all the instruments are printed at the top of each page above the flute

In the extract (**left**) the "*p*" tells us that the note is to be played *piano*, the hairpin ⊏ that the music is to get louder until it is eventually *forte* ('f'). The dot beneath the note heads shows that the notes must be played in a crisp 'staccato' manner, and the curved lines that each group should be played with one stroke of the bow.

part, and also above the strings (and sometimes above the brass section), in the manner of the first such indication at the beginning of a movement. Here too, at irregular intervals throughout the score, appears either a series of letters or a series of numbers. These are 'cues' which enable the conductor to pick up the music again if he has had to stop during a rehearsal. The same cues appear in the individual parts from which the instrumentalists play. Thus all the conductor need say is "Begin five bars after letter R", and everybody knows precisely where they are. Imagine how impossible it would be if the only reference he could give was something like "Begin at bar two hundred and three"! Very occasionally you find each bar laboriously numbered in this way, and then, of course, the number reference can be taken up.

A page of a typical orchestral full score, the slow movement of Parry's Symphony in E minor, beautifully engraved by Novello & Co in 1912, is shown on p. 107.

Although Parry's signs and directions may seem to lay down the manner of performance in great detail, it must always be remembered that musical notation is only precise up to a point. A composer may ask for a passage to be played *forte*, but he cannot say exactly how loud that *forte* is to be. It will vary with each performance, and even with each concert hall (a small room will not take a large sound as kindly as a large one). A *crescendo* may be required, but how exactly should it be graded? There are a thousand decisions of this sort that must be left to the conductor. The score may be a blueprint, but it is a blueprint that has to be *interpreted*.

When reading a full score, the following pointers may be helpful in finding your way about.

In the woodwind section the flutes, oboes and clarinets use the treble clef. The bassoon uses the bass clef, but sometimes, if it climbs very high, it changes to a tenor clef. The clarinet will always have a different key signature from the others, because it is a transposing instrument.

In the brass section, horns and trumpets use the treble clef. Horns also use the bass clef for their lower notes. As may be expected, tenor trombones use the tenor clef and bass trombones use the bass clef. Tubas remain with the bass clef, and their music is sometimes printed on the same stave as the bass trombone. Trumpets are transposing instruments and therefore have a key signature which is different from the key of the piece (unless they are 'C' trumpets, as in the Parry example page 107). Horns, however, use no key signature whatsoever, even though they are transposing instruments. This convention makes their lines easy to spot. It also means that their notation must be adjusted as it goes along – for it is still written five notes higher than it sounds.

In the string section, the violins use the treble clef, and the cellos and basses the bass clef (note, however, that the basses sound an octave lower than they are written). The viola uses the alto clef, and sometimes, for its higher notes, the treble clef.

Timpani appear at the required pitch in the bass clef; and the untuned percussion may be written either as a rhythm on a single line, or as a rhythm on certain fixed notes in the stave.

When reading a score it is best to let the eye 'scan' the page and pick up general information about what is happening and not try to concentrate on any one part at a time. Gradually the eye will grow accustomed to hopping from one important line to another as the dominant musical ideas appear in the different instruments. Practice first with a record and a simple score – a Haydn, Mozart or early Beethoven symphony, say. In works of this period the main burden will be taken by the strings, with woodwind and brass making only an occasional interjection on their own account. You can then move to more complicated scores.

Parts

Orchestral players do not, of course, play from a full score but from individual parts. These are single lines of music that reproduce all the notes exactly as they appear in the full score, except that a group of several consecutive bars rest will not be printed as individual bars but as one large bar with a number over it to indicate how many actual bars it is supposed to represent. If there are a great many bars rest at this point (as is often the case with percussion instruments) a 'cue' is given just before the player is to come in – a few notes from another instrumental part, such as will be very audible to the waiting player.

The key to Clefs

Clefs are simply signs that show how the set of five lines and four spaces that make up the 'stave' are to be read — that is to say, which line or space corresponds to which note in sound. Between them the treble and bass clefs cover the main range of notes in general use.

Middle C

Middle C

Middle C

The choice of clef is merely a convenience which enables notes to be written within the stave without having to go outside it too often.

Key to the full score example:

1. List of instruments used in this particular work, printed in Italian.
2. Clefs – the 'key' to each stave, telling you which lines and spaces represent which notes.
3. Time signature. The upper number shows how many beats there are in each bar, and the lower number the type of beat – in this case a crotchet. The figure 2 indicates beats of a minim's length (♩), 4 shows crotchets (♩), and 8 shows quaver beats (♪). 16, which is somewhat rare, would indicate semiquaver beats(♬).
4. General indication of speed. *Adagio* means a slow speed. *Molto adagio* means 'very slow'.
5. Dynamics: p = *piano* (soft), mf = *mezzo forte* (between loud and soft), and f = *forte* (loud).
6. Dynamic changes: *crescendo* and *diminuendo* (growing louder and growing softer). The 'hairpin' shape is a graphic suggestion of what takes place in the sound. The word *cresc.* is short for *crescendo* and indicates a gradual overall increase in tone and excitement.
7. *Unison* and *Divisi*. If two or more instruments that normally play the same notes are to divide into two separate parts (as do the cellos in bars 3-4), the word *divisi* (meaning 'divide') is used as a warning sign. When they come together again, the warning word is *unison*. *Unison* can be shortened to *unis.*, and *divisi* to *div*.

   In the case of the violas and cellos in bars 1-2, the word *unis.* is a warning that what at first sight may seem to be music played by divided instruments is in reality to be played by *all* the instruments in unison, using double-stopping.
8. Rests: used to show the moments where instruments are silent.
9. Accents and types of articulation. The accents (>) indicate that these notes require a little extra pressure, and the *staccato* dot (♩•) shows that the note must be short and crisp.
10. Bowing and phrasing. On stringed instrument parts these curves indicate that the notes contained within the curve are to be played with one bow stroke. With woodwind and brass, the same curves show that the notes are to be taken with one breath.

The Orchestras

The individual histories of a handful of the world's great orchestras constitute in many respects a history of the social attitudes adopted by the various countries towards the art of music. Sometimes these attitudes have been grudging, sometimes almost too enthusiastic, but always the growth of a great orchestra is a source of excitement and inspiration.

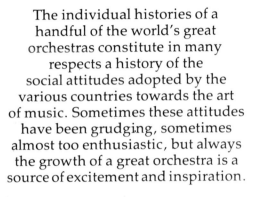

Left: the Concertgebouw Orchestra, at home in Amsterdam.

The World of the Orchestra

EHIND EVERY orchestra, generally unseen by the audience and unsung by the critics, there is a team of men and women whose sole task it is to see that its day-to-day administration runs smoothly and efficiently. There is no one way of doing this. Each orchestra tends to set up its administrative procedures according to the concert-giving traditions of the country and to its own historical origins and experience. But administration there must be – for an orchestra is a collection of highly individual artists who are called upon to carry out an exacting task, often amid nerve-wracking conditions. The conductor may assume responsibility for the music, but someone must ensure that this work can be carried out in the best possible atmosphere.

The man who organizes the orchestra's daily life is the General Manager. He may, of course, go under some other similar title, such as the Managing Director or the General Administrator. It is his task to see that everything runs smoothly and efficiently – whether it be the arrangement of an engagement for the orchestra to appear for a single evening in a neighbouring town, an extended foreign tour, or the ticklish business of sorting out a player's private grievances. There is virtually no limit to what he may be called upon to do. He is the orchestra's representative, its agent, its servant, and, if need be, its whipping boy.

He has, of course, a team of helpers – the number depending on the orchestra's financial situation and, to some extent, on the custom of the country. The London Symphony Orchestra, for example, has to make do with half the staff required to run the Boston Symphony Orchestra. There will therefore be Assistant Managers, secretaries, a Publicity Manager, an accountant, a Concerts Manager, and so on.

Most orchestras, however, have a Board of Management elected annually from the playing members themselves. It is this board that shapes the general policy – in consultation, probably, with any Board of Trustees that may exist (a board largely concerned with the orchestra's financial stability). This policy is then handed on to the General Manager to implement.

The board may also have a say in choosing what the orchestra is to play

The box office at this Barcelona concert hall (**left**) takes literally Andrew Marvell's phrase 'music, the mosaic of the air'?

– this time in consultation with the conductor and whichever concert-promoter happens to have engaged them.

No orchestral concert would ever take place if it were not for the Librarian. His job is probably one of the least regarded, even though it is one of the most crucial. He ensures that the music is sitting on each player's desk at the moment when it is wanted, and in the condition it should be in. If the orchestra's own library does not contain the necessary score and parts, then the librarian must find out where the music can be hired from. And then, when it arrives, he must check it carefully – just as he does his own library's stock.

During the course of a rehearsal the players will pencil in any instructions their conductor may give them: changes of bowing and phrasing, modifications to the dynamics, slight adjustments to the tempo, and a thousand other things that will help to remind them of that conductor's 'interpretation' of the work in question. These interpretations will change from conductor to conductor, and the librarian may often have to use his eraser simply to make sure that the music remains legible. He will also find himself having to check notes against the printed score – for misprints occur even in the orchestral parts of what one might suppose to be established and proven classics! Altogether his is an exacting, time-consuming and finicky sort of job. Moreover, the more efficiently he carries it out, the less likely anyone is to notice what he has done!

No orchestral concert would take place without the work of the Orchestral Attendants – or 'porters' as they used to be called. It is their duty to see that the chairs and music stands are in exactly the right position for the players. They also arrange the transport of all the instruments that are not actually carried by the players themselves – packing and unpacking them and generally seeing to their safety. On tours, which may after all embrace several different countries and transport in plane, train, and bus, their vigilance is crucial.

Except in special circumstances orchestral rehearsals take place in the morning, starting at ten. They last up to three hours. In that short time everything has to be sorted out for the evening performance. For an orchestra working with its 'permanent' conduc-

Every orchestral performance is founded on a vital structure of dedication and expertise. Those who make up this structure are likely to have the requisite love of music, but they will only create the optimum conditions for a performance if between them they combine administrative ability and management sense with sound financial know-how.

Orchestra
Conductor
Librarian
Porters
General Manager
Assistant Manager, Secretaries
Accountant
Concerts Manager
Publicity Manager
Board of Management
Board of Trustees

tor this may prove to be a relatively straightforward matter. Certain frequently performed works may need no more than a quick dusting down. Time can then be devoted to pieces that are less familiar, or even totally new. When the programme is very full, or the works particularly exacting, a conductor may arrange for more than one rehearsal. This costs money and can therefore not be expected as a matter of course, except perhaps in the largely state-supported orchestras of Europe.

A rehearsal will be carefully planned in advance: not only to make the best use of the time available, but also to avoid wasting a player's time. If one work makes use of players who will

Absorbtion in the non-musical (**above right**), in the midst of the musical. Silence while you work for the porters (**right**). **Far right:** the focal point takes time off for private reflection.

not be needed in the rest of the programme, then a sensible conductor will either rehearse this work first and then let the players go, or tell them in advance exactly when he intends to rehearse it so that they can turn up when they are needed. Everything good in music is the result of courtesy and co-operation.

Each rehearsal will have a short break in the middle. It would be asking too much of any human being to give the total concentration that good playing requires for a solid three hours.

Auditions to join an orchestra are carried out in a variety of different ways. The most usual is for the newcomer to be heard by a small panel consisting of the conductor, the leader of the orchestra, the orchestral manager, and several orchestral players. Their task is not only to assess his ability as a performer, but also to decide whether he is likely to fit in with the orchestra itself. There is no point in engaging someone who sticks out as an uncompromising individual or a wild eccentric, however good his playing may be. The members of an orchestra have to be able to sink their differences and blend together as one unit.

Perhaps the most gruelling of all orchestral auditions is that set by the Berlin Philharmonic. Here, by tradition, the entire orchestra listens to the newcomer. Then they vote. If he receives a majority of votes he is accepted for a probationary year. He will then be voted on again by a select and representative group of players before he can become a permanent member of the orchestra. The conductor can veto this final decision – but no conductor has ever yet dared!

With all its manifold and complex workings an orchestra is a world of its own, in some ways not unlike a ship. If everybody does his job and pulls in the same direction, then the passage will be smooth and enjoyable. But if things go wrong too often and the handling is inefficient and vexatious, then the ship will certainly sink. The individual player's devotion to music will not save it, nor will money, nor the photogenic good-looks of a star conductor. Every cog must run smoothly and efficiently in its own right: for music is not made without a tremendous outpouring of nervous energy. To work at all, the mixture must be explosive.

British Orchestras

Colin Davis leads a Proms concert (**right**) in inimitable style. The summer season of Promenade Concerts at the Albert Hall in London has long provided one of the most adventurous exciting and varied, programs of music available to any listening public. The glee and froth of the last night traditionally provide an opportunity for the expression of a cheerful and innocent kind of patriotism.

ITH THE exception of the various BBC orchestras, whose members are engaged on a salaried basis and are paid whether they are working or not, British orchestral players earn their living in the market place. The burden of musical patronage in the United Kingdom has devolved almost entirely upon private initiative. Royal purses have not played a significant part in the foundation and development of orchestras, and the State has only felt an obligation to lend a helping hand in comparatively recent years. State subsidy began at the beginning of the Second World War, when it was realized that normal sources of patronage and encouragement were in danger of collapse and that 'music and the arts' was an important element in keeping up national morale. Since that time subsidies have increased – but they are still woefully behind what is considered normal in Europe.

The British orchestral musician is virtually a free-lance performer who seeks engagements where and when he can on a contractual basis. And British orchestras must depend for the major part of their incomes on what they can earn: from the box office returns at public concerts, from work in film and recording studios, from broadcasts, and from foreign tours. In addition, most run various supportive schemes – subscription concerts, societies of 'friends' of the orchestra, and so on. The industrial and business world seems increasingly interested in sponsoring orchestras.

From an artistic point of view this is not necessarily a healthy situation. Eyes must always be fixed firmly on the box office, and programs therefore tend to rely too heavily on a limited number of sure-fire classics. Rehearsals have to be kept to a minimum in order to save money. And while good players may be sure of regular and well paid employment, they are denied the security and comfort of long-term permanent engagements.

Nevertheless, this rather harsh climate has its positive side. British orchestral players are resourceful, and particularly skilled at sight-reading. They tend to put up remarkable performances at short notice, and seem unperturbed by the style of music they are required to play. As craftsmen they are very much on their toes.

ROYAL PHILHARMONIC SOCIETY

Since 1813 an important part of London's musical life has come about through the activities of the Philharmonic Society, which, next to Leipzig's Gewandhaus Concerts, is the second oldest concert organization in the world.

Before that date London enjoyed the rather selective services of an organization known as the Concerts of Ancient Music, which had been established in 1776 and whose constitution forbade the performance of any music less than twenty years old. In practice its programs consisted (as the founders intended) mainly of Handel's music, and its audiences were restricted to the wealthy and aristocratic members of society. This situation so displeased the more enlightened professional musicians that thirty of them banded together as a Philharmonic Society (a society of 'friends of music'). The prefix 'royal' was not granted until 1912. Their intention was "to promote the performance, in the most perfect manner possible, of the best and most approved instrumental music . . ." Membership was by subscription (four guineas for eight concerts) and the orchestra was assembled from the best professional and amateurs willing to give their services. We are told that:
"The most eminent members of the profession took the whole affair into their own hands, and entered upon their duties strong, and justly strong, in their own strength. They merged all claims of rank and precedence in one great object – the love of their art. Men of the highest rank were content to occupy subordinate stations in the orchestra. Every man put his shoulders to the wheel . . ." *

The first concert was held in the Argyll Rooms, Regent Street, on 8 March 1813.

Though never itself an 'orchestra', the Philharmonic Society was always the vehicle for bringing an orchestra into existence for its concerts. The standard was generally very high, for it was felt to be a great honor to be asked to participate in the Society's activities. It was also something of an adventure, for it was at these concerts that all the latest music came to be known in England. The list of its conductors

*Henry F. Chorley, music critic (1808-72)

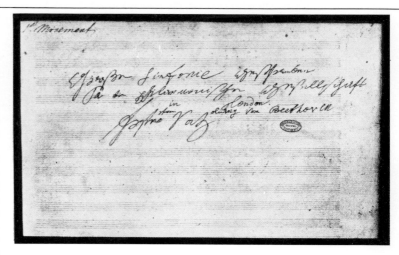

embraces a number of great composers, from Mendelssohn, Weber, and Wagner, to Sterndale Bennett, Sullivan, and Elgar, besides most of the important professional conductors of the day. The list of works performed is equally impressive. It was the Philharmonic Society that commissioned a symphony from Beethoven in 1825, and then sent him £100 when he lay on his deathbed and it was feared that he might be in want. It now treasures a manuscript dedicated to the Society.

The policy of recruiting an ad hoc orchestra for the season changed only in 1932, when Sir Thomas Beecham and the newly formed London Philharmonic Orchestra undertook the Society's work. One reason for the formation of Beecham's orchestra lay in the upheavals caused in London orchestral life when the BBC announced its intention of forming Britain's first fully salaried orchestra (see p126). The Society, which was in some financial difficulty at this time, soon found itself unable to attract the best musicians for its necessarily limited season, and consequently thought it more practical to employ an already existing orchestra. Beecham served the Society in this capacity until 1939.

During the Second World War, in which the Society's concert hall, Queen's Hall, was destroyed (10 May, 1941), activities continued under various conductors, including Sir Adrian Boult, Sir Malcolm Sargent, Sir John Barbirolli, Sir Henry Wood and Basil Cameron, and with various orchestras, including the BBC Symphony, the Hallé and the Liverpool Philharmonic. Since 1946 the Society has been served by another Beecham foundation: the Royal Philharmonic Orchestra.

Top: Beethoven's handwritten dedication of his Ninth Symphony to the London Philharmonic Society. It reads, 'Grosser Symphonie geschrieben für die Philharmonische Gesellschaft in London, Erster Satz.' **Above:** the Philharmonic Rooms where the Society held concerts between 1833 and 1869. **Right:** the program of the concert which included the first performance in England of Beethoven's Ninth Symphony.

UNDER THE IMMEDIATE PATRONAGE OF

His Majesty.

PHILHARMONIC SOCIETY.

THIRD CONCERT, MONDAY, MARCH 21, 1825.

ACT I.

Sinfonia Letter T. - - - - - - -	*Haydn.*
Terzetto, " Tutte le mie speranze," Madame CARADORI, Miss GOODALL, and Mr. VAUGHAN (Davide Penitente) - - - - -	*Mozart.*
Quartetto, two Violins, Viola, and Violoncello, Messrs. SPAGNOLETTI, OURY, MORALT, and LINDLEY - - - - - - -	*Mozart.*
Song, Mr. VAUGHAN, " Why does the God of Israel sleep," (Samson) -	*Handel.*
Quintetto, Flute, Oboë, Clarinet, Horn, and Bassoon, Messrs. NICHOLSON, VOGT, WILLMAN, PLATT, and MACKINTOSH - - - -	*Reicha.*
Recit. ed Aria, Madame CARADORI, " Per pietà," (Cosi fan tutte) -	*Mozart.*
Overture, Les deux Journées - - - - - -	*Cherubini.*

ACT II.

New Grand Characteristic Sinfonia, MS. with Vocal Finale, the principal parts of which to be sung by Madame CARADORI, Miss GOODALL, Mr. VAUGHAN, and Mr. PHILLIPS (composed expressly for this Society) - *Beethoven.*

Leader, Mr. F. CRAMER.—Conductor, Sir G. SMART.

To commence at Eight o'clock precisely.

The subscribers are most earnestly entreated to observe, that the Tickets are not transferable, and that any violation of this rule will incur a total forfeiture of the subscription.

It is requested that the Coachmen may be directed to set down *and take up* with their horses' heads towards Piccadilly.

The door in Little Argyll-street will be open after the Concert, for the egress of the Company.

The next Concert will be on MONDAY, APRIL 11.

TERZETTO.—*Mozart.*	RECITATIVE accompanied— Mr. VAUGHAN.
Tutte, le mie speranze	(Samson.)—*Handel.*
Ho tutte riposto in te !	
Salvami oh Dio	Justly these evils have befall'n thy son :
Dal nemico feroce	Sole author I, sole cause. My griefs for
Che m'insegue, e m' incalza	this
Oh Dio salvami.	

ROYAL PHILHARMONIC ORCHESTRA

Despite its title and the fact that it has served the needs of the old established Royal Philharmonic Society, the orchestra is of recent foundation. It was created, literally in a matter of weeks, by Sir Thomas Beecham, who on his return from America after the Second World War found himself without an orchestra, having failed to come to an agreement with Walter Legge and the Philharmonia. It gave its first concert on 15 September 1946 at the Davis Theater, Croydon, and within a few years was acknowledged as one of the finest orchestras in Europe.

Beecham had secured financial backing in England and America, plus a number of lucrative recording contracts, to which he later added film contracts. As always he ran things on intensely personal and autocratic lines. From 1948 the orchestra played at the Glyndebourne Festival opera season, and in 1950 it undertook an arduous tour of America – the first British orchestra to visit that country since the LSO's visit in 1912. By 1960, however, even Beecham had begun to realize that his career was coming to an end, and in that year he appointed Rudolf Kempe as his Associate Conductor. And so, when he died in 1961, Kempe was able to take over.

For a while Beecham's company, the Anglo-American Music Association, continued to manage the orchestra, but problems soon arose and Kempe felt obliged to resign. The management committee of the Royal Philharmonic Society also began to express doubts and finally withdrew from its association with the orchestra – which, for a time, put its very name in question. At last, in 1963, the members of the orchestra decided to assume control for themselves, and on 24 May 1964 the newly-constituted, self-governing orchestra gave its first concert, under the baton of Sir Malcolm Sargent.

Despite the superlative quality of its playing, the orchestra had to walk a financial tight-rope until the British government was finally persuaded that all four London orchestras should receive a more generous measure of public subsidy. This decision saved the RPO (as indeed it saved the other orchestras) which, with industrial backing, a wise recording policy, and all the other contrivances that British orchestras have to resort to, has continued to flourish.

Rudolf Kempe remained the orchestra's Principal Conductor until the year before his death in 1976, having been persuaded back shortly after his resignation in 1962. He was succeeded by Antal Dorati. The orchestra varies in strength according to the needs of the concert, but can rise to about 90 players for its main concerts. Though it is not a full-time orchestra, most of the players have contracts which assure them of an adequate year's work and so the RPO has first call on their service.

Sir Thomas Beecham decided to form the Royal Philharmonic Orchestra in 1946, but left the vital selection of players until four days before the first performance (**right**). In spite of this rather unusual beginning, the orchestra quickly became one of the most respected in the world. **Left:** the Royal Philharmonic Orchestra at the Herrod Atticus Theater during the Athens Festival in 1975. Colin Davis is the conductor.

LONDON SYMPHONY ORCHESTRA

The London Symphony Orchestra was founded in 1904 by four orchestral players who were worried by Sir Henry Wood's announcement that he would no longer tolerate the use of deputies in the orchestra of his Queen's Hall Promenade Concerts. Though he offered his players a retainer for the exclusive use of their services he could not offer them work throughout the year. This meant that if they were no longer allowed to supplement their incomes by accepting favorable engagements when and wherever they turned up, his players would find it impossible to make a decent living. Eventually some fifty of them broke away to form their own orchestra. They gave their first concert on 9 June 1904 at Queen's Hall.

From the very beginning the orchestra was established on a democratic footing. It was owned by the players and they promoted its concerts. They were not paid a salary, but by the concert. They were free to send deputies. Most important of all, perhaps, was their decision to appoint their own conductor – always with an eye to his standing as a box office draw. The first man to occupy this position was Hans Richter, whose credentials as a Wagner conductor were impeccable.

With the success of its first season the orchestra set itself up as a company, issuing £1,000 in £1 shares and allotting them to the players in £10 blocks. A Board of Directors was also set up, consisting of the four musicians who had started the orchestra (the 'Originators') and five members of the orchestra, elected annually.

The early years went smoothly and successfully. Famous guest conductors came from all over the world, as did famous soloists. In 1906 the orchestra visited Paris, and in 1908 Antwerp. In 1912, narrowly missing the fatal maiden voyage of the *Titanic*, it made a lengthy and highly successful tour of Canada and the United States, and thereafter it toured regularly – as it does today.

The constitution of the orchestra, however, had certain inbuilt weaknesses. It was soon discovered that although a player could be sacked, a player who was also a shareholder could not be so easily dismissed. The practice of using deputies also became

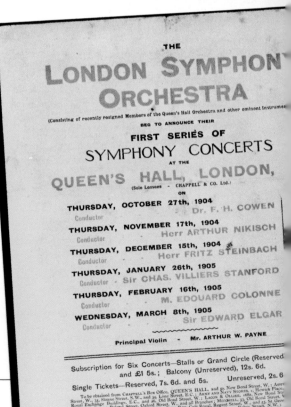

When Sir Henry Wood, the conductor of the Queen's Hall Orchestra, told his musicians that he could no longer agree to their supplementing their incomes with freelance work, they refused to accept his terms, arguing that they did not make enough money to live on from Queen's Hall alone. At the time, the only permanent British orchestra was at Bournemouth, so the players decided to form their own orchestra. They would own and run it themselves, along the same democratic lines which worked so well with the Berlin and Vienna orchestras. They had to promote their concerts as well as perform at them, as the poster (**right**), advertising their first season of symphony concerts, shows. **Above**: the orchestra in 1912, during their annual season in Queen's Hall, where they appeared under Nikisch (inset).

THE

LONDON SYMPHONY ORCHESTRA

(Consisting of recently resigned Members of the Queen's Hall Orchestra and other eminent Instrumen

BEG TO ANNOUNCE THEIR

FIRST SERIES OF

SYMPHONY CONCERTS

AT THE

QUEEN'S HALL, LONDON,

(Sole Lessees - CHAPPELL & CO. Ltd.)

ON

THURSDAY, OCTOBER 27th, 1904
Conductor - Dr. F. H. COWEN

THURSDAY, NOVEMBER 17th, 1904
Conductor - Herr ARTHUR NIKISCH

THURSDAY, DECEMBER 15th, 1904
Conductor - Herr FRITZ STEINBACH

THURSDAY, JANUARY 26th, 1905
Conductor - Sir CHAS. VILLIERS STANFORD

THURSDAY, FEBRUARY 16th, 1905
Conductor - M. EDOUARD COLONNE

WEDNESDAY, MARCH 8th, 1905
Conductor - Sir EDWARD ELGAR

Principal Violin - Mr. ARTHUR W. PAYNE

Subscription for Six Concerts—Stalls or Grand Circle (Reserved and £1 5s.; Balcony (Unreserved), 12s. 6d,

Single Tickets—Reserved, 7s. 6d. and 5s. Unreserved, 2s. 6

L. G. SHARPE, Concert Agency, 61, Regent S
Telephone: 5564 GERRARD.

a bone of contention – players who were not often asked to play elsewhere resented the absence of their colleagues, especially when some of them began to blossom as soloists. Moreover, such absences made it hard to maintain the highest standards of orchestral playing. In the end a delicate system of 'permissions' was worked out, to ensure that everybody had a fair chance of work outside and that nobody was away too often.

As a self-supporting organization the London Symphony Orchestra was naturally subject to many financial ups and downs. Sometimes they accepted help from a financial backer, such as F. J. Nettlefold of Courtaulds – only to find that he interfered too much in the orchestra's artistic policy and its choice of conductor. Sometimes it was outside engagements that kept things afloat – film recordings were especially profitable in the 1930s and 40s, and recordings for gramophone companies (in particular for Decca at the introduction of long-playing records) were also lucrative. Eventually State patronage

gave a helping hand, and from about 1963 help came from industrialists – led by the tobacco firm of Peter Stuyvesant.

In 1948 the London Symphony Orchestra reconstituted itself as a 'non-profit-distributing' concern, the better to claim exemption from various taxes. But its original policy of paying its members by the concert and not on a salaried basis remains, and this causes it to compete as one of the most hard-working orchestras in the country – or, indeed, in the whole world.

Its musical standing, at present very high indeed, has varied over the years according to the morale of the orchestra and the ability of the conductors most closely associated with it. Sometimes the conductor has happened to be just the right man for a limited period – as Albert Coates was in the 1920s, and Pierre Boulez in the 1970s. Sometimes the association has been more lasting. Among the great names that have worked with the LSO are: Artur Nikisch, Sergei Kussevitsky, Leopold Stokowski, Felix Weingartner,

The first season of the orchestra was successful enough for the players to set up the London Symphony Orchestra as a limited company. The shares (**above**) were allocated to the players in £10 blocks. A total of one thousand £1 shares were issued.

The era of LSO inter-continental tours almost ended before it began. The 1912 version of the orchestra (**right** aboard the *SS Baltic*), planning to break new ground across the Atlantic, booked its passage on the *Titanic*. Their New York agent brought forward the start of their tour by two days, thus forcing them to sail on the *SS Baltic* (**below**). The orchestra toured with Artur Nikisch as conductor and earned rave reviews. After opening in New York, the tour took in towns including Boston, Philadelphia, Washington and Baltimore.

L.S. Orchestra.
BALTIC
American Time
on Board 1912

Fritz Steinbach, Wilhelm Furtwängler, Bruno Walter, Thomas Beecham, Adrian Boult, Antal Dorati, Georg Solti – the list could go on almost to infinity. Great composers have also been invited to direct their works – Sir Edward Elgar, Carl Nielsen, Richard Strauss, Gustav Holst, Ralph Vaughan Williams, Sir William Walton, Sir Arthur Bliss, Aaron Copland and Benjamin Britten among them. Certain conductors have worked with the orchestra on a more permanent basis – among them, Pierre Monteux (1961-64), Istvan Kertesz (1965-68), and André Previn, whose association from 1968 to 1979 constitutes a record. The present conductor is Claudio Abbado and the orchestra numbers 95 players.

The London Symphony Orchestra is no stranger to touring, and it has played in a variety of venues, from famous concert halls to famous streets. **Above right:** the orchestra rehearsing for a performance of Berlioz's *Symphonie Fantastique* in the Champs Elysées, Paris, in May 1980. Amongst the more orthodox places it has played is the Carnegie Hall. A memorial concert for Pierre Monteux, in 1964, is announced (**above**). **Right:** the London Symphony Orchestra took part in the Granada Festival, in Spain in 1974.

PHILHARMONIA ORCHESTRA

The Philharmonia Orchestra was formed in London in 1945 by Walter Legge (1906–79), who had long cherished an ambition to create a world-class orchestra whose primary function would be to make superlative recordings under the direction of great conductors. As he was head of the EMI recording company's 'Columbia' label, he was in a position to offer lucrative contracts to conductors and soloists, and also guarantee regular work for the orchestra. And having spent the war years organizing concerts for ENSA, he had been able to keep track of the many fine players (including those who had fled to Britain from occupied Europe) who were now coming out of the forces. When the Philharmonia made its first appearance, at the Kingsway Hall in October 1945 in a concert directed by Sir Thomas Beecham, it was clear that Legge had succeeded and that London was possessed of another orchestra of international importance.

At first it seemed as if Beecham might become the orchestra's Principal Conductor, but his ambition was to run it for himself with Legge merely as manager. This was not acceptable and Beecham departed to found the Royal Philharmonic Orchestra, leaving the Philharmonia to strike roots under another baton. This it did, largely through the help of Wilhelm Furtwängler and the conducting genius of Herbert von Karajan. In 1959 Klemperer succeeded Karajan and the process continued.

In 1964, however, Walter Legge suddenly announced that he "could no longer maintain the orchestra as he wished" and would therefore withdraw from all involvement with it. Since it was his creation, and in many ways his personal property, the blow was catastrophic. For a time it seemed as if the orchestra would disband completely. But the musicians decided otherwise. They organized themselves into a self-governing body and, under the inspired leadership of Dr Klemperer, fought their way into a continued existence. Only the name was changed, and from 1964 until 1977 the orchestra was known as the New Philharmonia.

When Klemperer retired in 1971, Lorin Maazel became the orchestra's Associate Principal Conductor, and

The founder, and two important conductors in the history of the Philharmonia:**(above right)** Walter Legge, who formed the orchestra in 1945, with the intention of making recordings that were second to none. Otto Klemperer (**above**) took over the position of Principal Conductor in 1959, and was elected President of the New Philharmonia, as it was then called, in 1964. He is seen with the Orchestra and Chorus at the Royal Festival hall in 1970, in a performance of Beethoven's Ninth Symphony. **Top:** the Italian conductor Riccardo Muti became Principal Conductor of the orchestra in 1973, and Musical Director in 1977. He is conducting at a concert that took place in 1979, in memory of Walter Legge.

then, on Klemperer's death in 1973, Riccardo Muti was appointed Principal Conductor. In 1979 he was appointed Music Director. Among the other conductors closely associated with the orchestra, now and in the past, have been Guido Cantelli, Carlo Maria Giulini, Andrew Davis and Simon Rattle.

The Philharmonia Orchestra is governed by a Council of Management elected every two years from the playing members. The Council controls its financial policy, its choice of program, conductors and soloists, its engagements, tours and recording contracts, and together with a paid Executive Staff generally manages every aspect of its affairs. Apart from the government help it gets for its London engagements, through the London Orchestral Concerts Board, the orchestra looks to its box office receipts, recording contracts, and the sponsorship of various business and industrial firms. Associated with the orchestra are the 250-strong Philharmonia Chorus (founded 1957), a chamber group, The Philharmonia Ensemble (1975), and the Philharmonia Brass Ensemble (1976). The orchestra itself numbers 75 players.

BBC SYMPHONY ORCHESTRA

The various orchestras of the British Broadcasting Corporation, of which the BBC Symphony is the crown, are the only musical bands in the United Kingdom to be paid a guaranteed salary, with holidays, sickness benefits, and a compulsory pension scheme. The security thus offered gives an enviable sense of permanence, and leaves the players and their conductors free to concentrate on achieving artistic excellence. At least this is the theory – for critics say that the absence of competition has sometimes induced a sense of complacency! Whatever the truth of the matter may be, the result has been the formation of a fine orchestra which, under its various conductors, has achieved an international reputation. Not least among the feathers in its cap is the fact that it is able to explore a wider repertoire than any other British orchestra – for the simple reason that it does not depend upon the box office, and its audience is both enormous and very select: drawn, in fact, from the whole country.

The BBC Symphony Orchestra was founded in 1930 as the result of a general feeling that the concert scene in London rested on a far from satisfactory basis. Good as the London orchestras were, they were limited by uncertain and fluctuating financial considerations, by their tendency to employ a series of short-term guest conductors, and a free-lance system which led to a constant change of personnel.

What was needed was a permanent orchestra of musicians recruited on a salaried basis, whose loyalty would therefore go unquestioned and who could be given adequate rehearsal time under the direction of one man. The need for such a body was emphasized by the London concerts of the Berlin Philharmonic in 1927 (their first visit since the 1914-18 war) and the subsequent visit of the Budapest Philharmonic in the following year. Both orchestras worked in conditions of permanence and security and the excellence of their playing came as a revelation.

At first the BBC explored the possibility of creating a joint orchestra with Sir Thomas Beecham and the Royal Philharmonic Society. But since this scheme would probably have meant the disintegration of the London Symphony Orchestra, many of whose members played free-lance for Beecham, it was vigorously opposed and eventually dropped. In the end the BBC went ahead by itself – much to the concern of the existing London orchestras. They felt that unfair competition was being introduced into their musical world, even though they agreed that artistically that world was far from satisfactory.

Under the somewhat ungainly title of The Wireless National Orchestra, the original BBC orchestra consisted of 119 players and was carefully designed to meet the requirements both of studio broadcasts and live performances in the concert hall. It could, in effect, be divided into two pairs of smaller self-

Sir Adrian Boult (**left**) was conductor of the BBC Symphony Orchestra for the first twenty years of its life. **Above:** he takes charge in one of its first ever performances, at Queen's Hall in September 1930. **Below:** he directs a radio broadcast in 1942, on the 450th anniversary of Columbus' landfall. Music was by William Walton.

Above: Rozhdestvensky with the BBC Symphony Orchestra. Rozhdestvensky has managed to bring the orchestra to the highest international standards, while at the same time continuing his work with the Moscow Chamber Opera. Both Russian and English composers feature prominently in his symphonic canon: Elgar, Tippet and Britten as well as contemporary Russian composers such as Lokshin and Schnittke.
Left: Sir Malcolm Sargent, Chief Conductor of the BBC Symphony Orchestra from 1950-57, and of the Proms from 1950-1966.

contained orchestras: one pair of 80 and 39 players, and the other of 71 and 48 players. Thus in all there were five possible orchestras available from the overall complement of players. This meant that the same musicians could tackle a very wide variety of music, from the small orchestral resources appropriate to Haydn and Mozart, to the gigantic forces demanded by Strauss and Mahler.

The conductor responsible for planning the original orchestra and then developing it into the fine body of musicians it soon became was Sir Adrian Boult. He remained in charge until 1950, when a bureaucratic attitude to retirement forced his premature resignation. During his time the idea

of a flexible, multi-purpose group of players was abandoned and the BBC Symphony Orchestra became an indivisible unit of close on one hundred players.

Boult was succeeded by Sir Malcolm Sargent (1950-57), Rudolf Schwartz (1957-62), Antal Dorati (1963), Colin Davis (1967-71), Pierre Boulez (1971-75), and most recently (1978) Gennadi Rozhdestvensky. The orchestra gives a series of public concerts each year, besides its studio work. It also appears at the Promenade Concerts at the Royal Albert Hall each summer, and tours both in this country and abroad. Its first overseas visit was made to Brussels in 1935, and since 1956 it has toured almost every year.

Orchestral movement

欢迎英国伦敦爱乐管弦乐

The London Philharmonic Orchestra has a distinguished record of touring. It was not only the first British orchestra to tour the Soviet Union and India, but was the first non-Communist Western orchestra to perform in the People's Republic of China. Other countries visited by the orchestra include Germany, Australia, Switzerland, Hong Kong, Canada, Mexico and the Philippines. Apart from building national prestige abroad, touring helps to build an orchestra's sense of its own identity — so that it can be argued that home audiences benefit indirectly from these ventures also.

LONDON PHILHARMONIC ORCHESTRA

The LPO was created in 1932 by the indefatigable Sir Thomas Beecham. After securing agreements to serve with The Royal Choral Society, the Courtauld-Sargent Concert Club, Sir Robert Mayer's children's concerts scheme, and finally The Royal Philharmonic Society, Sir Thomas assembled an orchestra of first-rate musicians, registered them as a limited liability company and, after twelve rehearsals, appeared at Queen's Hall on 7 October 1932 in a program of works by Berlioz, Mozart, Delius and Richard Strauss. The result was a triumph. One critic, the influential Ernest Newman, wrote "nothing so electrifying had been heard in the London concert hall for years. The tone was magnificent, the precision perfect, the reading a miracle of fire and beauty."

Typically, Sir Thomas had placed, and continued to place, artistic perfection before everything else – even before financial stability. Work, however, was not difficult to find. The orchestra played at the Royal Opera summer seasons at Covent Garden, at many of the provincial festivals, made successful tours abroad and in Great Britain, undertook recording and broadcasting work and generally earned for itself an enviable international reputation. In 1935 the players were put on a regular salaried basis.

Below: the engagements of the 1973 LPO tour of China in Peking, Shanghai and Canton. **Above:** almost the whole of a species plays for the orchestra. **Left:** Chinese leaders congratulate the LPO after their final concert in Canton.

London Philharmonic Orchestra

四十周年演出季

首次访问中华人民共和国

伦敦交响乐团

The orchestra toured the Soviet Union in 1956, with Sir Adrian Boult as conductor. **Above:** Boult conducting at the magnificent Great Hall of the Moscow Conservatoire. Sightseeing **(right)** is an inevitable part of exotic travel. **Below:** the LPO in Bombay in 1962. Sir Malcolm Sargent is the conductor.

In 1970 the London Philharmonic Orchestra toured the United States of America, with Bernard Haitink (**left**), who was then the Principal Conductor. He held the appointment for 12 years, longer than any other conductor, and is the Musical Director of the Glyndebourne Festival Opera, at which the LPO is the resident orchestra. He has been Principal Conductor of the Concertgebouw since 1964.
On the 1970 US Tour he received the Bruckner Medal from the Bruckner Society of America.

In 1939, however, the war brought about a considerable disruption of concert life and the normal methods of funding it. The LPO soon found itself in difficulties. Beecham's company went into liquidation and he himself left for America. The members of the orchestra thereupon decided to reorganize themselves and, under the title of Musical Culture Limited, became a self-governing independent orchestra, not unlike the LSO. The London Philharmonic has since continued in this way, promoting its own concerts, engaging its own conductors, and generally pursuing its own artistic style and policy.

A number of distinguished musicians have held the position of Principal Conductor and have accordingly been able to help mould and refine the LPO's distinctive voice. Among them are Eduard van Beinum (1949–50), Sir Adrian Boult (1950–57), John Pritchard (1962–66) and Bernard Haitink (1967–79). The present Principal Conductor and Artistic Director is Sir Georg Solti.

The LPO was the first British orchestra to tour the Soviet Union (1956), India, Ceylon, Hong Kong, Australia and the Philippines (1962), and China (1973). It plays frequently for radio and television, and since 1964 has been the resident orchestra at the Glyndebourne Festival Opera from May to August each year.

It consists of 90 players.

ROYAL LIVERPOOL PHILHARMONIC ORCHESTRA

In the strictest sense the Royal Liverpool Philharmonic did not come into existence until 1943, when it was established on a full time basis as a permanent orchestra. But in one form or another an orchestra of this name has existed since 1840 when the Philharmonic Society of Liverpool (it did not become 'royal' until 1957) was established to promote concerts on a subscription basis.

The Society began in a small way, first in 'Mr Lassell's Saloon' (a dancing academy), and then (1843) in the hall of the Collegiate Institute. The orchestra was part-amateur and part-professional and the concerts a mixture of orchestral items, songs, madrigals and operatic choruses. An older body, the Festival Choral Society (1839), also made regular contributions to the meetings.

Such was the success of the venture that in 1849 a sumptuous and very spacious new hall was built – it could seat 2100 and an orchestra and chorus of 250. It was generally held to be one of the finest concert halls in the whole of Europe, and remained the Society's home until 1933, when it was destroyed by fire.

The Liverpool Philharmonic Society's concerts flourished throughout the 19th century on a very grand scale, involving artists of international repute and maintaining a remarkable adventurousness in its choice of program. Among its principal conductors were Zeugheer Herrmann (1843-65), Sir Julius Benedict (1867-79), Max Bruch (who enjoyed a brief and rather disastrous season in 1882), Sir Charles Hallé (1883-95), Sir Frederick Cowen (1896-1913), and Sir Malcolm Sargent (1942-48), together with many distinguished guest conductors from all over the world.

With the destruction of the Philharmonic Hall in July 1933 it became possible to rethink the Society's policies, which had remained unchanged since 1840. Subscribers to the 1849 hall had been invited to purchase boxes, which then became their property in perpetuity (a similar scheme was operated by the builders of London's Albert Hall). Evening dress was obligatory, and only a small area of the hall (the two upper side galleries) was open to the general public. The new Philhar-

One of the finest concert halls in Europe, the Philharmonic Hall (**left**) was completed in 1849 for the Liverpool Philharmonic Society. Seats on the two upper side galleries were available to the general public. The rest were sold outright to subscribers. The Liverpool Philharmonic Society played here until 1933, when the building was completely gutted in a fire. **Above**: to celebrate the Queen's Silver Jubilee in 1977, the orchestra (now 'royal') performed Mahler's Symphony No 8 at the Liverpool Cathedral.

monic Hall was opened in June 1939. It proved to have excellent acoustics, and every seat was now available to the paying public.

Strangely, it was the war that turned the old Philharmonic Orchestra into the new Royal Liverpool Philharmonic Orchestra. It was soon found that players could not travel freely from different parts of the country to make up the orchestra (as they had done for years, largely from Manchester and the Hallé). Moreover, another Liverpool orchestra, the Merseyside, which had been directed by the violinist Louis Cohen since 1930, also found itself depleted. The two decided to combine and form a new orchestra of some 60 players. The Liverpool Corporation agreed to purchase the Philharmonic Hall and entered into a unique partnership whereby it promised the orchestra generous financial support. From this moment the Liverpool Philharmonic Orchestra, conductor Sir Malcolm Sargent, became a reality.

It has never looked back, and is now rightly regarded as an orchestra of international significance. Among its permanent conductors have been Hugo Rignold (1948-54), John Pritchard (1954-63), Sir Charles Groves (1963-77) and Walter Weller (1978-80). Its present conductor, David Atherton, was appointed in 1980. The orchestra serves not only the needs of Liverpool, but of the surrounding area and makes regular tours throughout Britain and abroad. It has a large number of excellent recordings to its credit – particularly of British music. Its present strength is about 75 players.

In addition to the Orchestra, the Liverpool Philharmonic Society now administers its own Philharmonic Choir and Philharmonic Club, as well as the Merseyside Youth Orchestra and the Rodewald Chamber Music Society (founded in 1911).

Conductors of the Royal Liverpool Philharmonic Society past and present: Walter Weller (**above**) was Principal Conductor and Artistic Adviser of the orchestra from 1977-1980. He is shown (**right**) with the orchestra in the second Philharmonic Hall, opened in 1939. David Atherton (**below**) succeeded him in September 1980, having performed with every British orchestra.

HALLÉ ORCHESTRA

The Hallé Orchestra grew out of a musical society that had been founded in 1770, known as the Gentlemen's Concerts. Like many such organizations it was really an amateur orchestra. (Legend has it that the original twenty-four members all played the flute!) But its concerts flourished, doubtless with professional help, and as early as 1806 it was able to boast performances of at least one Beethoven symphony. By the middle of the 19th century orchestral concerts were a valued feature of Manchester life, but it was felt that standards needed to be improved. To this end the orchestra of the Gentlemen's Society turned to Charles Hallé (1819-95), a German-born pianist who had enjoyed a considerable success in London and Paris, and asked him to undertake the duties of permanent conductor and general manager. He began the task on 1 January 1850 with all the thoroughness of a new and very enthusiastic broom. By March he had engaged an almost entirely new orchestra of forty players.

In 1857, however, he was asked to assemble a special orchestra to take part in the celebrations that were to accompany a great Art Treasures Exhibition. Such was the success of this new orchestra (partly recruited from the orchestra of the Gentlemen's Concerts) that Hallé decided to keep it in existence. He took over personal responsibility, gave it his own name, and launched upon a series of public concerts. The first of these took place on 30 January 1858. In the strictest sense, then, the Hallé is the oldest orchestra in Britain, and the fourth oldest in the world.

Hallé's orchestra was his own property, and though the profits from his first sixteen concerts were minimal (about one penny a concert!) they *were* profits and came from a genuinely popular support, and not from the subscriptions of a private and rather exclusive club, as was the case with the Gentlemen's Concerts. Throughout his career Hallé sought to introduce good music to as wide an audience as possible. He introduced the principle of cheap seats for a proportion of the audience, insisted on a high standard of performance, and offered an interesting and varied selection of music. By the time he died (1895) his orchestra

Sir Malcolm Sargent was Director of the Royal Liverpool Philharmonic Orchestra from 1942-1948, during which time he was knighted. In the 1940s he conducted the orchestra in a historic recording of Elgar's *The Dream of Gerontius* (1900). **Left:** Sargent conducting the orchestra in 1944 at a concert attended by many members of the armed forces.

Sir Charles Hallé (**left**) gave his name to the orchestra he formed to take part in the celebrations for a large Art Treasures Exhibition. It was such a success that he decided it should continue, and took over the responsibility for this himself. Throughout his life he aimed to bring good music to as many people as possible. He tried to ensure that there were always some cheap seats at his concerts.
In addition to his orchestral work, he helped found Manchester's Royal College of Music and was its first Principal.

had become a successful and popular institution. Three years later a Hallé Concerts Society was founded to maintain the orchestra at the standard he had left it, and in 1899 Hans Richter (considered by many to be the greatest conductor of his day) was invited to come from Vienna to take charge. He remained the orchestra's conductor until 1911.

The most important permanent conductor to follow Richter was Sir Hamilton Harty, who remained with the orchestra from 1920 to 1933. A brief spell with Michael Balling (1912-14) had no significant effect, but Sir Thomas Beecham's work during the 1914-20 period was extremely valuable, even though it was not carried out on a permanent basis. Sir Malcolm Sargent

was also valued as a regular guest conductor in the years 1933-43.

In 1943, however, it was decided that the orchestra was in need of a thorough reorganization, and Sir John Barbirolli, who had made a considerable impression as a guest conductor some ten years earlier, was called upon to undertake the task. For the first time the orchestra was put on a permanent basis – each player receiving an annual contract which made him independent of the kind of summer engagements (on seaside piers and the like) previously necessary to supplement his income when the orchestra's two main seasons were over. Sir John remained the orchestra's conductor until 1968, when he became its Conductor Laureate. He died two years later. During his last

Above: Hallé with the Hallé Orchestra at the Free Trade Hall, Manchester, with his wife, Madame Wilma Norman Neruda as violin soloist. Madame Neruda worked with the orchestra for many years and was generally regarded as the greatest woman violinist of her day. Another famous conductor of the Hallé was Sir Hamilton Harty. He is seen **(right)** at a Northern Promenade concert at the Free Trade hall in 1930. The Free Trade Hall itself was built in 1843. Bombed in 1940, it was rebuilt in 1951.

Hans Richter (**below**) took over the orchestra in 1899 after the death of Hallé, and continued as conductor until his retirement in 1911. **Right:** Sir John Barbirolli rehearsing with the orchestra at Kingsway Hall, Holborn. He was asked to reorganize the orchestra in 1943. He put all the players on an annual contract. The Scottish conductor James Loughran (**bottom**) became Principal Conductor and Music Adviser in 1971. His recordings of Brahms and Beethoven symphonies have won high praise. He is well known at the London Proms.

years with the orchestra he was helped by various associate conductors, including George Weldon (1952-63) and Maurice Handford (1966-71). Since 1971 James Loughran has been the orchestra's Principal Conductor and Music Adviser. In this role he has more than maintained the Halle's standing.

The Hallé Orchestra subsists on the income it derives from its playing, helped out by grants from the Manchester City Corporation, the Arts Council of Great Britain, and a certain amount of industrial and business sponsorship. Its permanent home is the Free Trade Hall, built originally in 1843, but rebuilt in 1951 after destruction by incendiary bombs in 1940. It has excellent acoustics and seats about 2,500 people.

CITY OF BIRMINGHAM SYMPHONY ORCHESTRA

Although not of international standing, the CBSO shows the way in which local enthusiasm can, despite many setbacks, and in the teeth of local apathy, lead to the foundation of an institution of considerable excellence.

The orchestra dates from 1920, but Birmingham had enjoyed a flourishing musical life for at least a century before that date. This centered mainly around various choral activities, though there were many attempts to promote regular orchestral concerts. Of these the most important were those under George Halford at the turn of the century.

The new 'City Orchestra', as it was at first called, grew directly out of the interest created by Halford's concerts and the subsequent formation of a Birmingham Philharmonic Society in 1911, which also began to sponsor concerts of its own. In 1918 Appleby Matthews, a local pianist, choir conductor and director of the Birmingham Police Band, commenced a series of Sunday Orchestral Concerts. They caught the public imagination and two years later

Top: George Halford and violin soloist Fritz Kreisler with the City Orchestra in 1910. **Above left:** Neville Chamberlain, Beecham and the then Lord Mayor with the Philharmonic Society's orchestra in 1917 at the Birmingham Town Hall. **Above:** the first conductor of the City of Birmingham Orchestra, Appleby Matthews. **Facing page, top:** the present orchestra playing in Birmingham. **Bottom:** Simon Rattle, new Principal Conductor.

it was agreed that a city of Birmingham's size and importance should have an orchestra of its own. An annual grant was voted from the rates, and various donations were collected from private citizens. Thus, with Appleby Matthews as its first conductor, the CBSO was under way.

At first it gave six 'symphony' concerts each year, plus six 'popular' concerts on Saturdays, and two dozen Sunday concerts. It also gave special concerts for children on Saturday afternoons. Important guest conductors were regularly invited to conduct the symphony concerts. Appleby Matthews was succeeded by Sir Adrian Boult (1924-30), Leslie Heward (1930-43), George Weldon (1943-51), Rudolf Schwartz (1951-57), Andrzej Panufnik (1957-60), Hugo Rignold (1960-68), Louis Frémaux (1969-78) and Simon Rattle (appointed 1980).

In addition to the support given by the local authorities the orchestra now receives government grants and industrial sponsorship. It became a full-time orchestra in 1943 and has since undertaken several European tours. Its present strength is about 72 players.

BOURNEMOUTH SYMPHONY ORCHESTRA

Though not perhaps a 'great' orchestra by international standards, the Bournemouth Symphony Orchestra occupies a unique place in the musical and social history of Great Britain. It was founded in 1893 as a band of thirty players engaged to play on the pier and in the old Winter Gardens Pavilion, as part of the general amenities of a flourishing and popular seaside resort. It was fortunate in its first conductor: Dan Godfrey (1868-1939), a former military bandmaster. In 1895 he began a weekly series of symphony concerts and soon attracted attention by the standard of his work and the encouragement he gave to young British composers. He remained in charge until 1934, when his place was taken by Richard Austin (1934-40). After a

difficult period during the war, the orchestra was enlarged in 1947 and Rudolf Schwarz became its conductor (1947-51). He was followed by Sir Charles Groves (1951-61), Constantine Silvestri (1961-69), Paavo Berglund (1972-79) and Uri Segal (appointed in 1980).

The Bournemouth Symphony Orchestra was the first permanent municipal orchestra to be established in Great Britain. It is a remarkable example of what can be done where local enthusiasm is strong enough. It became an orchestra in its own right in 1954, though municipal aid continues to play a part in its funding. It consists now of about 115 players and has a useful offshoot in the shape of the Bournemouth Sinfonietta. Although it made its first foreign tour in 1965, the orchestra's chief function is to serve the south and west of England.

The Bournemouth Symphony Orchestra playing at home in Bournemouth.

THE
Co

SCOTTISH NATIONAL ORCHESTRA

Formed under its present name in 1950, the Scottish National Orchestra can be said to have grown indirectly out of an orchestra which had been founded in 1874 to accompany the activities of the Glasgow Choral Union. This orchestra also gave a limited number of purely orchestral concerts, both in Glasgow and Edinburgh. Its first conductor was the director of the Choral Union itself, Henry A. Lambert (1874–75), but he was followed by Sir Arthur Sullivan (1875–76), Hans von Bülow (1877–78), Julius Tausch (1878–79), and Sir August Manns (1879–94). By the 1890s it had grown into a band of some 90 players, and though its activities were restricted to the winter season they had spread over a fairly wide area in Scotland.

In 1891 certain music-lovers who

Above left: Sir Alexander Gibson conducting the orchestra on the Last Night of the Promenade Concerts in the Usher Hall, Edinburgh. The soloist is Kenneth McKellar. **Left:** Frederic Cowen and the Scottish Orchestra at the time of the Glasgow International Exhibition in 1901. Gustav Holst (indicated) played trombone with the orchestra.

thought the Choral Union's orchestral season too short formed their own Scottish Orchestra Company, Ltd. and set out to run a six month season in Glasgow, under the baton of Sir George Henschel. By 1894, however, it had become clear that there was really only a sufficient public to support the work of one orchestra, and so both contenders agreed to amalgamate into a new body of some 80 players operating under the title: the Choral and Orchestral Union. The first conductor of this new venture was Sir George Henschel (1894–95). He was followed by Willem Kes (1895–98), who did much to establish its artistic reputation, Wilhelm Bruch (1898–1900), Sir Frederick Cowen (1900–1910), and Emil Mlynarski (1910–16).

Concerts were discontinued during the period 1916–19 and began again under Sir Landon Ronald (1919–23). The 1920s and 30s were a period of considerable uncertainty, and it was only the enthusiasm and determination of such guest conductors as Sir John Barbirolli and George Szell that kept the orchestra in existence at all. Despite a more settled period under Warwick Braithwaite (1940–45), it did not really achieve stability and permanence until it was reformed under Susskind in July 1950 as the Scottish National Orchestra.

Since then it has flourished as an orchestra of some 75 players, working on a full-time permanent basis and with financial support from the cities of Glasgow and Edinburgh (and other Scottish towns), as well as the Scottish Arts Council, and business and industrial sponsorship. It now gives about 150 concerts each year, and tours both in England and on the continent as well as providing for the musical needs of Scotland. Among its more recent conductors have been Karl Rankl (1952–56), Hans Swarowsky (1957–59) and Sir Alexander Gibson (appointed in 1959).

In 1898 the Scottish Orchestra toured the Netherlands (**above, left**) under the baton of Willem Kes (**left**) who helped to establish the reputation of the Scottish Orchestra as well as that of the Concertgebouw.

ЅH ORCHESTRA.
² FREDERIC COWEN.

„The Scottish Orchestra"
Conductor: WILLEM KES.
Solo-Violist: ELKAN KOSMAN.
Impresa: „DE NIEUWE MUZIEKHANDEL"
Leidschestraat 46, Amsterdam.

Concert-Tournée in Nederland,
1–6 Februari 1898.

European Orchestras

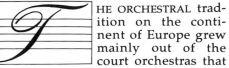 HE ORCHESTRAL tradition on the continent of Europe grew mainly out of the court orchestras that came into existence in the 18th century. Many of these, as we have seen in earlier chapters, were orchestras of considerable magnificence – large, and lavishly supported by music-loving kings and princes. Their fortunes, of course, varied over the years and were always subject to the whims of the royal paymaster. They began to fade during the second half of the 19th century when political changes (in particular the unification of Germany) upset the old pattern of small, autonomous states. But some survived for a surprisingly long time – until the First World War, in fact. It is astonishing to think that a composer who died as late as 1949 (Richard Strauss) could have begun his conducting career with the Court Orchestra of the Duke of Meiningen!

Fortunately, when kings and princes gave way to government by the state, the orchestral habit had become so ingrained that it was thought proper, at least in Germany, for every large city to support an orchestra (and an opera house) out of the public purse. And so today the number of fine orchestras in central Europe is quite remarkable. In countries that depended more on a central monarchy (France, for instance) the situation tended to be rather different. The descendants of their ancient orchestras often owe more to private initiative – the setting up of philharmonic and orchestral societies. The habit of backing such enterprise from the public purse, however, has been widespread from the first, and doubtless owes its origins to the earlier habit of royal patronage. In Communist countries orchestras are wholly state-supported as a matter of course. And if considerable surveillance is placed over what they may or may not play, and where they may or may not travel, the standard of their playing is unaffected.

Herbert von Karajan (**left**), records with the Berlin Philharmonic Orchestra in the Jesus Christus Kirche, Berlin. The partnership of orchestra and conductor has lasted over a quarter of a century.

DRESDENER STAATSKAPELLE

In the very broad sense of its forming an official part of 'music at Dresden', the State Orchestra can claim to be the oldest foundation of its kind still in existence in Europe. But it must be stressed that it is only in the last hundred years or so that Dresden's music has been anything other than an affair of the Royal Court. Dresden was the capital of Saxony, and the idea of 'municipal music' could therefore not arise until the process of German unification was well under way.

Music in the royal court can be traced back to 1548 when a body of singers was set up as the official 'Chapel'. Instrumentalists only began to play an important part with the arrival of Heinrich Schütz as Director of Music in 1617. Schütz had studied in Italy and was anxious to explore the new 'concerto' style – combining and contrasting vocal and instrumental groups, as he had learned to do under Gabrieli in Venice. Although his efforts were disrupted by the events of the Thirty Years War, even to the point where he found himself having to pay his musicians' salaries out of his own pocket, Dresden under Schütz became recognized as an important center of music-making. This fame increased after 1731, when Johann Adolph Hasse came to direct the court music of the Elector Augustus II, who was now also King of Poland. Hasse's activities were largely concerned with the court opera, but its accompanying orchestra soon became renowned throughout Europe.

The Dresden Royal Orchestra began to play a part in the municipal scene after 1858, when it commenced a regular series of subscription concerts open to the general public. It is from this date that it can be counted as an orchestra in the usual sense of the word, and under the guidance of Ernst von Schuch during the period 1877–1914 it achieved international fame. Thereafter it attracted the allegiance of a number of major conductors, notably Fritz Reiner (1914–22), Fritz Busch (1922–33), and Karl Böhm (1934–40). Its work with the Dresden State Opera (with which, of course, it is still fundamentally linked) was also much admired. Many of Strauss's greatest operas (including *Salome*, 1905; *Electra*, 1909; and *Der Rosenkavalier*, 1911) received first performances in Dresden.

After the Second World War, during

Heinrich Schütz (**left**) led the orchestra to its first taste of European fame. He acquired the tag of 'most excellent musician of the century' and during the Thirty Years War earned the appellation 'father of the orchestra' for his protective efforts. He is shown (**above**) in 1662, surrounded by singers in Dresden castle.

Johann Adolf Hasse (**below**) came to the Dresden court of Elector Augustus II (**bottom**) in 1731, and was instrumental in establishing Dresden as a European center of Italian operatic art. Under Ernst von Schuch (**right**) the Dresden Opera emerged onto the international scene.

which Dresden was almost totally destroyed by bombing, the orchestra was reassembled under the baton of Joseph Keilberth (1945–50), Rudolf Kempe (1950–54) and Franz Konwitschny (1954–62), rapidly regaining much of its former eminence. It now figures as the most outstanding orchestra in the German Democratic Republic.

The Dresden State Orchestra gives a dozen symphony concerts and a dozen chamber concerts each season. Its members regularly form small ensembles – including the *Cappella Sagittariana*, which specializes in performances on ancient instruments. Since 1923 it has run a special Orchestral School for training young musicians. Its main center is the Kulturpalast, opened in 1969, which seats some 2,400 people, but it also makes regular tours abroad and serves the needs of the State Opera.

Karajan and the Dresden State Orchestra (**above**) record Wagner's *Meistersingers* in a Dresden recording studio.

Because of this dual function as symphony and opera orchestra the Dresdener Staatskapelle is rather larger than average – at present numbering 128 musicians. Recent Principal Conductors include Otmar Suitner and Kurt Sanderling, and, since 1974, Herbert Blomstedt.

Countless German operas have been given premiers in Dresden, the first being *Dafne* by Heinrich Schütz. **Above:** the second Dresden opera house to be designed by Gottfried Semper, and home of the Opera between 1878 and 1945. **Left:** Karl Böhm, conductor between 1934 and 1940.

Many players have formed ensembles with the intention of playing chamber music. The Capella Sagittariana (**below**) plays ancient instruments.

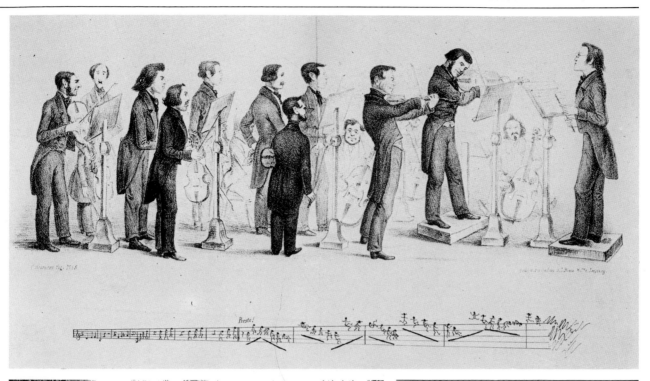

LEIPZIG GEWANDHAUS ORCHESTRA

The orchestra is so named after the ancient market-hall of the Leipzig linen-merchants, where regular concerts began to be given in 1781. These concerts followed on a series which started in 1743 but were subject to several major interruptions – including the events of the Seven Years War (1756–63). The first Gewandhaus concert took place on 29 September 1781, with Johann Adam Hiller as its director. It was backed by a board of governors, headed by the Lord Mayor, Karl Wilhelm Müller, who may be considered to be the founder of the institution in its present form. It was Müller who, a year or so earlier, had insisted that a new hall suitable for balls and concerts be added to the Gewandhaus itself. The September concert was a success and the first of a series of 24 subscription concerts commenced on 25 November.

Hiller's duties were taken over by Johann Gottfried Schicht in 1789, and then by Johann Philipp Schulz (1810–27) and Christian August Pohlenz, who remained the director until 1835. In that year the Gewandhaus Orchestra met its first genuine 'conductor' in the modern sense of the word, the composer Felix Mendelssohn. Under his superior musicianship and meticulous

The Leipzig Gewandhaus Orchestra (**top**) rehearses under Julius Rietz in about 1850. The drawing is by cellist Carl Reimers, and the notation represents Beethoven's Leonora No.3 Overture. **Above:** a concert in the original Gewandhaus in about 1846. Most of the 800 seats in the hall faced the center gangway, in the manner of choir stalls. **Left:** the second Gewandhaus concert hall, in 1891. Built in 1884 it was fully the equal of the first in acoustics and aesthetics.

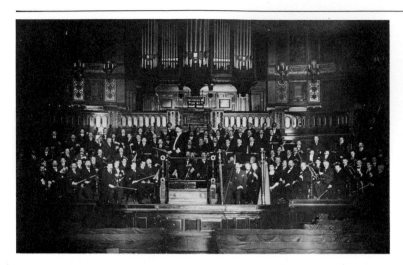

attention to detail the orchestra flourished as never before. Mendelssohn made Leipzig a center for the exploration of contemporary music, and set the pattern for the type of purely orchestral symphony concert we are now accustomed to. He remained at Leipzig until 1843 and was followed by Ferdinand Hiller, who was in turn succeeded by the young Danish composer Niels Gade (1844–48).

Of the conductors who have followed in Mendelssohn's footsteps perhaps the most influential have been Arthur Nikisch (1895–1922), Wilhelm Furtwängler (1922–30), Bruno Walter (1930–33), and Hermann Abendroth (1934–45). During their tenure of office the Gewandhaus Orchestra has been at its most brilliant – though in view of their remarkable talents this is perhaps not surprising.

Concerts were given in the original Gewandhaus building until 1884, when a fine new concert hall was opened. This superb building, in the classical style, contained a large concert hall, able to seat 1,700 people, and a smaller hall of about one third the size. The acoustics of both were exceptional. It was destroyed during the bombing of the Second World War. At the time of writing a new hall is under active construction, and it promises to be every bit as worthy as its predecessor.

Among the more recent conductors of the Gewandhaus Orchestra have been Herbert Albrecht (1946–48), Franz Konwitschny (1949–62), Václav Neumann (1964–68), and Kurt Masur (appointed in 1970). The orchestra is now, of course, wholly supported by the state.

The oldest existing photograph of the Leipzig Gewandhaus Orchestra (**above**) dates from 1893. Nikisch's work with the orchestra spanned twenty-seven years. He can be seen with them (**top**) in 1904. Bruno Walter (**left,** in the Lucerna Hall, Prague) directed the orchestra for three years in the thirties. Kurt Masur (**facing page** and **right**) was with the East Berlin Komische Oper for four years, and is as respected for his operatic work as his concert work.

Rudolf Kempe (**right**) conducts the Vienna Philharmonic. The many tours made by this orchestra throughout the world, coupled with its outstanding gramophone records under a whole galaxy of great conductors, have made it one of the most admired of all orchestras.

VIENNA PHILHARMONIC ORCHESTRA

The first performance given by the Vienna Philharmonic Orchestra took place in the Redoutensaal of the Royal and Imperial Palace on 28 March 1842. The orchestra consisted of players from the Court Opera, and the conductor was Otto Nicolai – still remembered as the composer of *The Merry Wives of Windsor* (1849). Before that date most Viennese public concerts had been given by a mixture of amateur and professional players in such places as the Augarten (the open-air pleasure grounds) and were, to say the least, intermittent and of variable artistic worth. Of these the most important were the concerts sponsored by the Gesellschaft der Musikfreunde (the Society of Friends of Music, or 'Philharmonic' Society), which was founded in 1813 and still promotes concerts to this day. An earlier attempt to form a professional orchestra, also using members of the Court Opera, had been made in 1833 by Schubert's friend Franz Lachner. But this had failed through lack of drive. Nicolai suffered from no such inhibitions and within a remarkably short time had won the allegiance of players and audience.

Although the players were committed to their work at the Court Opera, what they did in their free time was their own affair. The Vienna Philharmonic therefore emerged, right from the start, as a self-governing body, dependent on no patron and able to do as it liked with its finances. Nicolai arranged that provision should be made for pensions, and later a special annual benefit concert was inaugurated to provide funds for his scheme. It still takes place each year and is called, appropriately, the 'Nicolai-Konzert'.

As long as Nicolai remained with the orchestra, which he did until 1847, its success seemed assured. But with his departure its fortunes wavered and by the late 1850s had reached a very low ebb indeed. Matters were not improved by the political uprisings that culminated in the 1848 Revolution. In 1860, however, Karl Eckert, the orchestra's conductor (1854–60), hit upon the idea of introducing a subscription scheme for its concerts. Instead of the single concert every so often, music-lovers could now buy a ticket for a series of four. The scheme proved so attractive that a fifth concert had to be added to

The standard of musical entertainment available in Vienna at such venues as the Augarten (**below**) was rather uneven until Otto Nicolai formed the Vienna Philharmonic Orchestra. After his departure the orchestra lost its sense of direction, but Karl Eckert (**right**) supervised a revival in its fortunes which culminated in a move to the Kärntnertor theater.

the first series. At the same time the orchestra moved out of the Redouten-saal and into the Kärntnertortheater (the home of the Court Opera). By the end of 1860 the Vienna Philharmonic had regained its self-confidence, and with a new conductor, Otto Dessoff (1861–75), was able to face the future. By 1879, during the conductorship of Hans Richter (1875–98), it was even able to raise the funds necessary to build a magnificent concert hall of its own: the Grosser Musikvereinsaal.

Since then the story of the Vienna Philharmonic has been one of almost continuous success – though like all great orchestras it has had periods when things have not gone too well. Richter was succeeded by Gustav Mahler (1898–1901), and then by the competent but rather unmagnetic Joseph Hellmesberger. Various distinguished conductors shared the direction of the orchestra after Hellmesberger's retirement in 1903, including Nikisch, Richard Strauss, Bruno Walter, Felix Mottl, Franz Schalk, and Karl Muck, but it was not until 1908 that a satisfactory permanent conductor could be found. This was Felix Weingartner, who guided the orchestra through the difficult period of the First World War and the even more difficult period that followed. After Weingartner, in 1927, came Wilhelm Furtwängler who,

though he remained only until 1930, did much to raise the orchestra's standards and sense of enthusiasm.

During the 1930s it became the policy to have more than one 'main' conductor, and therefore after Clemens Krauss's tenure of office (1930–33) some great names run concurrently: Bruno Walter and Wilhelm Furtwängler during the 1933–38 period, with frequent appearances by Arturo Toscanini.

Uncertainties arose again after 1938 when Austria became an appendage of the German Reich. But, thanks to the efforts of Furtwängler, the orchestra was able to retain its identity and independence. Within two weeks of the end of the Second World War it was back in business, with Clemens Krauss again as its conductor.

Since then there can be few conductors of any importance who have not been eager to work with the Vienna Philharmonic, and it is one of the most admired of all orchestras. Its most recent conducting appointment, following on that of Claudio Abbado (1971–77) is that of Karl Böhm.

Left: Bernstein and the orchestra acknowledge the applause of the audience in the splendid Grosser Musikvereinsaal, home of the orchestra since 1879. **Above:** Karl Böhm, with a Vienna Philharmonic of more classical proportions, in the serenity of the Hofburgkapelle in Vienna.

The self-contained, amiable and elegant Artur Nikisch (**right**) provided a sharp contrast of personality with his predecessor at the Berlin Philharmonic, the fervent and single-minded Hans von Bülow. Nikisch said that he allowed the 'stimulating power of music' to work upon him, so that he could relay it to others with the same force. Tchaikovsky described him as 'wonderfully calm, and at the same time remarkably powerful, energetic and full of self-control. He doesn't conduct, rather it seems as if he indulges in a certain mysterious magic.'

In five years Hans von Bülow (**right**) established sound foundations for the Berlin Philharmonic. His intense personality embodied the extremes of a fiery and at times bitingly ironic temperament and a selfless dedication to a composer's intentions. Brenner (**far right**) was the first conductor of the orchestra created by Bilse's rebel musicians.

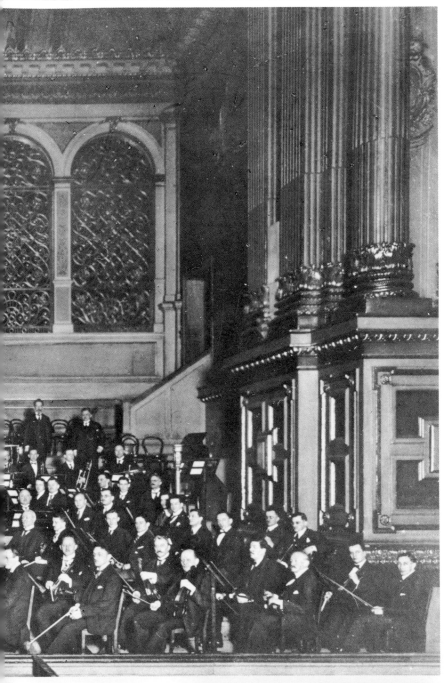

BERLIN PHILHARMONIC ORCHESTRA

In the early years of the German Empire the musical life of the capital city was not particularly impressive, and certainly could not be compared with that of the days of Frederick the Great. Perhaps the most interesting orchestra of the period was that owned, run and conducted by Benjamin Bilse, which had given concerts since 1868.

In 1882, however, Berlin was suddenly made aware of its musical inadequacies by a series of concerts given by Hans von Bülow and the Meiningen Court Orchestra. And when, a few months later, fifty of Bilse's musicians resigned because of low wages and the indignity of being required to travel fourth class instead of third on the railways, what could have been more natural than that they should decide to form themselves into a new, self-governing orchestra: an orchestra dedicated to the pursuit of the artistic standards of the Meiningen Orchestra.

They chose Ludwig von Brenner as their conductor and gave their first concert on 17 October 1882. Their courage was rewarded and the season that followed was remarkably successful. Of particular importance was their series of 'Philharmonic Concerts' devoted to major symphonic classics and conducted by Franz Wüllner, director of the famous Dresden Court Orchestra.

But in spite of its artistic success the orchestra met with severe financial problems. These came to a head in 1886 and were only averted by the generosity ·and financial expertise of the wealthy Mendelssohn family. At the same time the orchestra put itself in the hands of a new conductor: Hans von Bülow. He was determined to aim for the highest possible level of technical and artistic achievement. And this, over the period 1887–93, is what he attained.

The old Philharmonie (**left**) was built as a roller-skating rink in the mid-nineteenth century. Splendid interior decoration did not quite eradicate the feeling of a multi-purpose hall, but it was still the musical center of Europe in the 1920s. Furtwängler (**above left,** in the old Philharmonie) saw his role as a conductor as one of allowing a composer's creative processes to unfold again in performance, thus 'laying bare the soul of a work.' Some found this approach too subjective.

Since Bülow's reforms the orchestra has gone from strength to strength, always remaining a self-governing, democratic body that appointed its own conductors and ordered its own affairs. Bülow was succeeded, after a series of guest conductors, including Richter, Mottl, Levi, and Richard Strauss, by Artur Nikisch (1895–1922), and then Wilhelm Furtwängler (1922–45).

During the 1920s and 30s the Berlin Philharmonic, in common with the rest of Germany, suffered many financial troubles – though during this period it came to be subsidized by the government, the City of Berlin, and the Berlin State Radio. It also had to fight the various restrictions that the Nazi Party sought to place on its choice of guest conductor and the kind of music it wished to play. Anything or anybody with Jewish connections was anathema to the Nazis, whether it was Mendelssohn or Mahler, Menuhin or Huberman! Unlike many artists of his stature

Furtwängler stayed on in Nazi Germany, keeping his orchestra alive and in the government's good books.

The first concert after the Second World War took place on 26 May 1945 in the Titania Palast – a former cinema, literally the only reasonably sized hall left standing in a devastated Berlin. The Philharmonic's own concert hall, the Philharmonie (remodelled from an old roller-skating rink and used by the orchestra from 1882) had been destroyed in 1944. By August 1945 the orchestra had a new conductor – the young Sergiu Celibidache. Though inexperienced, he proved to be a good choice and remained with the orchestra long enough to re-establish its sense of self-respect. Gradually the exiled musicians began to return as guests, and even Furtwängler was able to rehabilitate himself, taking over official leadership in 1952. He was succeeded by the orchestra's present conductor, Herbert von Karajan, in 1954.

When Karajan accepted *'mit Tausend Freuden'* the invitation to become the Berlin Philharmonic's Permanent Conductor, it was the fulfilment of a fifteen-year ambition. **Above:** he records a Bruckner symphony in the Jesus Christus Kirche, Berlin. His characteristic underscoring of Bruckner's majestic work with measured, unhurried tempi has won much admiration, as has his deep understanding of Brahms. **Right** and **center:** the Philharmonie, built in 1953. Architect Hans Scharoun tried to abolish the division between performer and audience and place the music at the center of attention. Many find that this structure does indeed lend the music greater communicative power. The design also allows the possibility of having music sound from all sides, and this makes the Philharmonie particularly suitable for modern music.

CONCERTGEBOUW ORCHESTRA AMSTERDAM

Until the formation of the Concertgebouw Orchestra, the Wagner Vereniging (Wagner Society) and the Toonkunst Organization (a society for the promotion of choral singing) towards the end of the 19th century, the city of Amsterdam was not noted as a center of European music. Its earliest promotional institution, the Felix Meritis Society, had been founded in 1777 and was concerned with the cultivation of the arts in general. It sponsored regular winter concerts and continued its operations until 1889. Various orchestras were formed in Amsterdam in the middle of the 19th century, the most notable being the Park Orkest, conducted by Willem Stumpff, and then, after 1883, by Willem Kes. This gradually developed into an impressive body, much helped by the musicianship of the violinist and conductor Johannes Verhulst.

In 1883 a group of music-lovers formed themselves into the Concertgebouw Gezelschap – the Concert Building Society. Their intention was to found a suitable orchestra and promote a series of first-class concerts throughout the year. In fact the 'concert building' they had in mind was not yet in existence, but this did not deter them. The first program to be played in the new Concertgebouw was given on 11 April 1888, under the conductor Henri Viotta. In the following autumn the first series of subscription concerts commenced, this time conducted by Willem Kes, who remained the

Henry Viotta (**left**) conducted the first ever concert (announced **above**) in the hall from which the Concertgebouw Orchestra takes its name.

Society's Principal Conductor until 1895.

Within a short time the Concertgebouw Orchestra could fairly claim to be *the* national orchestra of Holland, and well on its way to becoming an orchestra of international importance. Willem Kes was succeeded by Willem Mengelberg (1895–1938), who then worked in partnership with Eduard van Beinum until he eventually retired in 1941. Van Beinum was the orchestra's Principal Conductor until 1959, and was followed by Eugen Jochum (1961–63), and Bernard Haitink (appointed in 1964).

The Concertgebouw Orchestra consists of approximately one hundred players. It began making regular European tours under Mengelberg and these are now continued on a world-basis. Guest conductors make frequent appearances, and there can be scarcely any musician of international standing who has not felt it a privilege to appear in one of its concerts.

The Concertgebouw Orchestra seems able to form extremely resilient relationships with its conductors. Mengelberg (**top**) was Principal Conductor for forty-three years and van Beinum (**above** and, **left,** with the orchestra) for eighteen. Bernard Haitink, (sixteen years to date) records (**right**) in the Concertgebouw in 1979. The session brought together violinist Itzhak Perlman and cellist Mstislav Rostropovich.

Among the many major recordings made by Haitink and the Concertgebouw are the complete symphonies of Bruckner and Mahler.

CZECH PHILHARMONIC ORCHESTRA

Although the Czech Philharmonic gave its first concert on 4 January 1896, it came into existence as the result of a strike for improved conditions staged on 1 January 1894 by the members of the National Theater Orchestra. One of their decisions was to found a Philharmonic Orchestral Society that would "raise the artistic standards of music-making in Prague to a level befitting so ancient and historic a city." The first concert to be given by the National Theater Orchestra on behalf of the Society consisted of works by Dvořák

and was conducted by the composer himself. In February 1901 the musicians of the National Theater Orchestra went on strike again, but this time they were dismissed. They promptly reorganized themselves as an independent orchestra under the name of the Czech Philharmonic.

Despite many setbacks and financial crises the new orchestra flourished. Its first important conductor was Vilém Zemánek (1903-18) who, together with a frequent guest-conductor Oskar Nedbal, established a firm artistic basis. Even during this early period several important artists were invited to conduct the orchestra, including Mahler,

In 1919 Václav Tálich (**above**) became Principal Conductor of the Czech Philharmonic. It was largely as a result of his outstanding gifts that the orchestra was able to achieve international importance. He was an effective champion of Czech composers and brought world-famous conductors to Prague. Kubelik (**right**) steered the orchestra on a steady course through the 1940s, but in the 1950s found that the opera houses of London and New York afforded a more congenial environment.

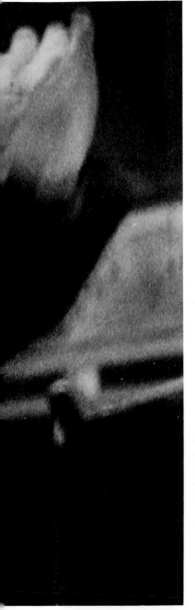

After Kubelik left the Czech Philharmonic it was directed jointly by Václav Neumann (**above** and **left**) and Karel Sejna. In 1950 Karel Ancerl became Principal Conductor but when he left in 1968 Neumann returned to the orchestra. From 1970-73 he combined this role with that of Music Director of the Stuttgart Opera.

Grieg, and Richard Strauss.

The years 1918-45 saw the Czech Philharmonic assume the status of a world-class orchestra. The main credit for this must go to Václav Tálich, who directed its fortunes from 1918 to 1941. He was succeeded by Rafael Kubelik (1942-48), who guided the orchestra through the difficult years of the Second World War.

The Czech Philharmonic became a State Orchestra on 22 October 1945, and from that moment its financial problems were over. The players were now placed on a salaried basis, with pensions, paid holidays, and sickness benefits, and consideration given to the importance of adequate rehearsal time.

In 1948, however, political upheavals arose once more, and Kubelik left in protest at the Russian domination of his country. For a while the orchestra was directed by Václav Neumann and Karel Šejna, but in 1950 Karel Ančerl was appointed Principal Conductor and another great era began. Ančerl remained in charge until 1968 and was succeeded by Václav Neumann. The orchestra's present strength is about 115. It has toured widely, visiting Great Britain for the first time in 1902 and America in 1965. It has been conducted by most of the world's great conductors.

ORCHESTRE DE LA SUISSE ROMANDE

This orchestra was founded by the Swiss conductor Ernest Ansermet in 1918 for the express purpose of giving concerts in the French-speaking part of Switzerland (the 'Suisse Romande'). At that time there was no symphony orchestra resident in that part of the country. Despite many organizational and financial problems, Ansermet managed to persuade the cities of Geneva and Lausanne, together with some of the smaller towns in the area, to give financial support to the venture.

Until 1938 the orchestra was active only during the winter months, but it was then adopted as the regular broadcasting orchestra for the French region, and this consolidation of its financial support has enabled it to extend its activities throughout the year. Besides its regular public concerts and work for Swiss Radio, the orchestra serves the needs of the Geneva Opera House, whose productions in recent years have been particularly striking and adventurous. It has toured widely, both in Europe and America, as well as Japan and South Korea. Its present strength is about 115 players.

Ernest Ansermet retired in 1966 and was succeeded by Paul Kletzki who, for reasons of health, remained with the OSR for only two years. He, in turn, was followed by Wolfgang Sawallisch, and then, in 1980, by Horst Stein.

The Suisse Romande orchestra was founded by Ernest Ansermet (**right**) in 1918. By the time of his retirement in 1966 it had become one of the most respected and versatile in Europe. **Above:** Wolfgang Sawallisch conducting the orchestra at its home, the Geneva Opera House. Horst Stein (**left**) became Conductor in 1980.

PARIS CONSERVATOIRE ORCHESTRA

The Orchestre de la Société des Concerts du Conservatoire came into existence in 1828 when the German-born violinist François Habenek, who had already distinguished himself as director of the amateur concerts known as the 'Concerts Francais' and the professional 'Concerts Spirituels', proposed to form a society which would be a focal point for the performance of orchestral music. In conception it owed much to the London Philharmonic Society, founded in 1813.

The first concert took place on 9 March 1828 in the theater of the Conservatoire. The orchestra numbered nearly one hundred players, and the program contained, among other items, Beethoven's Third Symphony, the *Eroica*. Habenek directed the proceedings in the old-fashioned way, from his seat as leading violin. The concert was a success and the way was paved for a regular series of similar events.

Habenek remained in charge of the Concerts du Conservatoire until 1848 and was followed, successively, by Narcisse Girard (1849–60), Théophile Tilmant (1860–63), François Hainl (1864–72), Edouard Deldevez (1872–95), Jules Garcin (1885–92), Paul Taffanel (1892–1901), Georges Marty (1901–08), the composer André Messager (1908–18), Philipp Gaubert (1919–38), Charles Munch (1938–47), and André Cluytens (1947–67).

The orchestra is managed by a committee of seven of its members, who elect the conductor. Many of its concerts are given in the Théâtre des Champs Elysées. It has worked under important guest conductors and made fine recordings.

Left: Berlioz directs a performance at the *Circe Olympique* in the Champs Elysées, Paris. Many French composers, including Berlioz, Debussy, Ravel and Messiaen, have been outstanding masters of orchestration. **Above:** André Cluytens was Conductor at the Conservatoire for twenty years.

ISRAEL PHILHARMONIC ORCHESTRA

Organized musical life in Israel began in 1909 with the building of the city of Tel-Aviv. The first symphony orchestra was that of a small Music School established in 1910. Opera arrived in 1923, and in 1933 a Conservatory of Music and Dramatic Art was founded. In the face of this evidence of a genuine music-loving public, the presence of a major symphony orchestra became a necessity.

The Israel Symphony Orchestra was founded in 1936 by Bronislaw Huberman who, apart from artistic considerations, wished to create a refuge for distinguished Jewish musicians who were being forced, as he had been, to flee from Nazi persecution. The first concert was conducted by Arturo Toscanini, and it soon became very clear that a world-class orchestra had come into existence.

For a brief period (1946-48) the orchestra was known as the Palestine Philharmonic, but when the British Mandate ended in 1948 it adopted its present name: the Israel Philharmonic Orchestra. Its headquarters is the Frederick R. Mann Auditorium in Tel-Aviv, but it shares its main concert-series with Haifa and Jerusalem and gives concerts throughout Israel. It is an independent institution, sponsored by the Ministry of Education and Culture, the America-Israel Cultural Foundation, and the Friends of the Israel Philharmonic Orchestra – a society which operates in Britain, Australia, and Switzerland. Besides its regular subscription series, it is involved in special concerts in kibbutzim and military camps. It has toured throughout the world, and appears regularly at the Israel Festival. Its present Music Director and Adviser is Zubin Mehta.

The IPO takes its role in the musical and moral life of the nation very seriously. Apart from its worldwide tours it gives concerts throughout Israel, taking in kibbutzim and military camps. **Above:** Nativity Square, Bethlehem. Zubin Mehta (**below** and **right**) is present Music Director.

LENINGRAD PHILHARMONIC ORCHESTRA

In comparison with other major European countries, Russia was slow to develop an organized concert life that involved permanent orchestras. Although music had played a part in the Tsarist court, it tended to be imported—usually in the form of Italian and French opera. The most distinctly Russian form of music-making was to be found in the Imperial Chapel, whose choir had been developed in 1713, by order of Peter the Great, from a smaller group of singers that had existed in one form or another since 1479. This choir, of men and boys, achieved great renown, and after the 1917 Revolution continued as a choir of mixed voices affiliated to the Leningrad Philharmonic Society and now known as the Academic Glinka Choir.

During the 19th century, when the great school of Russian Nationalist Composers came into existence, it was to private enterprise that 'orchestras' owed their foundation. For example, when Anton Rubinstein commenced his series of Russian Musical Society Concerts in 1859, he drew his forces partly from the professional musicians attached to St Petersburg's theaters and opera house, and partly from the more accomplished amateur musicians in the city. Similarly Belayev's series of Russian Symphony Concerts, established in 1885 and devoted exclusively to the performance of Russian music, depended on an ad hoc assembly of amateur and professional musicians.

In these and similar enterprises it was St Petersburg, the Tsarist capital, that led the way—with Moscow, which became the Soviet capital in 1918, some distance behind. To that city, renamed Petrograd in 1914 and Leningrad in 1924, belongs what is certainly the oldest and probably the best known of Russia's present-day orchestras: the Leningrad Philharmonic.

In its present form the orchestra dates from 1917 when, as the Petrograd State Orchestra, it continued the work of the St Petersburg Court Orchestra, which had been founded in 1882. In the difficult years immediately after the revolution it was directed by Serge Kussevitsky (1917-20) and Emil Cooper (1920-22), with the assistance of certain conductors from the Maryinsky Theater (the former Imperial Opera House), including Nikolai Malko, Albert Coates, and Gregor Fitelberg. It changed its name in 1920 to the State Philharmonic Orchestra, and finally in 1924 to the Leningrad Philharmonic. From 1933 to 1937 it was conducted by the Austrian conductor Fritz Stiedry, and during the Second World War came under the direction of Yevgeni Mravinsky, who remained its Principal Conductor for more than thirty years.

The Leningrad Philharmonic has been associated with many important

The Great Hall of the Leningrad Philharmonic Society (**left**), belonged to the Nobles' Club of St Petersburg until the October Revolution, and was accessible only to the aristocracy. It lays claim to the best acoustics in Europe. The Leningrad Philharmonic Society was the first of many similar societies created after 1917 to take charge of the musical affairs of the larger Soviet cities.

first performances of Soviet music, notably the symphonies of Shostakovich. The famous wartime premiere of his Seventh Symphony, composed during the siege of Leningrad and performed under the direction of Karl Eliasberg on 9 August 1942 to the sound of German gunfire, was, however, undertaken by members of the Radio Orchestra—the Philharmonic having been evacuated to the safety of Novosbirsk.

The orchestra now forms part of the Leningrad Philharmonic Society—the first of the many 'Philharmonics' to be set up after 1917 to administer the musical activities of the main Soviet cities. It is large enough to be able to break down into two full orchestras, and also subdivides into a 17-man chamber orchestra, and various quartets and quintets. Part of its duties is to accompany the Kirov Ballet and the Opera. It tours widely within Soviet

Yevgeny Mravinsky (**above, left**) first became conductor of the Leningrad Philharmonic during the Second World War, and remained with the orchestra for more than thirty years. **Left:** Yevgeny Svetlanov, People's Artist of the USSR, conducts at the Moscow State Conservatory. **Above:** Play it again, Mstislav. Composer Shostakovich (left) performer Rostropovich (center) and conductor Rozhdestvensky (right) discuss a point in Shostakovich's Cello Concerto. **Right:** Veronika Dudarova conducts the Moscow City Symphony Orchestra in the Hall of Columns at the House of Trade Unions in Moscow.

Russia itself, and has also made tours abroad—notably to America in 1962. All its decisions are made by a council of fifteen playing members.

In recent years several of its younger assistant conductors, such as Eduard Sarov and Igor Blazhkov, have attempted to broaden its rather conservative repertoire by exploring avant-garde music. But in July 1968 Blazhkov was dismissed for his pains. Under the threat of this kind of artistic interference from an all-powerful and somewhat capricious government, it is hard to see how an orchestra of international repute can hope to maintain the vitality that alone can guarantee true excellence. Total State subsidy, and a consequent low price of admission, may ensure large and enthusiastic audiences and enviable working conditions, but it is available at an artistic price that most Western orchestras would be loathe to pay.

American Orchestras

*S*INCE THE UNITED States of America has had the good fortune to have been forced to invent herself, as it were from scratch, many of her institutions have been able to raise themselves on a more rational basis than was permitted to European societies, with their double-edged attribute of a historical and cultural heritage reaching back into the mists of time. The American orchestra has availed itself of this opportunity for rationality as much as any other American institution. Though in certain instances its model is to be found in the typical European 'Philharmonic Society' tradition, the less hidebound atmosphere of the United States has combined with its capacity for creating enormous wealth (for society at large, and individuals in particular) to place the average orchestra on a solid financial footing, backed by the socially-conscious enthusiasm of a significantly large section of the public.

It was to America, moreover, that large numbers of professional musicians turned – either to escape the political upheavals that shook Europe in the 18th and 19th centuries, or to rid themselves of its ridiculous and cramping social systems. Some went merely on a visit, returning in due course content with the profits they had made. Others went to stay – and work. From all their efforts, permanent or transitory, perhaps the greatest cross-fertilization of talents that the world has ever known took place. Talent, money, and freedom! It is scarcely surprising that the American orchestra has emerged as fully the equal of any of its European ancestors.

Perspectives on a New World: Toscanini refused to perform under German or Italian Fascism, and came to New York to take charge of the New York Philharmonic. Persuaded out of retirement at the age of 70, he conducted the NBC Symphony Orchestra till he was 87. He is seen (**far left**) with Phillip Sacci, editor of the Italian publication *La Stanza* during a US tour in May 1950. **Above:** the Hollywood Bowl, one of the world's largest natural amphitheaters. It also enjoys one of the world's most magnificent climates and shares with its environs one of the world's largest quotas of glamor and romance. **Left:** the memorial to Antonin Dvořák, near Pribràm in Czechoslovakia. During his visit to America Dvořák was fascinated by American folk music and suggested that American composers might find it a source of inspiration.

NEW YORK PHILHARMONIC SYMPHONY ORCHESTRA

The present orchestra derives its somewhat awkward name from the fact that it originated in the union of two old-established New York concert-giving societies: the Philharmonic Society, founded in 1842, and the New York Symphony Society, founded in 1878. The amalgamation took place in March 1928. Thus the present orchestra may fairly claim to be the oldest body of its kind in continuous existence in America, and the third oldest (next to the Philharmonic Societies of London and Vienna) in the world.

The New York Philharmonic Society came into existence as the result of a meeting of professional musicians, under the chairmanship of Ureli Corelli Hill, on 2 April 1842. Their intention was to bring to New York the same standard of music-making enjoyed by comparable cities in Europe, and they set about it in the same way – by developing a supportive Society that would sponsor an orchestra specially gathered together for the purpose. The first concert took place on 7 December 1842 at the Apollo Rooms. If the occasion sounds as if it might have taken place in London it is hardly surprising, for many of the founding musicians were Englishmen: Charles Horn, William Wallace, Edward Hodges, and George Loder, for example.

Regular seasons, each consisting of three concerts at a cost of ten dollars a series, followed this first meeting. The orchestra worked on a co-operative basis, paying its musicians out of the box-office receipts (which naturally varied from season to season!). It was not until 1909 that a guaranteed salary structure was introduced.

In the early years the elected president of the Society (always a professional musician) directed the performances, and fortunately several 'presidents' turned out to be effective conductors. Among the most interesting and influential were Theodore Eisfeld (1852–56), Carl Bergman (1856–76), Leopold Damrosch (1876–77), Theodore Thomas (1878–91), and Anton Seidl (1891–98). Thomas and Seidl were particularly successful in guiding the Society's artistic and financial policies. By the end of the 19th century the season included more than a dozen concerts, and in 1891 the Philharmonic moved into its own concert hall, the

Music Hall (built by the generosity of the millionaire Andrew Carnegie) which remained its home for seventy years.

After a certain falling off in popular interest during the early 1900s, the Society invited a series of famous guest conductors to come over from Europe. They included Henry J. Wood (London), Felix Weingartner (Munich), Richard Strauss (Berlin), Willem Mengelberg (Amsterdam) and Edouard Colonne (Paris). The scheme came to an end in 1906 when Vassily Safonov was engaged as sole conductor for three years. He was followed by Gustav Mahler (1909–11) and Josef Stransky (1911–21). By this time the season lasted twenty-three weeks and embraced fifty-four concerts.

Meanwhile a new organization, the New Symphony Orchestra, had appeared in April 1919. Its intention (at least in the beginning) was to provide a platform for contemporary music. The orchestra was renamed the National Symphony in 1920, but the venture proved too costly. In April

Right: A program from the first concert the orchestra gave, in December 1842 at the Apollo Rooms. Its home today is in the Lincoln Center for the Performing Arts. **Top** and **above:** the interior and exterior of the Avery Fisher Hall, part of the Center. **Far right** (from left to right): Walter Damrosch, guest conductor of the orchestra, with Paul Whiteman, who ran several dance bands in New York and was known as the 'King of Jazz', and Leonard Bernstein, who combines a career as a conductor with one as a composer.

1921 an amalgamation with the Philharmonic Society was announced. Two years later a further amalgamation took place – this time with the City Symphony Orchestra, which had enjoyed a brief existence giving concerts at low admission prices.

From now on the expanded Philharmonic Society engaged Principal Conductors and Guest Conductors, the 'principal' conductorship often being shared. For example, Willem Mengelberg and Josef Stransky shared the regular conductorship in the 1922–23 season, with Willem van Hoogstraten as guest conductor. Hoogstraten then joined Mengelberg as principal conductor for 1923–24 and 1924–25.

In the meantime a New York Symphony Society had been founded in 1878 by Leopold Damrosch. In 1885 the Society's artistic policy was determined by Walter Damrosch (Leopold's son), and he conducted most of the concerts. Though largely successful, its fortunes varied somewhat over the years. In 1903 it changed its name to the New York Symphony Orchestra and reorganized itself on a co-operative basis – profit and loss being shared by the players themselves. But this proved unsatisfactory and in 1907 a 'Symphony Society' was formed, which assumed all financial responsibility and put the performers on a salary.

The cost of maintaining both the Philharmonic Society *and* the Symphony Society proved too much, even for New York, and in March 1928 they amalgamated. Toscanini and Mengelberg became the new regular conductors, with Walter Damrosch as one of several guest conductors. The first season lasted twenty-eight weeks and offered a subscription schedule of 103 concerts – about two thirds the number given by the two independent organizations in the previous year.

Since then the orchestra's history has been one of continuous and growing success under a steady procession of great conductors, including Sir John Barbirolli (1937–40), Artur Rodzinski (1942–47), Leopold Stokowski (1949–50), Dimitri Mitropoulos (1949–58), Leonard Bernstein (1958–69), who was then created the orchestra's first 'Laureate Conductor', Pierre Boulez (1971–77), and, since 1978, Zubin Mehta. The orchestra consists of 105 players, operates on an annual budget of more than 9 million dollars, and provides a round-the-year season of some 200 concerts. Since September 1962 it has had a permanent home in the splendid Philharmonic Hall of New York's magnificent Lincoln Center for the Performing Arts.

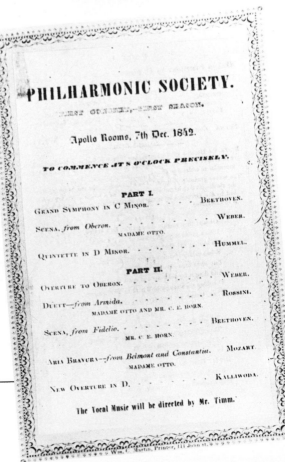

Above: the original Boston Symphony Orchestra at Music Hall in 1882. **Top left:** Munch; **top right:** Kussevitsky; **mid-right:** Monteux; **right:** Leinsdorf. With Rabaud (1918) Monteux marks the beginning of the French-oriented tradition of the BSO. In Kussevitsky's twenty-five years with the orchestra he led the first concerts in the Berkshires (1936). An energetic man, of eclectic musical taste, he contributed to the formation of the summer academy for young artists at Tanglewood. Munch introduced much contemporary music, particularly from France. Leinsdorf restored many forgotten works to the repertory. His noteworthy recordings include a Prokofiev cycle.

BOSTON SYMPHONY ORCHESTRA

The orchestra was founded in 1881 by Henry Lee Higginson, a wealthy soldier and amateur musician who wished to give his fellow Bostonians the chance to hear regular concerts of good music at a low price. Higginson assembled an orchestra of about 70 players, and engaged the German-born singer and composer George Henschel (who became a naturalized Englishman and pursued much of his career in England) as conductor. The first con-

cert took place on 22 October 1881 at the Music Hall. It was a great success and the entire season sold out.

Henschel was succeeded by a series of German-born conductors: Wilhelm Gericke (1884-89), Artur Nikisch (1889-93), Emil Pauer (1893-98), Wilhelm Gericke again (1898-1906), Karl Muck (1906-08), Max Fiedler (1908-12), and Karl Muck again (1912-18). By 1918, however, an anti-German feeling had grown up because of the First World War (which America entered in 1917), and Karl Muck was followed by two French conductors: Henri Rabaud

(1918-19) and Pierre Monteux (1919-24). Thereafter the orchestra's policy toward the appointment of conductors became more catholic: Sergei Kussevitsky (1924-49), Charles Munch (1949-62), Erich Leinsdorf (1962-69), William Steinberg (1969-72), and now Seiji Ozawa (appointed in 1973). Of all the Boston conductors perhaps Karl Muck, Pierre Monteux, Sergei Kussevitsky and Charles Munch have been most influential in moulding its style and reputation.

In Higginson's original scheme were included concerts of light music. The

Seiji Ozawa, (**above**) born in China of Japanese parents, became the thirteenth Music Director of the Boston Symphony Orchestra in 1973, having spent the previous year as Music Adviser. In 1976 he led the orchestra on a European tour, encompassing most major cities, and followed this with a triumphant tour of Japan in 1978. He was then invited to work with the Peking Central Philharmonic Orchestra.

In 1938 the Boston Symphony Orchestra took up summer residence at Tanglewood in Berkshire. The large estate (**above**) originally belonged to a Boston banker.

first of these was given in July 1885 and was followed by a series of spring concerts which gradually became a tradition – the famous Boston 'Pops'.

Until 1918 Henry Lee Higginson met the annual financial deficit out of his own pocket. But with the crisis that arose out of the war-fevered dismissal of Karl Muck, Higginson handed over responsibility to a Board of Trustees. Soon they had to face the fact that the orchestra was not only unhappy with the wages it was getting, but resented never having been allowed to join the Musicians Union. Thirty players resigned in a body, and Pierre Monteux had to do the best he could by bringing in retired musicians and anyone who was willing to accept the existing conditions. Despite this the orchestra's reputation continued to grow and it was not until 1942 that the Trustees finally capitulated and allowed the players to become Union members. It was the last important orchestra to come into the fold!

The Boston Symphony Orchestra began making recordings with RCA in 1917, and with the coming of radio began to broadcast regularly. In 1938, under Kussevitsky, it took up annual summer residence at Tanglewood, and there, two years later, founded the now famous Berkshire Music Center – an annual summer academy for young musicians.

The orchestra has toured throughout America and much of the world, including the USSR and China. It gives more than 250 concerts each year, and its annual budget has grown from Higginson's estimated 115,000 dollars to more than 12 million. It receives both federal and state grants, besides benefiting from a great many business foundations and individual patrons. The present orchestra consists of 102 players, and its Boston concerts are given at Symphony Hall (opened 1900).

CHICAGO SYMPHONY ORCHESTRA

The Chicago Symphony Orchestra was founded in 1891 by the German-born violinist and conductor Theodor Thomas and is therefore the third oldest orchestra in the United States. Thomas, whose family settled in America in 1845, organized his first concert-orchestra in 1864 and travelled the country giving concerts of an extremely adventurous kind. It was not until he settled in Chicago, however, that he was able to realize his ambition of founding a full-time orchestra on a permanent basis. Backed by a group of wealthy citizens he established his Chicago Orchestra (as it was then called) and in 1904 was able to move it into its permanent home: the Orchestra Hall.

Thomas died in 1905 and was succeeded by another German-born musician, Frederick Stock. At the same time the orchestra was renamed in his memory. It remained the Theodor Thomas Orchestra until 1913, when it

Theodor Thomas (**right**), the founder of the Chicago Symphony Orchestra, was an acknowledged authority on acoustics. He helped Daniel Burnham, the architect of Orchestra Hall, in the planning of the building. The picture of the orchestra in the Hall (**far right**) is from 1953. Fritz Reiner is the conductor. Stock (**bottom right**) directed the orchestra for thirty-eight years and founded the Civic Orchestra of Chicago in 1919. This was the first training orchestra in the United States to be affiliated to a major orchestra.

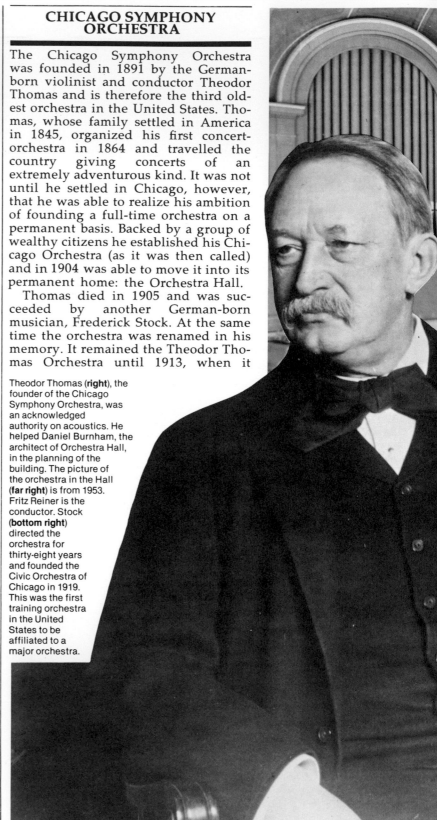

MPHONY ORCHESTRA
Conductor
253

OSCAR
CHICAGO

finally became the Chicago Symphony Orchestra.

Stock was its director for 38 years, during which time he founded a training orchestra for young musicians (the Civic Orchestra of Chicago, 1919) which was the first of its kind in America, and established a series of 'popular' concerts, and subscription concerts especially for children. He also added a pension fund for his players. Stock was the first conductor to make recordings with his own orchestra (1916), and in 1941, to celebrate the orchestra's fiftieth birthday, he commissioned a remarkable series of new works – including Stravinsky's Symphony in C, Milhaud's Symphony No. 1, Roy Harris's *American-Creed*, Kodaly's *Concerto for Orchestra*, and Sir William Walton's overture *Scapino*.

Stock died in 1943. He was followed by Artur Rodzinsky (1947-48), Rafael Kubelik (1950-53), Fritz Reiner (1953-63), Jean Martinon (1963-68), and Sir Georg Solti (appointed in 1969). Since 1962 the orchestra has also enjoyed the services of a Principal Guest Conductor – the first being Giulini (1969-72).

The Chicago Symphony Orchestra consists of 106 players. Its main 30-week season begins in the autumn, presenting a series of five subscription concerts each week. Since 1911 it has taken part in the annual Ravinia Festival, held in Highland Park, some 25

The Orchestra Hall (**left**) was built in 1904 with funds provided by 'ten gentlemen of Chicago'. The trustees' intention was to build 'a Music Hall pure and simple, monumental in character, without proscenium or scenery, and also without stores or business adjuncts of any kind.' Burnham emulated the architecture of 'the best period of the Italian Renaissance, that noble and well settled style..' Sir Georg Solti (**above** and **right**, with the orchestra in the Hall) is present Music Director.

miles north of Chicago. It undertook its first international tour in 1971, and tours frequently throughout the United States. Under Solti's guidance it has become recognized as one of the world's great orchestras. Not least among its achievements has been a long line of commissions and world premieres – one of the most recent being Sir Michael Tippett's Symphony No. 4 (1977). It has won two awards for its services to contemporary music, and its recordings of Mahler symphonies, under Solti, have been universally acclaimed. The Chicago Symphony Orchestra's library is one of the largest and most comprehensive collections of scores and parts in the world.

PHILADELPHIA ORCHESTRA

Although Philadelphia, the state capital of Pennsylvania, has enjoyed a long history of musical activity (its oldest musical organization, The Musical Fund Society, was founded in 1820), the Philadelphia Orchestra did not come into existence until 1900.

At the end of the 18th century and during the first half of the 19th, Philadelphia's musical life was vigorous and self-sufficient. But gradually it found itself dependent on visits from the superior orchestras of New York and Boston. But civic pride called for something more personal, and when the German-born conductor Fritz Scheel visited Philadelphia in the summer of 1899 three amateur music societies agreed to pay his expenses for conducting two concerts with a professional orchestra. These were given in the spring of 1900 and were so successful that it was decided to found a new orchestra with Scheel as its permanent conductor. The first concert took place in November in Philadelphia's historic Academy of Music (1857) and the Philadelphia Orchestra was born.

Scheel remained with the Philadelphians until his death in 1907, during which time he recruited new and better players and gradually built his forces into a well-drilled ensemble. He was succeeded by Carl Pohlig (1907-12), and then by Leopold Stokowski (1912-36). And it is to the remarkable Stokowski that the orchestra owes its rise to world eminence. His unfailing, though sometimes rather questionable, sense of showmanship made the Philadelphians the talk of America. But his fine musicianship could not be denied, and under his guidance much excellent work was done.

Stokowski was followed by the orchestra's present chief conductor: Eugene Ormandy. He had appeared as a guest conductor in 1931, and within a few years the Board of Directors had begun to consider him as a possible co-

Under the baton of Eugene Ormandy (**left**), the Philadelphia Orchestra has developed the largest recorded repertoire of any orchestra. In 1976, 297 records by the orchestra with Ormandy were listed as available. On two occasions, Ormandy and the orchestra won the Grammy Award. **Far left:** Ormandy conducting the orchestra during a recording at the Old Met in New York.

The Philadelphia Orchestra was founded after Fritz Scheel (**above**) conducted two concerts in the city. They were so successful that an orchestra was created for Scheel. Leopold Stokowski (**left**) made the orchestra famous using his unique blend of showmanship and fine musicianship. Amongst the works Stokowski premiered with the orchestra were Stravinsky's *Rite of Spring* (1913), Shostakovich's First Symphony (1925) and Mahler's Eighth Symphony (1907). Each summer the orchestra performs in the open-sided pavilion in Robin Hood Dell (**top**), recently renamed the Mann Music Center, in Fairmount Park.

conductor with the controversial Stokowski. His appointment in 1936 was therefore a foregone conclusion. It also proved to be a wise decision, and the 'Ormandy-Philadelphia' sound has since become a legend.

Ormandy will retire at the end of the 1979-80 season, handing over the title of Music Director to the orchestra's current Principal Guest Conductor, Riccardo Muti. He will retain a link with the orchestra, however, by becoming its Conductor Laureate.

The backbone of the orchestra's year is its series of subscription concerts at the Academy of Music. This consists, on average, of nearly 90 concerts. In the summer the orchestra performs in the Mann Music Center, a magnificent open-sided pavilion at Robin Hood Dell in Fairmount Park. During August the orchestra moves to the Saratoga Performing Arts Center, and in winter it gives concert seasons in New York, Washington, Baltimore and Wilmington, Delaware.

Since 1904 the orchestra has enjoyed the unstinting services of a Women's Committee – the first of its kind – which raises substantial and necessary funds, entertains visiting artists, and generally sees to it that the 106 playing members of the orchestra can pursue their work in the best possible conditions.

DETROIT SYMPHONY ORCHESTRA

As has often been the case in the history of American cultural enterprises, the impetus towards the formation of the Detroit Symphony Orchestra came from a group of public spirited ladies who decided to launch a 'trial' concert in the hope of arousing local enthusiasm and the promise of financial support. Their concert, which took place on 26 February 1914 under the baton of a local musician, Weston Gales, was successful enough to allow them to plan a full season on a budget of 16,000 dollars. Thus the history of the Detroit Symphony Orchestra began, in November 1914.

Weston Gales remained its conductor until 1918. He was followed by Ossip Gabrilowitsch, who held the position until 1935 (he died in the following year). It was his flair and musicianship that put the orchestra on the map. Part of his original contract contained a clause which insisted that the orchestra

The first conductor of the Detroit Symphony Orchestra was Weston Gales (**top**). His successor, Ossip Gabrilowitsch (**right**), accelerated the orchestra's rise to fame.

removed its activities to a brand new Orchestral Hall. This remained its headquarters until 1939.

After Gabrilowitsch's death the orchestra was served by a series of guest conductors, of whom Fritz Reiner was perhaps the most distinguished. Four years later it lost its home in Orchestra Hall and underwent a series of internal difficulties which were compounded by the inevitable restrictions of wartime. In 1943, however, it was reconstituted on lavish lines as an orchestra of 110 musicians – claimed to be the 'largest in the world'. Three years later it bought and refurbished a new Music Hall (formerly the Wilson Theater). But more troubles followed and in September 1949 the orchestra was actually disbanded.

It came into being again in the autumn of 1951, this time funded by the motor manufacturer John B. Ford's famous 'Detroit Plan' – a league of sponsors, each contributing a maximum of 10,000 dollars annually, whether they were industrial or business foundations, or private citizens. After a series of famous guest conductors, the Frenchman Paul Paray became the orchestra's permanent conductor (1951-63). He was followed by Sixten Ehrling (1963-73), Aldo Ceccato (1973-77), and most recently by Antal Dorati (appointed in 1977). The orchestra now consists of 97 players engaged on a full year's contract, and operates on a budget of about five million dollars. It gives over 200 concerts each year, has made important records, and broadcasts regularly over Michigan State's ten radio stations.

Since October 1956 the Detroit Symphony Orchestra has had a permanent home in the Henry and Edsal Ford Auditorium, which holds nearly 3,000 people. And since 1964 it has spent the summer months at the Meadow Brook Music Festival.

There were no Detroit Symphony Orchestra concerts in 1942-43, or in 1949-51. The chemical industrialist John B. Ford (**above right**) re-established the orchestra in 1951. Five years later the orchestra had a permanent home at the white marble Henry and Edsal Ford Auditorium (**right**). Early acoustical problems here were not really solved until 1974. Antal Dorati (**left** and, **above**, with the orchestra) is the present Director.

CLEVELAND ORCHESTRA

During the late 19th century several organizations were established in Cleveland to promote concerts and raise orchestras. The most successful was the Musical Arts Association (1902), which existed to present concerts by visiting orchestras. In 1918, however, the Association joined forces with a wealthy music-lover, Mrs Adella Prentiss Hughes, and established the Cleveland Orchestra on a permanent basis, with Nikolai Sokoloff as its first conductor and Mrs Prentiss Hughes as manager. The first concert was given on 11 December 1918 at Gray's Armory, Cleveland.

The Musical Arts Association is still the orchestra's parent organization and its affairs are managed by a Board of Trustees, who are responsible for fund-raising activities. The annual budget is nearly 10 million dollars.

Nikolai Sokoloff remained the orchestra's conductor until 1933, when he was succeeded by Artur Rodzinski (1933-43), Erich Leinsdorf (1943-46), George Szell (1946-70), and Lorin Maazel (appointed in 1972). During the 1970-71 season Pierre Boulez acted as Musical Adviser and Principal Guest Conductor.

The Cleveland Orchestra consists of 91 players. It has two homes: during the winter, the Severance Hall (opened in 1931) at Cleveland itself, and in the summer, from July to September, the Blossom Music Center (1968), a splendid park and recreation center on the

The Cleveland Orchestra was formed when Mrs Adella Prentiss Hughes (**far left**) agreed to provide funding additional to that made available by Cleveland's Musical Arts Association. She became first manager of the orchestra and Nikolai Sokoloff (**left**) first conductor. The Severance Hall (**center** and **above**, interior and exterior) was a gift from local philanthropist John Long Severance. Erected in 1931, it was rebuilt in 1958 to perfect the acoustics.

In the inaugural week of the Sydney Opera House the Cleveland Orchestra appeared in its Concert Hall (**left**) under Lorin Maazel. The Blossom Music Center (**right**) is the orchestra's permanent summer home. It gave its first concert there in 1968, as part of its Fiftieth Anniversary Season. The Center is named after the Dudley Blossom family, whose activities on behalf of the orchestra span several decades. Dudley S Blossom (**above**) held many posts in the Musical Arts Association, which raised most of the money for the orchestra's Endowment Fund. The Center's Pavilion was built at the base of a natural bowl. The convex, fan-shaped roof has no interior columns, but Is supported by specially shaped tubular steel pipe trusses which do not distort or reflect sound.

banks of the upper Cuyahoga River. A magnificent open-sided performing pavilion has been built here, which seats nearly 5,000 people. A further 13,500 can sit on the sloping grass lawns outside, within sight and sound of the performing area.

The Cleveland Orchestra took some time to establish itself, but was finally able to offer its players a full year's contract in 1967, which it now honors with some 200 concerts each year. At least two dozen of these are given especially for children. The orchestra is supported by a 'Sustaining Fund', established in 1970, which also receives help from the fund-raising activities of The Women's Committee of the Cleveland Orchestra (formed in 1921) and the Junior Committee of the Cleveland Orchestra (which dates from 1968). Money is also earned from recording contracts and radio broadcasts.

Members of the Cleveland Orchestra have made a speciality of dividing themselves into small ensembles – a String Quartet, a Woodwind Octet, a String Orchestra, and so on. These groups appear in regular concerts alongside the main orchestral series. Touring has always been a part of its policy – the first extended US Tour being made in 1921, and the first European Tour following in 1957. Tours of Canada began in 1922 and have been a permanent feature of the orchestra's activities. The Cleveland Orchestra is now regarded not only as one of the country's finest, but as one of the finest in the world.

Lorin Maazel (**far left**) became the fifth Music Director of the Cleveland Orchestra in 1972. He has led the orchestra on many international tours, conducted approximately one hundred concerts, and made numerous recordings. In 1960 he was the youngest conductor and first American to conduct at Bayreuth. The Cleveland Orchestra String Quartet (**left**) is one of the many ensembles from the Cleveland Orchestra which play at the Chamber Music Festival at Severance Hall.

LOS ANGELES PHILHARMONIC ORCHESTRA

In 1919, when Los Angeles was a relatively quiet city of about 350,000 people, William Andrews Clark, an amateur musician, art patron and bibliophile, who happened also to be the son of a multi-millionaire copper baron, decided to give the city a permanent symphony orchestra. There had been orchestras in Los Angeles during the previous forty years, but the Philharmonic was the first to be founded on a secure financial basis and with an eye to performing for every music-lover and not merely a select coterie of wealthy patrons. It was, said Clark, to be "the incarnation of an ideal and not a display of wealth." He started with a gift of one million dollars, and went on, during the remaining fifteen years of his life, to support it with a further two million.

The orchestra of 94 musicians – the largest Los Angeles had ever seen – gave its first performance on 24 October 1919, under the direction of Walter Henry Rothwell. The first season consisted of twelve pairs of subscription concerts, fourteen 'popular' concerts, and nine 'special' concerts (including some for schools). Its success was beyond question.

The first concerts were given in the Methodist Trinity Auditorium, but this soon proved too small and in 1920 the orchestra removed to a building that

Carlo Maria Giulini (**right**) began his musical career as a viola player in the Augusteo Orchestra, and first conducted it in June 1944, in a concert to celebrate the liberation of Rome. In 1951 Toscanini heard a broadcast of Haydn's *Il mondo della luna* by Giulini. He arranged a meeting and the friendship lasted.

became known as the Philharmonic Auditorium.

When Clark died in 1934, however, the Philharmonic was in financial trouble, despite his generosity. The public began to realize that it would be lost altogether if something was not done. A civic non-profit corporation was therefore set up, a Board of Trustees appointed, and a vigorous policy of fund-raising was set in motion that continues successfully to this day.

Although the orchestra's first conductor was a capable musician, and perhaps an ideal one for establishing firm foundations, he has been followed by men of international repute. First the Finnish Georg Schneevoigt (1927-29), then Artur Rodzinski (1929-33), Otto Klemperer (1933-39), Alfred Wal-

lenstein (1943-56), Eduard van Beinum (1956-59), Zubin Mehta (1962-78), and Carlo Maria Giulini (appointed in 1978). Various guest conductors were appointed to cover the years 1939-43 and 1959-62.

The Los Angeles Philharmonic consists of 86 players and operates on an annual budget of about 10 million dollars. Since December 1964 its winter home has been the Dorothy Chandler Pavilion, which seats an audience of nearly 3,200 and is part of Los Angeles' luxurious Civic Center Mall. In the summer the orchestra performs at the famous Hollywood Bowl – an open air auditorium built in 1922 in a natural amphitheater and park. Here more than 17,000 people can be seated. The orchestra gives approximately 230 concerts each year, and undertakes two annual tours – one in America, and one abroad.

The Los Angeles Philharmonic's first concerts were at the Methodist Trinity Auditorium, under the baton of Walter Henry Rothwell (**top**). Since 1964 the orchestra has had a winter home at the Dorothy Chandler Pavilion (**above**), and each summer it performs at the world-renowned Hollywood Bowl (**left**). The inset shows the setting of the open air auditorium.The main picture shows the Los Angeles Philharmonic and the Los Angeles Bureau of Music, with Carlton Martin conducting, performing the Berlioz Requiem at a concert in the late 1950s. It marked the orchestra's official Memorial Day, and was thought to be the first time that the work had been performed in its full score.

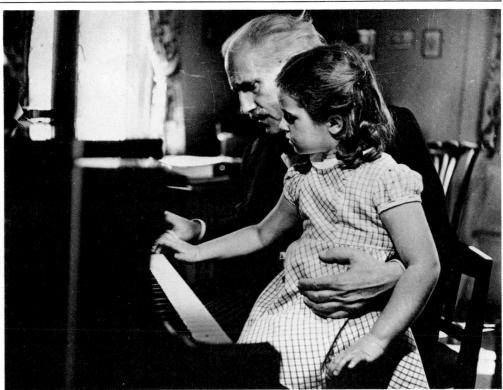

NBC SYMPHONY ORCHESTRA

The American Broadcasting Company's Symphony Orchestra was formed in October 1937 expressly for the seventy-year old Arturo Toscanini, who had been persuaded to emerge from retirement after resigning from the New York Philharmonic in 1936. The initial training was undertaken by Artur Rodzinsky, who was then Principal Conductor of the Cleveland Orchestra. The first broadcast was made on 13 November 1937 under Pierre Monteux, and Toscanini directed it for the first time in a broadcast on Christmas night the same year.

Toscanini became the NBC Symphony Orchestra's permanent conductor in 1938 and, save for a brief period 1941–42, remained with it until his final retirement (aged 87) in 1954. He conducted his last concert on 7 April that year. During the 1941–42 interim Leopold Stokowski acted as Principal Conductor. Throughout the orchestra's history distinguished guest conductors made frequent appearances – among them Sir Adrian Boult, Fritz Reiner, Alfred Wallenstein, George Szell, Ernest Ansermet, and Guido Cantelli.

During Toscanini's reign the full orchestra of about 100 players gave twenty-six Saturday studio concerts during each winter season, and a smaller orchestra of about 60 gave concerts of lighter music during the spring and summer seasons. Toscanini also directed one major opera each season. When finally the orchestra was dismissed by NBC, on Toscanini's retirement, the players attempted to keep it in existence on a co-operative basis. In this form, under the title 'Symphony of the Air' it continued for about ten years, but finally collapsed altogether.

Arturo Toscanini conducted the NBC Symphony Orchestra for 14 years. He began his work with them on Christmas night, 1937 (**left**) in the NBC Studios. **Top:** Toscanini with his grand-daughter Sonia, in his home in Riverdale, New York. His daughter Wanda married the Russian pianist Vladımır Horowitz. **Above:** the Milan newspapers of 15 January 1957 announce the death of one of Italy's greatest conductors.

The Conductors

A hundred years ago the conductor was scarcely the figure that today's audiences revere. Helped by the proliferation of orchestras and the widespread dissemination of music through radio and recordings, his word is now musical law. What makes a 'great' conductor is, perhaps, open to argument, but here are the biographies of a handful whose excellence is in no doubt.

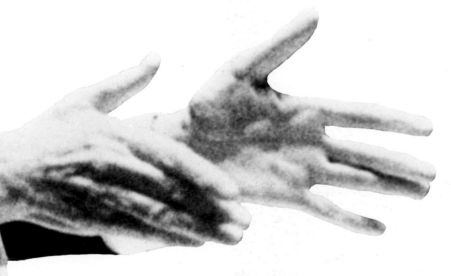

Left: Stokowski, hands in the spotlight, without baton.

101 Conductors

CLAUDIO ABBADO
b.1933

Italian conductor. Studied piano and composition in Milan, and conducting in Vienna. In 1958 he won the Kussevitsky Prize, which led to engagements with a number of important orchestras in Europe and America. Further conducting prizes followed, including the Phillips Prize at the 1966 Salzburg Festival for his performance of Mahler's 2nd Symphony with the Vienna Philharmonic. He has conducted the Vienna Philharmonic Orchestra (1971–77), and the London Symphony Orchestra (first as Principal Guest Conductor, and then, from September 1979, as Principal).

KAREL ANCERL
b.1908

Czech conductor. He studied at the Prague Conservatory and, after two years as assistant to Hermann Scherchen in Berlin (1929–31), became conductor of the Liberated Theater in Prague, and later (1933) of the Czech broadcasting organization. He was imprisoned during the Second World War, but returned to direct the Smetana Theatre (1946) and the Czech Broadcasting Orchestra (1947–50). He was appointed Artistic Director of the Czech Philharmonic in 1950, a position he held until 1968.

ERNEST ANSERMET
1883–1969

Swiss conductor. Studied at Lausanne University and later taught mathematics there. In 1914 he took charge of the Montreux Casino Concerts and in the following year became the conductor of Diaghilev's Russian Ballet Company. In 1918 he founded the Orchestre de la Suisse Romande, the first permanent orchestra in the French-speaking part of Switzerland. He continued to direct it until his retirement in 1966.

DAVID ATHERTON
b.1944

British conductor. After studying at Cambridge University he joined the music staff of Covent Garden (1967) and, at the age of twenty-four, became the youngest conductor ever to appear there. He later became Resident Conductor. In 1967 he formed the London Sinfonietta, remaining its Musical Director until 1973. In September 1980 he became the Principal Conductor and Artistic Adviser of the Royal Liverpool Philharmonic.

Sir JOHN BARBIROLLI
1899–1970

British conductor of Italian parentage. He studied at the Royal Academy of Music and began his career as a cellist, playing in orchestras, chamber groups, and as a distinguished soloist. He began conducting in the early 1920s and in 1926 joined the British National Opera Company. He later directed performances at Covent Garden (1929) and conducted various London Symphony Orchestra and Royal Philharmonic Society concerts. From 1933–37 he directed both the Scottish Orchestra and the Northern Philharmonic. International recognition came in 1936 when he succeeded Toscanini as conductor of the New York Philharmonic (1936–43). He returned to England as Conductor and Musical Director of the Hallé Orchestra, becoming its Conductor Laureate when he retired in 1968. He was also Conductor-in-chief of the Houston Symphony Orchestra (1962–67). He was knighted in 1969.

Sir THOMAS BEECHAM
1879–1961

British conductor. He was the son of a wealthy industrialist, to whose baronetcy he succeeded in 1916, having himself been knighted for services to music in 1915. He was largely self-taught and made his first important appearance in 1905 with a series of concerts at the Wigmore Hall. From 1910 he financed and directed a series of operatic seasons in London, and in 1911 presented Diaghilev's Russian Ballet at Drury Lane. Two years later he sponsored a season of Russian opera. This became the pattern of his life, and he used his wealth to promote music that was new to England, often conducting performances himself. In this way he founded the

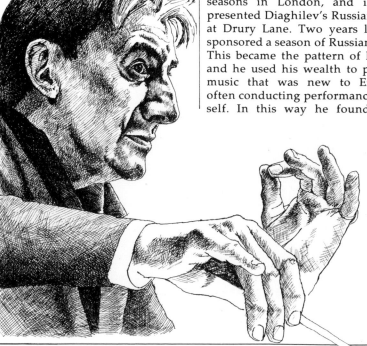

Sir John Barbirolli

Sir Thomas Beecham

short-lived Imperial League of Opera (1932), presented the great Delius Festival (1929) and the Sibelius Festival (1938), and founded two major orchestras: the London Philharmonic (1932) and the Royal Philharmonic (1946). He was Artistic Director of Covent Garden (1933–40), directed opera at Glyndebourne and the Met, and appeared as guest conductor with major orchestras throughout the world. As a personality he was larger than life, as famous for his wit as for his impeccable musicianship.

EDUARD van BEINUM
1901–1959

Dutch conductor. He studied at the Amsterdam Conservatory and in 1921 became conductor of the Toonkunst Choir at Schiedam (1921–30). He then directed the Haarlem Orchestra (1927–31), after which he became assistant conductor to Mengelberg and the Amsterdam Concertgebouw Orchestra. His career was interrupted by the war, but in 1945 he was able to return to the Concertgebouw, this time as Conductor-in-chief. He directed the Los Angeles Symphony Orchestra from 1956–59. He was then appointed Principal Conductor of the London Philharmonic but was obliged to resign almost immediately because of ill-health.

LEONARD BERNSTEIN
b.1918

American conductor, pianist and composer. Studied at Harvard University, and the Curtis Institute of Music, Philadelphia. He was Kussevitsky's assistant at Tanglewood in 1942, and Assistant Conductor of the New York Philharmonic in the following year. When illness prevented Bruno Walter from conducting on one occasion he won immediate fame. Since then he has appeared with every major orchestra throughout the world, and in many leading opera houses, including the Vienna State Opera and the Met. He was Principal Conductor of the New York Philharmonic from 1958–69. His compositions range from symphonies – the *Jeremiah* (1942) and *The Age of Anxiety* (1949) – to the *Fancy Free* ballet (1944) and the enormously successful musical *West Side Story* (1958).

LEO BLECH
1871–1958

German conductor. After studying in Berlin he held posts in Aachen and Prague, before becoming conductor of the Court Opera in Berlin (1906–23). In 1923 he became Artistic Director of the Deutsches Opernhaus (Berlin), and of the Berlin Volksoper (1924). In 1926 he

returned to the Court Opera (now the Berlin State Opera). He left Germany in 1937 because of the political situation, and later became conductor of the Royal Opera, Stockholm (1941–49). On his return to Germany he became conductor of the West Berlin Civic Opera Orchestra, a post which he held until his retirement in 1954. He was also a composer of some distinction.

KARL BÖHM
b.1894

Austrian conductor. Studied in Graz and Vienna, but originally intended to make a career in law. Quite by chance he became coach at the Graz Opera House (1917), and within three years was promoted to the position of Principal Conductor. He then moved, in the same capacity, to the following Opera Houses: Munich (1917–27), Darmstadt (1927–31), Hamburg (1931–34), Dresden (1934–43), the Vienna State Opera (1943–45), and again (1954–56), Buenos Aires (1950–53). He is now Principal Conductor of the Vienna Philharmonic Orchestra.

PIERRE BOULEZ
b.1925

French composer and conductor. Although primarily known as an avant-garde composer of great importance, Boulez has also made a name as a conductor of 20th century music. Among his more important and fruitful appointments have been those as conductor of the BBC Symphony Orchestra (1971–75), and of the New York Philharmonic (1971–77). He now heads a special

Pierre Boulez

acoustical research center in Paris: the Institut de Recherche et de Coordination Acoustique-Musicale, or IRCAM for short.

Sir ADRIAN BOULT
b.1889

British conductor. After studying at the Leipzig Conservatoire under Nikisch, he made his name conducting several Royal Philharmonic Society concerts in 1918–19. He was conductor of the City of Birmingham Orchestra (1924–30), and the first conductor of the BBC Symphony Orchestra (1930–50). From 1950–57 he was Principal Conductor of the London Philharmonic Orchestra, and continued to work with them, both in the recording studio and the concert hall, until his 80th year. In 1965 he was made President of the London Philharmonic Orchestra. He has appeared with most major orchestras of the world and is especially renowned for his championship of English music, in particular that of Elgar and Vaughan Williams.

HANS von BÜLOW
1830–1894

German conductor. After early training as a pianist he studied law, but returned to music in 1850, undertaking his first concert tour in 1853. He then taught piano at the Berlin Conservatory (1855–64), but gradually became known as a conductor. From 1864–69 he directed the Royal Opera in Munich, and there championed the cause of Wagner's music. In 1869, however, his wife Cosima (Liszt's daughter) left him for Wagner, whom she later married. His greatest work as a conductor was with the Duke of Meiningen's Court Orchestra (1880–85), and as director of the Berlin Philharmonic (1887–92). He is the only man ever to have resigned from the Berlin orchestra, after creating a scandal by publicly announcing his admiration for Bismark, who had just been dismissed as Chancellor by Kaiser Wilhelm II. This action was typical of his steadfast and uncompromising character, which showed clearly in his work as a conductor.

FRITZ BUSCH
1890–1951

German conductor. Studied at the Cologne Conservatory, and in 1909 was appointed conductor of the municipal theater in Riga. He also at this time made several tours as a concert pianist. In 1918 he became conductor of the Stuttgart Opera, and in 1922 succeeded Fritz Reiner at the Dresden State Opera. He remained there until 1933, also conducting the Dresden State Orchestra, but then left Germany because of the rise of the Nazi Party. After a brief period in South America he settled in England as conductor of

Leonard Bernstein

the Glyndebourne Opera (1934–51), which he turned into a company of world importance. He was also conductor of the Danish Radio Symphony Orchestra, and the Stockholm Philharmonic (1937–40).

GUIDO CANTELLI
1920–1956

Italian conductor. He trained at the Milan Conservatorio and in 1943 became conductor of the Teatro Coccia, Novara. He was obliged to join the Italian army, however, and was then interned in a German labour camp for openly objecting to the Nazi regime and its influence on Italy. After the war he obtained conducting engagements at La Scala, Milan, and with many European orchestras. Just as his career was beginning to blossom he was killed in an air disaster.

SERGIU CELIBIDACHE
b.1912

German conductor, of Rumanian birth. Studied at the Berlin Conservatory and the University of Berlin (1939–45). Though inexperienced he was appointed conductor of the Berlin Philharmonic in 1945 and did remarkable work in re-establishing the orchestra in the bleak days immediately following the war. In 1948 he shared the concerts of the orchestra's visit to America with Furtwängler, but was not appointed Principal Conductor on the latter's death in 1954. He has since worked with major orchestras throughout the world, and is Principal Conductor of the Munich Philharmonic. He is also a distinguished philosopher.

ANDRÉ CLUYTENS
1905–1967

Belgian conductor who worked mainly in France. His first appointment, however, was at the Theater Royal, Antwerp (1922–27). He became conductor of the Paris Opéra in 1944 and of the Opéra Comique five years later. He was the first conductor of the French school ever to direct opera at Bayreuth (in 1955, 1956, 1957, 1958, and 1965). From 1947 until his death he was Principal Conductor of the Paris Conservatoire Orchestra.

Sir MICHAEL COSTA
1808–1884

Born and trained in Italy, he made his first mark as a composer of opera. He came to England in 1829 and found work as a composer and conductor. In 1846 he became conductor of the Philharmonic Society's orchestra and of the Italian Opera at Covent Garden. Thereafter he was much in demand as a conductor, particularly at the various provincial choral festivals (for example, the Birmingham Festival, 1849–82). As conductor of the Sacred Harmonic Society he directed the great Handel Festivals in London, 1857–80. He was knighted in 1869.

Sergiu Celibidache

LEOPOLD DAMROSCH
1832–1885

He was born in Germany and trained as a doctor, but later studied music and became a concert violinist and conductor. He led the Court Orchestra at Weimar (under Liszt) and was conductor of the Breslau Philharmonic Society (1850–60). In 1871 he settled in New York, where he founded the Oratorio Society (1874) and the Symphony Society (1878), which he directed until his death. In 1881 he conducted the first great music festival ever held in New York, and in 1884 presented the first great season of German Opera at the Met.

WALTER DAMROSCH
1862–1950

Son of Leopold Damrosch. He succeeded his father as conductor of the New York Oratorio and Symphony Societies, and in 1894 organized a Damrosch Opera Company. From 1899–1901 he conducted at the Metropolitan Opera House. He directed the New York Philharmonic Society (1902–03), and in 1903 helped in its reorganization. In later years he was famous for his broadcasts of symphonic music, becoming Music Adviser to the National Broadcasting Company in 1927. His compositions include four operas, of which *The Scarlet Letter* (1896), and *Cyrano de Bergerac* (1913) were the most successful.

Sir COLIN DAVIS
b.1927

British conductor, knighted in 1980. He studied clarinet at the Royal College of Music and began to make his name as the conductor of two London groups, the Kalmar Orchestra, and the Chelsea Opera Group. In 1957 he was appointed Assistant Conductor of the BBC Scottish Orchestra. He has been Musical Director of the Sadler's Wells Opera Company (1961–65), Chief Conductor of the BBC Symphony Orchestra (1967–71), and Music Director of Covent Garden (appointed in 1971). He is widely admired for his interpretations of

Karl Böhm

Sir Adrian Boult

music by Berlioz and Sir Michael Tippett. His Berlioz cycle was awarded the Grosse Deutschen Schallplattenpreis in 1978.

ANTAL DORATI
b.1906

Hungarian-born conductor. Studied at the Budapest Academy of Music and then worked as an operatic-coach and assistant conductor in Budapest and Dresden. He was conductor of the Münster Opera House (1928-33), and Musical Director of the Ballet Russe de Monte Carlo (1934-41). He made his American debut in 1937, and from 1941-42 was Director of the New York Opera Company. Thereafter his work has mainly been with orchestras: as Principal Conductor of the Dallas Symphony Orchestra (1945-49), the Minneapolis Symphony Orchestra

(1949-60), the BBC Symphony Orchestra (1963-67), the Stockholm Philharmonic (1967-74), the Royal Philharmonic Orchestra (appointed 1975), and the Detroit Symphony Orchestra (appointed 1977). He also directs the National Symphony Orchestra of Washington, DC.

JÁNOS FERENCSIK
b.1907

Hungarian conductor. Ferencsik has appeared with most important European orchestras and several major opera companies, including the Vienna State Opera during its post-war years at the Theater an der Wien. He has been most noted for his remarkable work in turning the old Budapest Municipal Orchestra (founded in 1923) into the present Hungarian State Symphony Orchestra, which he has conducted since its foundation in 1952.

FERENC FRICSAY
1915-1963

Hungarian conductor. He was a pupil of Bartók and Kodály, and later became known as an interpreter of their work. He was appointed Musical Director of the Berlin City Opera (1948), and then of the Munich State Opera. He was a notable conductor of the RIAS Orchestra, broadcasting from Berlin after the Second World War.

Antal Dorati

WILHELM FURTWÄNGLER
1886-1954

German conductor. Studied in Munich and gained early experience as an opera-coach and chorus-master in Zürich and Munich, and as an operatic conductor in Strasbourg, Lübeck and Mannheim. There then followed a series of important appointments: as conductor of the Berlin State Opera Orchestra (1920-22), Director of the Museum Concerts in Frankfurt, and Director of the Vienna 'Tonkunstler' Orchestra (1919). In 1922 he became conductor of the Leipzig Gewandhaus Orchestra, and of the Berlin Philharmonic, with whom he remained until 1934. He was then required to resign by the Nazi Party because of the support he gave to the 'banned' composer, Paul Hindemith. He was restored to favor in the following year, however, and remained the Philharmonic's conductor until January 1945. He conducted the Bayreuth Festivals in 1936-37, and 1943-44, and the Vienna Philharmonic Orchestra in 1927, 1928-30, 1933-38, and 1938-45. Furtwängler again became official Director of the Berlin Philharmonic in 1952, and though his powers were but a shadow of what they had been he continued to conduct until two months before his death.

CARLO MARIA GIULINI
b.1914

Italian conductor. Studied at the Accademia di Santa Cecilia, Rome, and worked first as an orchestral viola player. He then studied conducting at the Chigi Academy of Siena. After a brief period of unwilling military service he became Deputy Conductor of the Rome Radio

Sir Colin Davis

Wilhelm Furtwängler

Orchestra and began to appear also as guest conductor outside Italy. He became Principal Conductor at La Scala, Milan, in 1954. His American debut, with the Chicago Symphony Orchestra, was made in the following year. He has been Principal Conductor at the Rome Opera House, Music Director of the Vienna Symphony Orchestra, and Principal Guest Conductor of the Chicago Symphony Orchestra. He is now Music Director of the Los Angeles Symphony Orchestra (appointed in 1978).

Sir EUGENE GOOSSENS
1893–1962

British conductor, of Belgian descent. He studied at the Bruges Conservatory, the Liverpool College of Music, and the Royal College of Music, London. His first appointments were as an orchestra violinist, but after 1915 he appeared with various London orchestras and operatic ventures as a conductor. At the same time his own compositions began to achieve success. In 1923 he went to America as conductor of the Rochester Philharmonic Orchestra (1923-31) and then of the Cincinnati Symphony Orchestra (1931-46). He then moved to Australia, becoming

Director of the Sydney Conservatoire (1947-56) and Resident Conductor of the Sydney Symphony Orchestra.

Sir CHARLES GROVES
b.1915

British conductor. He studied at the Royal College of Music and then joined the BBC as an accompanist and chorus master. He became conductor of the BBC Northern Symphony Orchestra (1944-51) and of the Bournemouth Symphony Orchestra (1951-61). In 1961 he became Director of the Welsh National Opera Company, but resigned in 1963 to take up the post of Musical Director of the Royal Liverpool Philharmonic Society, 1963-77. He has since been Associate Conductor of the Royal Philharmonic Society (1967), and Musical Director of the English National Opera (1978-79).

VITTORIO GUI
1885–1975

Italian conductor. After studying composition at the Liceo Musicale di Santa Cecilia in Rome, he first appeared as a conductor in 1907 at the Teatro Adriano. He held con-

ducting posts in the Turin Opera House (1922-27) and at La Scala, Milan (1923-28), where he also conducted the Società dei Concerti Sinfonici. He became permanent conductor of the Teatro di Torino, Turin (1925-27), and in the following year (1928) formed the Orchestra Stabile at Florence. From this grew the Teatro Communale, which he conducted until 1943. In 1933 he also helped to found the Maggio Musicale Fiorentino. He made his debut at Covent Garden in 1938, and at Glyndebourne ten years later.

FRANCOIS HABENEK
1781–1849

French violinist and conductor, of German descent. He became conductor of the Opéra in 1824, and taught at the Paris Conservatoire from 1808-16 and again after 1825. In 1828 he founded the *Société des Concerts du Conservatoire*, which he conducted for twenty years. He introduced Beethoven's symphonies to France (against great opposition) and became famous for his strict orchestral discipline and the force and delicacy of his interpretations. His compositions include two violin concertos. He is the first important French conductor.

BERNARD HAITINK
b.1929

Dutch conductor. Principal Conductor of the Netherlands Radio Philharmonic Orchestra (1955-61), and Permanent Conductor of the

Carlo Maria Giulini

Amsterdam Concertgebouw since 1964. He was Principal Conductor of the London Philharmonic Orchestra (1967-79) and has been a guest conductor of almost all the major world orchestras. Haitink has directed opera at Glyndebourne (where he is now Musical Director) and at Covent Garden. In 1977 he was knighted for his services to British music.

Sir CHARLES HALLÉ
1819–1895

He was born in Germany and became known there as a prodigy pianist. He settled in Paris in 1836, but fled to England during the 1848 revolution. He then made his home in Manchester, becoming conductor of the Gentlemen's Concerts in 1850 and of the St Cecilia Society in 1852. In 1857 he formed a special orchestra for the Manchester Exhibition, and in the following year turned it into the now famous Hallé Orchestra. As a pianist and conductor he appeared frequently in London and the provinces. He helped found Manchester's Royal College of Music and was its first Principal.

Sir HAMILTON HARTY
1879–1941

Irish conductor, pianist, and composer. Settled in London in 1900 and became known as an exceptionally fine accompanist and very capable composer. As a conductor he

worked with most British orchestras, including the Royal Philharmonic Society's orchestra and the London Symphony Orchestra, but is mainly associated with the Hallé, which he directed from 1920 to 1933.

JASCHA HORENSTEIN
1898–1973

Russian-born conductor. He left Russia when he was six and from 1911-19 studied the violin in Vienna and composition in Berlin . He made his debut as an orchestral conductor in Vienna (1923), and was later appointed to the Berlin Philharmonic Orchestra (1925-28), and the Düsseldorf Opera House (1928). With the rise of the Nazi Party he made Paris his home, but settled in America in 1941, where he conducted all the leading orchestras.

EUGEN JOCHUM
b.1902

German conductor, trained in Augsburg and Munich. He began his conducting career in the opera houses of Kiel and Mannheim, becoming Principal Conductor of the Duisburg Opera in 1930, and of

Sir Charles Groves

Bernard Haitink

the Hamburg State Opera and Philharmonic Orchestra in 1932. In 1949 he helped to reorganize the Munich Radio Symphony Orchestra. He conducted at Bayreuth in 1953 and 1954. In 1960 he was appointed conductor of Amsterdam's Concertgebouw Orchestra, remaining with them until 1963.

LOUIS ANTOINE JULLIEN
1812–1860

Eccentric, flamboyant French conductor who settled in England (1838) where he gave regular concert seasons at various London theaters. His programs included many classical pieces (even complete symphonies), but concentrated on the tuneful and spectacular. His own appearance and behaviour fascinated the public – he always conducted Beethoven in a fresh pair of white kid gloves and with a jewelled baton, both brought to him on a silver salver. For his concerts he wrote a series of 'Monster Quadrilles'. His opera *Pietro il grande* (1852) failed disastrously. After visiting America (1852-54) he lost most of his music in the Covent Garden fire of 1856. He ended his life bankrupt and in a lunatic asylum. Though essentially an entertainer, Jullien did much good work in creating a public for orchestral concerts.

HERBERT von KARAJAN
b.1908

Austrian conductor. He trained first as a pianist in the Vienna Academy for Music and the Salzburg

Eugen Jochum

Mozarteum, but soon turned to conducting, and after various minor appointments (at Ulm, and Aachen) gave his first concert with the Berlin Philharmonic in April 1938. His success on that occasion was followed by invitations to conduct the Berlin State Opera. He became internationally known after the Second World War – first as a conductor of the Vienna Philharmonic, and then, since 1954, as Permanent Conductor of the Berlin Philharmonic. He has also been appointed 'Concert Director for life' by the Vienna Gesellschaft der Musikfreunde'. He became director of the Salzburg Festival in 1964, and of the Vienna State Opera in 1976. Karajan appears as guest conductor with orchestras and in opera houses throughout the world, and is as much admired for his 'super-star' image as for his outstanding musicianship.

JOSEPH KEILBERTH
1908–1968

German conductor. Joined the Karlsruhe State Theater as an opera-coach in 1923 and by 1933 had become its chief conductor. He was Conductor of the Deutsche Philharmonie in Prague (1940-45) and Director of the Dresden State Opera (1945-51). He became conductor of the Hamburg Philharmonic Orchestra in 1951, and from 1952-56 conducted at the Bayreuth Festival.

RUDOLF KEMPE
1910–1976

German conductor. He trained as an oboist, later playing first oboe in the Leipzig Gewandhaus Orchestra (1928). As a conductor his first important appointment was as Musical Director of the Chemnitz Opera House, from which he progressed to the Dresden State Opera (1949-54). He made his debut at Covent Garden in 1953, the Met in 1954, and Bayreuth in 1960. He was Principal Conductor of the Zurich Tonhalle Orchestra (1965-72), and of the Royal Philharmonic Orchestra (1961-75) – this following a period as Beecham's 'Associate Conductor' in 1960. He was appointed conductor of the BBC Symphony Orchestra in 1975.

ISTVAN KERTESZ
1929–1973

Hungarian-born conductor. After a period of study in Budapest and Rome, he made his conducting debut in 1948. He settled in Germany in 1957, becoming well-known as an opera conductor. He was Music Director of the Augsburg Opera (1958-63), and of the Cologne Opera from 1964. He visited Great Britain on several occasions, becoming Principal Conductor of the London Symphony Orchestra (1965-68) in succession to Pierre Monteux.

Carlos Kleiber

CARLOS KLEIBER
b.1930

German-born conductor, the son of Erich Kleiber, now of Austrian nationality. He received his main education in Argentina, but made his conducting debut in Potsdam in 1954. He then gained experience as an opera-coach at the Deutsche Oper am Rhein. He began to make a name as an opera conductor in Germany from 1966, first in Stuttgart and then (1968) in Munich. International fame came in 1974 when he conducted at Bayreuth and then Covent Garden.

ERICH KLEIBER
1890–1967

Austrian-born conductor, later of Argentinian nationality. He studied at the Conservatory and University of Prague, and later became chorus-master at the German Opera. His early appointments were as an operatic conductor at: Darmstadt (1912–18), Barmen-Elberfeld (1919–21), Düsseldorf and Mannheim (1922–23), and the Berlin State Opera (1923–35). He left Germany in 1935 in protest against Fascism, settling in Argentina. He appeared as guest conductor in all the more important South American states. He also conducted in North America, and from 1947 toured extensively in Europe. He was one of the few conductors who appeared more concerned to express the composer's intentions, rather than display the charms of his own personality.

OTTO KLEMPERER
1885–1973

German conductor. He studied in Hamburg and Frankfurt, and at the Stern Conservatory, Berlin. His career began in 1907 when he was appointed Assistant Conductor to the German Opera in Prague. He moved to Hamburg in the same capacity (1910–12), and then to Barmen as Chief Conductor (1913–14). He was Deputy Music Director at the Strasburg Opera House (1914–17), and the Music Director at Cologne (1917–24) and Wiesbaden (1924–27). He was then appointed to the famous Kroll Opera in Berlin, which specialized in modern works

(1927–31). In the meantime his fame as an orchestral conductor also spread. After a period directing the Berlin State Opera (1931–33) the German political situation forced him to leave for America. There he became conductor of the Los Angeles Symphony Orchestra (1933–39). He founded the Pittsburg Symphony Orchestra in 1937, but handed over the conductorship to Fritz Reiner. After the war he toured Europe with the New York Philharmonic, becoming one of its conductors in 1959. From 1947–50 he was Musical Director of the Budapest State Opera, and in 1959 he was appointed Principal Conductor (for life) of the Philharmonia Orchestra in London. This honor was carried on by the New Philharmonia, who also elected him their President in 1964. He retired in 1972.

PAUL KLETZKI
1900–1973

Polish conductor. Studied at the Warsaw State Conservatory and the Hochschule in Berlin. He conducted the Dallas Symphony Orchestra (1958–61), and toured with the Israel Philharmonic. In 1966 he succeeded Ernest Ansermet as conductor of the Orchestre de la Suisse Romande, but was forced to retire in 1968 through ill-health.

HANS KNAPPERTSBUSCH
1888–1965

German conductor. Studied at the Cologne Conservatory and began his career in 1910 as an opera conductor at Mühlheim, then Elberfeld, Leipzig, and Dessau. He was Music Director of the Munich State Opera (1922–36), and after several guest appearances (1935–38) as conductor of the Vienna State Opera he was appointed its 'permanent' conductor (1938–45).

KIRILL KONDRASHIN
b.1914

Russian conductor. · Studied conducting at the Moscow State Conservatory from 1931, and in 1934 began to work as an assistant conductor at the Nemorovitch Dachenko Theater. He became conductor of the Academic Malyi Opera, Leningrad in 1936, and also worked with the Leningrad Philharmonic and Radio Orchestras. From 1943–56 he was conductor of the Bolshoi Theater, but after that date concentrated mainly on orchestral work. He has been Musical Director of the Moscow Philharmonic Orchestra (1960–75). He now lives in Amsterdam and is co-conductor of the Concertgebouw Orchestra with Bernard Haitink.

CLEMENS KRAUSS
1893–1954

Austrian conductor. He studied at the Vienna Conservatory and, after working with opera houses at Riga, Nuremberg, Stettin, and Graz, he became conductor of the Vienna State Opera (1922). In 1924 he went to the Frankfurt Opera House, but in 1929 returned to Vienna as Direc-

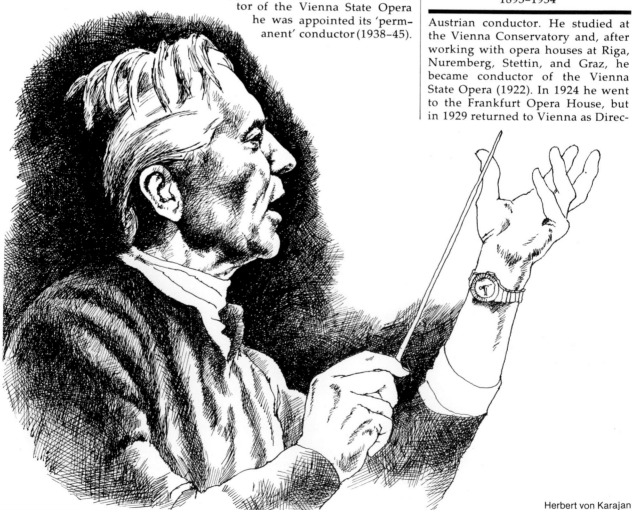

Herbert von Karajan

Rafael
Kubelik

tor of the State Opera. He became head of the Berlin State Opera in 1934, and then head of the Bavarian State Opera (1938). He was particularly sympathetic to the music of Richard Strauss and collaborated with him in the preparation of the libretto of his last opera, *Capriccio* (1942).

JOSEF KRIPS
1902–1974

Austrian conductor. He studied conducting at the Vienna Academy of Music under Weingartner, and received his first public appointment in 1921 at the Vienna Volksoper. After conducting opera in Dortmund and Karlsruhe he became Conductor of the Vienna State Opera (1933–38), and again after the war (1945–50). His work in Vienna was interrupted by the Nazis, as was the work that followed in Belgrade. In the post-war years he helped to re-establish the Salzburg Festival. In 1950 he was appointed conductor of the London Symphony Orchestra, remaining with them until 1954. He was then made Principal Conductor of the Buffalo Symphony Orchestra (1954–63), and of the San Francisco Symphony Orchestra (1963–70).

RAFAEL KUBELIK
b.1914

Czech conductor, the son of the composer Jan Kubelik (1880–1940). He studied at the Prague Conservatory and made his first important conducting appearance in 1934 with the Czech Philharmonic. In 1939–41 he was chief conductor of the National Theater at Brno, and from 1942–48 was Artistic Administrator of the Czech Philharmonic. In 1948,

however, he emigrated to England and thereafter devoted himself to an international conducting career. He became conductor of the Chicago Symphony Orchestra (1950–53).

SERGEI KUSSEVITSKY
1874–1951

Russian-born conductor. After graduating from the Philharmonic School of Music, Moscow, he appeared as a double-bass virtuoso, his fame spreading throughout Europe. He made his debut as a conductor in 1908, with the London Symphony Orchestra, and proved to be a fine interpreter of Russian music. He then studied with Nikisch in Berlin, and later formed his own orchestra in Russia (as well as a publishing company). After the 1917 revolution he settled first in Paris and then in America, where he was appointed Principal Conductor of the Boston Symphony Orchestra (1924–49).

CHARLES LAMOUREUX
1834–1899

After a successful career as a violinist, he founded, in 1873, the Société de l'Harmonie Sacrée (modelling it on London's Sacred Harmonic Society) and proceeded to give performances of oratorios. These revealed his talents as a conductor. He was appointed to the Opéra-Comique (1876–77) and the Opéra (1877–79), and from 1872–79 was sub-conductor of the Concerts du Conservatoire. After 1879 he preferred to remain independent, founding the Nouveaux Concerts (afterwards called the Concerts Lamoureux) in 1881. He was a great champion of Wagner's operas and gave first performances of many contemporary French pieces. Lamoureux's orchestra was renowned for its precision and warmth of expression.

ERICH LEINSDORF
b.1912

Austrian conductor. He began his conducting career as assistant to Bruno Walter and Toscanini at the Salzburg Festivals of 1934–37. He went to America in 1938, first as Assistant Conductor to Bodanzky at

the Metropolitan Opera House, New York, and then as conductor of its German repertoire. In between periods of military service he directed the Cleveland Orchestra (1943–46), and then the Rochester Philharmonic Orchestra. He returned to the Met in 1957, but resigned in 1962 to become Music Director of the Boston Symphony Orchestra (1962–69). Since then he has appeared as guest conductor with all the major world orchestras, and in many of the most important opera houses, including Bayreuth (1972).

HERMANN LEVI
1839–1900

Studied at Mannheim and Leipzig and began his career as a conductor in 1859. After working at Saarbrücken Rotterdam and Karlsruhe, he took up his most important appointment as director of the Court Theater in Munich (1872–96). He was famous as a Wagner conductor and directed the first performance of *Parsifal* at Bayreuth in 1882. He visited England in 1895, but conducted only one concert. In his last years he was prevented from conducting by ill health.

James Levine

Otto Klemperer (**above**); Rudolf Kempe (**above right**).

Soloist conductors

Such is the glamor of the conductor's art that many musicians already famous as soloists have been tempted into taking up the baton on their own account. Pianists, violinists, and even singers have succumbed, with varying degrees of success.

Among the most outstanding of today's 'part-time' conductors are the pianists Daniel Barenboim (**left**) and Vladimir Ashkenazy (**center**), and the 'cellist Mstislav Rostropovitch (**right**).

JAMES LEVINE
b.1943

American conductor. After studying the piano with Rudolf Serkin, he spent six years with the Cleveland Orchestra as George Szell's assistant. He made his conducting debut in 1970. He conducted at the New York Metropolitan Opera for the first time in 1971, was Principal Director (1973–76), and is now Artistic Director. Since 1973 he has been Musical Director of the Chicago Symphony Orchestra's Ravinia Festival, and from 1974–78 directed the May Festival at Cincinnati.

LORIN MAAZEL
b.1930

American conductor. He began his musical studies when he was five and first appeared as a conductor four years later. After studying at the University of Pittsburg, and in Italy, he began his career as a mature artist in 1953. Within a few years he had appeared with most major orchestras and in most major opera houses in the world. He has been Music Director of the Berlin Radio Symphony Orchestra, and the West Berlin Opera (1965–71), Associate Principal Conductor of the Philharmonia Orchestra of London (1970–72), and is currently Music Director of the Cleveland Orchestra (appointed in 1972). He is also Principal Guest Conductor of the Philharmonia Orchestra (1976) and the French National Orchestra (1977), and has directed opera in London, Paris, Vienna, Berlin, Milan, New York, and Bayreuth.

Sir CHARLES MACKERRAS
b.1925

Australian conductor. Studied at the Sydney Conservatory and the Prague Academy of Music. Came to England in 1946 and established himself as a conductor of opera and ballet. Conductor at Sadler's Wells Opera House (1948–54), of the BBC Concert Orchestra (1954–56), and the Hamburg State Opera (1966–69). He has been Music Director of the English National Opera (1970–78), and is now Principal Guest Conductor of the BBC Symphony Orchestra. He is known particularly for his

Lorin Maazel

interpretation of Janáček's operas, and for his ballet *Pineapple Poll* (arranged from music by Sullivan).

NICOLAI MALKO
1883–1961

Russian-born conductor. He was trained at the St Petersburg Conservatory under Rimsky-Korsakov and Glazunov, and studied conducting at Munich with Felix Mottl. He was conductor of the St Petersburg State Opera and Ballet (1908–18), and of the Leningrad Philharmonic Orchestra. He made many European tours and, for a while, settled in America. He was conductor of the Royal Danish Orchestra in Copenhagen. His last post was as Principal Conductor of the Sydney Symphony Orchestra (1956).

Sir AUGUST MANNS
1825–1907

German Bandmaster and conductor who came to London in 1854 as sub-conductor of the Wind Band at the Crystal Palace. He was appointed conductor there in 1855 and thereafter directed the daily music and the Saturday Concerts, as well as the special Festival performances for which the Crystal Palace became famous. In 1883 he followed Costa as director of the Handel Festivals. He was knighted in 1903. His considerable talents as conductor and organizer, and his willingness to perform new music (he was a great Schumann enthusiast) did much to develop the London concert scene.

JEAN MARTINON
1910–1976

French conductor, composer, and violinist. He studied violin and composition at the Lyons and Paris Conservatoires, and made his first name as a composer. But he also showed gifts as a conductor. After studying under Charles Munch he directed the Paris Conservatoire Orchestra (1944), the Bordeaux Symphony Orchestra (1946), the Lamoureux Orchestra (1951–57), the Chicago Symphony Orchestra

(1963–68), the Orchestre National de l'ORTF (1968–75), and the Hague Residentie Orchestra (1975–76). He also appeared as a guest conductor in Europe and America.

ZUBIN MEHTA
b.1936

Indian conductor. Studied conducting under Hans Swarowsky at the Vienna Academy of Music. He made his debut in 1958 and in the same year won the International Conductor's Competition in Liverpool. He was appointed Music Director of the Montreal Symphony Orchestra (1960–64), and of the Los Angeles Philharmonic (1962–78). His operatic debuts include the Salzburg Festival (1965), the Metropolitan (1965), La Scala (1974), and Covent Garden (1977). He is Music Director of the Israel Philharmonic and, since 1978, of the New York Philharmonic.

WILLEM MENGELBERG
1871–1951

Dutch conductor of German descent. He studied music in Utrecht and Cologne, and in 1881 was appointed municipal music director to the city of Lucerne. In 1895 he was appointed conductor of the Concertgebouw Orchestra, Amsterdam, remaining with them until 1941. He made many guest appearances in Germany, England and America, and toured frequently with the Concertgebouw Orchestra. After the Second World War he was charged with Nazi collaboration and forbidden to exercise his profession in public. He died in exile in Switzerland. Mengelberg was particularly noted for his performances of Mahler and Tchaikovsky.

DIMITRI MITROPOULOS
1896–1961

Greek conductor. He studied first in Athens, and later in Brussels and Berlin. He was appointed conductor of the Athens Symphony Orchestra in 1924 and of the Athens Concert Society (1925–27). He then directed the orchestra of the Athens Conservatory (1927–30). After appearing with great success in a concert with the Berlin Philharmonic (1930) he

was invited to conduct in many European countries. He went to America in 1936 as guest conductor of the Boston Symphony Orchestra, and in the following year was appointed conductor of the Minneapolis Symphony Orchestra (1937–49). He became Stokowski's successor at the New York Philharmonic Symphony Orchestra (1949–58). He was also known as a composer.

PIERRE MONTEUX
1875–1964

French conductor. Trained at the Paris Conservatoire and played viola in the orchestras of the Opéra Comique and the Colonne concerts. He was conductor of the Diaghilev Russian Ballet (1911–14, and 1917), and in 1913–14 conducted at the Paris Opéra. During the years 1917–19 he conducted the Metropolitan Opera, New York, and from 1919–24 was Principal Conductor of the Boston Symphony Orchestra. He was second conductor of the Concertgebouw Orchestra (1924–34), and founded and directed the Orchestre Symphonique de Paris (1929–38). He was Principal Conductor of the San Francisco Orchestra (1935–52), and from 1960 until his death he directed the London Symphony Orchestra.

FELIX MOTTL
1856–1911

Austrian composer and conductor. He studied in Vienna, where he soon became known as a conductor. In 1881 he was appointed to the grand-ducal opera house at Karlsruhe, where he remained until 1903,

giving many brilliant performances of operas by Berlioz and Wagner. He was also much admired as a concert conductor, directing the Philharmonic Society of Karlsruhe until 1892. He conducted Wagner at Bayreuth, Covent Garden and New York. In 1904 he was made a director of the Berlin Royal Academy of Music, and in 1907 he became director of the Opera at Munich. His own compositions are no longer performed.

CHARLES MUNCH
1891–1968

French conductor. He was trained as a violinist at the Strasbourg Conservatory and in Berlin. He did not make his debut as a conductor until 1933 – giving concerts with the Paris Symphony Orchestra, and the Lamoureux Orchestra. He then directed the Paris Philharmonic Orchestra, and succeeded Philippe Gaubert as conductor of the Société des Concerts du Conservatoire in

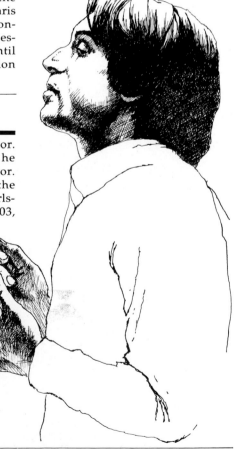

Riccardo Muti

1938. After 1945 he spent much time touring in Europe and America, and in 1949–62 was conductor of the Boston Symphony Orchestra.

RICCARDO MUTI
b.1941

Italian conductor. Studied at the Milan Conservatorio and won the Guido Cantelli International Conducting Contest in 1967. He became Principal Conductor of the Orchestra of the Maggio Musicale Fiorentino, Florence, in 1969, and of the Philharmonia Orchestra, London, in 1973. He has been Principal Guest Conductor of the Philadelphia Orchestra since 1977 and will succeed Eugene Ormandy as its Director at the end of 1980.

ARTUR NIKISCH
1855–1922

Austro – Hungarian conductor. After early appearances as a prodigy pianist he studied the violin at the Vienna Conservatory. He became a member of the Vienna Court Orchestra in 1874, but left after four years to become choral coach at the Leipzig Opera. By 1879 he had become conductor there. In 1889 he took over the Boston Symphony Orchestra, remaining with it until 1893. Appointments at the Budapest Opera and in London were followed by that of director of the Gewandhaus Concerts in Leipzig (1895–1911). From 1895 he was conductor

Artur Nikisch

Eugene Ormandy

of the Berlin Philharmonic. He also directed the Hamburg Philharmonic Concerts (from 1897) and the Leipzig Opera (1905–06). Nikisch visited London on many occasions, conducting the London Symphony Orchestra, which he took to America in 1912. He is generally considered to have been one of the greatest conductors of all time.

EUGENE ORMANDY
b.1899

Hungarian – born conductor. He began his musical studies when he was five, and four years later became a pupil of the violinist Jeno Hubay. After extensive tours as a soloist, and a teaching appointment at the Hungarian State Conservatory, he left for America (1921). He worked first as a violinist in cinema orchestras, but soon became the conductor of that of the Capitol Theater in New York. He also directed several broadcast concerts. In 1931 he deputized for Toscanini with the Philadelphia Orchestra and was then appointed Music Director of the Minneapolis Symphony Orchestra

(1931–36). He returned to the Philadelphia Orchestra as assistant to Stokowski and became its Principal Conductor in 1938. Having held that position longer than any other man, he will retire at the end of 1980. Ormandy took American citizenship in 1927.

SEIJI OZAWA
b.1935

Japanese conductor. Studied at the Toho School of Music, Tokyo, with Charles Munch at Tanglewood, and with Karajan in Berlin. He became an Assistant Conductor of the New York Philharmonic in 1961 and made his first professional appearance with the San Francisco Symphony Orchestra in the following year. He has been Music Director of the Chicago Symphony Orchestra (1965–69), and of the San Francisco Symphony Orchestra (1970–76). In 1973 he was appointed Music Director of the Boston Symphony Orchestra. He has also appeared as guest conductor with orchestras throughout the world – including the Peking Central Philharmonic Orchestra (1978).

Seiji Ozawa

ANDRÉ PREVIN
b.1929

American conductor, born in Berlin. He studied conducting with Pierre Monteux, but made a name for himself first as a pianist and then as a composer of film music. He has devoted himself to conducting since 1960 and has now appeared with every major orchestra in the world. He has been Music Director of the Houston Symphony Orchestra, and from 1968 to 1979 the Principal Conductor of the London Symphony Orchestra – holding that position longer than any other man. Since 1976 he has been Music Director of the Pittsburg Symphony Orchestra. He appears frequently as a pianist, and has a considerable reputation as a composer and television personality.

JOHN PRITCHARD
b.1921

British conductor. Worked at Glyndebourne under Fritz Busch and first conducted there in 1951. He was Music Director of the Royal Liverpool Philharmonic Orchestra (1956–63), and of the London Philharmonic Orchestra (1962–66). He was Principal Conductor at Glyndebourne (1963), and then Musical Director (1969–77). Operatic debuts include Covent Garden (1952), the Metropolitan (1971), and La Scala (1976). He was appointed Chief Conductor of the Cologne Opera in 1978.

FRITZ REINER
1888–1963

Hungarian conductor. He studied at the National Music Academy in Budapest, becoming conductor of the People's Opera in 1911. He conducted at the Dresden Opera in 1914 and from 1922–31 was conductor of the Cincinnati Symphony Orchestra. After working as head of the orchestral and opera departments of the Curtis Institute, Philadelphia, he became conductor of the Pittsburg Orchestra (1938–48), the Chicago Symphony Orchestra (1953–62), and the Metropolitan Opera House (1948–53). He toured widely in North and South America, and to a lesser extent in Europe. He visited England for the first time in 1924, conducting the London Symphony Orchestra.

HANS RICHTER
1843–1916

Austro – Hungarian conductor. Studied at Vienna Conservatory and worked first as an orchestral horn player, and then as copyist to Richard Wagner. His first conducting post was in Munich (1868), and in 1871 he became chief conductor of the National Theater in Pest. In 1875 he attracted attention with a concert in Vienna and was appointed director of the Court Opera and the Vienna Philharmonic concerts. In the following year he conducted the Bayreuth season. A series of Wagner concerts in London (1877) introduced him to England, and from 1879 the 'Richter Concerts' in London attracted much favorable attention. He became director of the Hallé Orchestra in 1879, and of the Birmingham Festival in 1885. Though mainly interested in German music (particularly Wagner), he also championed Elgar, whose First Symphony is dedicated to him.

André Previn

HANS ROSBAUD
1895–1962

Austrian conductor. Trained at Frankfurt-am-Main, and then held various positions as an opera and concert conductor at Mainz, Frankfurt, Munster, Strasbourg, and Munich, before becoming conductor of the Baden-Baden Radio Orchestra (1948). At the meetings of the International Society for Contemporary Music (ISCM), and the Donaueschingen and Aix festivals he did much to popularize the more advanced modern scores, particularly the music of Schoenberg.

GENNADI ROZHDESTVENSKY
b.1931

Russian conductor. After studying at the Moscow Conservatoire he was appointed as one of the conductors of the Bolshoi Theater (1956–60), Moscow's main opera house. From 1960–65 he was Chief Conductor of the USSR Radio and Television Symphony Orchestra before returning to the Bolshoi as Principal Conductor. He has toured in Europe with the Bolshoi Ballet Company. In 1978 he was appointed Principal Conductor of the BBC Symphony Orchestra, in succession to Pierre Boulez.

Gennadi Rozhdestvensky

VICTOR de SABATA
1892–1967

Italian conductor. After studying at the Milan Conservatory he became known as a composer, but gradually turned to conducting. Though he worked in the concert hall he was best known as an operatic conductor. Among his principal appointments were those with the Monte Carlo Opera and La Scala, Milan (1929–54). He conducted at Bayreuth in 1939. Ill-health led to his early retirement (1954).

PAUL SACHER
b.1906

Swiss conductor. Studied at the University of Basle and the Basle Conservatory. Conducted the Basle Male-Voice Choir (1929–34) and during that period founded the Basle Chamber Orchestra (1926) and Chamber Choir (1928), both specializing in pre-classical and contemporary music. In 1933 he also established the Schola Cantorum Basiliensis, whose object is to study old music and perform it in as authentic a manner as possible. In 1941 he became conductor of the Collegium Musicum, Zurich.

VASSILY SAFONOV
1852–1918

Russian conductor and pianist. His early career was that of a concert pianist, but he became known as a conductor after about 1890. He was Principal Conductor of the New York Philharmonic Orchestra (1904–09). He often conducted without a baton, and was much admired for his interpretations of Russian music – particularly that of Tchaikovsky.

Sir MALCOLM SARGENT
1895–1967

British conductor. He worked first as an organist and tried to make a career as a composer, but his gifts as a conductor soon led him into other paths. He worked with the British National Opera Company (1924) and D'Oyly Carte, and from 1928 became especially noted for his work with the Royal Choral Society. From 1942–48 he directed the Royal Liv-

erpool Philharmonic Orchestra, and from 1950–57 the BBC Symphony Orchestra. From 1950 to 1966 he was chief conductor at the Proms. His work in helping to establish the Robert Mayer Concerts for Children was also much admired. He was knighted in 1947, and although not perhaps a truly 'great' conductor was much loved by the general public.

WOLFGANG SAWALLISCH
b.1923

German conductor. After studying in Munich he began his career as a pianist specializing in chamber music, but was soon attracted by conducting. He was appointed a chorus-master at the Augsburg Opera House and Music-Director to the city. He then went to the opera houses of Wiesbaden (1958) and Cologne (1960) as Principal Conductor, and in 1961 was appointed Music Director of the Hamburg State Philharmonic Orchestra. In 1969 he succeeded Joseph Keilberth at the Bavarian State Opera, Munich; and in 1970 he took over the Orchestre de la Suisse Romande.

FRANZ SCHALK
1863–1931

Austrian conductor. He was a pupil of Bruckner, whose works he later did much to popularize (unfortunately in 'improved' versions edited by himself, and now discredited). After gaining early experience in various German and Austrian opera houses he succeeded

Hans Richter

Ferdinand Löwe as Director of the Vienna Court Opera (1918–29), where for some time he shared the direction with Richard Strauss (1919–24). He made his debut at Covent Garden and the Met in 1898, and his 1911 visit to Covent Garden was long remembered for a particularly fine 'Ring' cycle.

HERMANN SCHERCHEN
1891–1966

German conductor. Largely self-taught. He played viola in the Berlin Philharmonic Orchestra and made his debut as a conductor with them in 1901. In 1914 he was conductor of the Riga Symphony Orchestra, but was interned in Russia as a prisoner of war. In 1918 he returned to Berlin, founding the New Music Society and the Scherchen Quartet. Thereafter he held conducting posts in Leipzig, Frankfurt and Königsberg. He left Germany in 1932, becoming Musical Director of the Swiss Radio Orchestra at Beromünster and Zurich. He founded the Ars Viva Orchestra, which did much to introduce new music in Europe. He was a frequent conductor at the meetings of the International Society for Contemporary Music.

THOMAS SCHIPPERS
1930–1977

American conductor. He studied at the Curtis Institute and made his conducting debut in 1948. He was an outstanding operatic conductor, appearing for the first time with the New York City Opera (1951), and at La Scala and the Met in 1955. He conducted at Bayreuth in 1963, and later became Music Director of the Spoleto Festival. He was conductor of the Cincinnati Symphony Orchestra from 1970 until his death.

HANS SCHMIDT-ISSERSTEDT
1900–1973

German conductor. He studied composition in Berlin, and began his conducting career in the opera houses of Wuppertal, Rostock, and Darmstadt. He was appointed Principal Conductor of the Hamburg State Opera in 1935, and Director of the Deutsches Opernhaus (Berlin) in 1943. In 1945 he joined Radio Hamburg and was invited by the Allies to found the Nordwestdeutscher Rundfunk Symphony Orchestra. He was also Principal Conductor of the Stockholm Philharmonic (1954–63), and appeared as guest conductor with orchestras throughout the world.

CARL SCHURICHT
1880–1967

German conductor. Studied at the Berlin Hochschule für Musik, and after working in various provincial theaters he was appointed Director of Music at Wiesbaden (1911), a post which he held for more than thirty years. From 1930 he conducted the summer concerts at Scheveningen and was closely associated with various Dutch orchestras, including the Concertgebouw, and the Residentie Orchestra at the Hague. From 1944 he lived in Switzerland, but was a frequent guest conductor in England and America.

URI SEGAL
b.1944

Israeli conductor. Studied at the Rubin Academy in Jerusalem and the Guildhall School of Music, London. In 1961 he won the Dimitri Mitropoulos International Conducting Competition and was therefore appointed Assistant Conductor of the New York Philharmonic for one year, working with George Szell and Leonard Bernstein. Since making London his base in 1970 he has worked with most major European orchestras, including the London Philharmonic, the London Symphony Orchestra, the Berlin Philharmonic, and the Israel Philharmonic. He made his operatic debut in 1973 with the Santa Fé Opera Festival in America. He is now Conductor of the Bournemouth Symphony Orchestra.

TULLIO SERAFIN
1878–1968

Italian conductor. Studied at the Milan Conservatory and worked first as an orchestra violinist, turning to conducting in 1898. Known largely as an operatic conductor at: La Scala, Milan (1909–24), the Metropolitan, New York (1924–34), the Royal Opera, Rome (1934–56, and 1962). He also conducted opera in London, Paris, Chicago, Buenos Aires and Madrid.

CONSTANTIN SILVERSTRI
1914–1969

Rumanian-born conductor. His first important post was with the Bucharest Radio Symphony Orchestra, and he was later associated with the Bucharest Opera (1935–57). He left Rumania in 1957 as a refugee, and after several engagements with the London Philharmonic was appointed to the Bournemouth Symphony Orchestra (1961). He did much to improve its standards and increase its size. He was also a composer and pianist.

Sir GEORG SOLTI
b.1912

Hungarian-born conductor, now of British nationality (1972). He studied with Bartók, Kodály and Dohnányi and made his debut with the Budapest Opera in 1936. He was Assistant Conductor to Toscanini at the 1936 and 1937 Salzburg Festivals. He left Hungary in 1939 and worked in Switzerland as a solo pianist. He has been Music Director of the Bavarian State Opera (1946–52), the Frankfurt City Opera (1952–62), and Covent Garden (1961–71). He made his American

Sir Georg Solti

213

debut in 1953 with the San Francisco Opera Company and Symphony Orchestra. In 1970 he became Music Director of the Chicago Symphony Orchestra, and in 1979 of the London Philharmonic Orchestra – both of which posts he still holds. He was knighted in 1971.

HORST STEIN
b.1928

German conductor. Studied at the Academy of Music, Cologne. After working in the opera houses of Wuppertal, Hamburg and Berlin, he became joint-director of music at the Hamburg State Opera (1961), and then Director of the Mannheim Opera (1963). He returned to the Hamburg Opera in 1972, remaining in charge until 1977. In 1980 he was appointed Chief Conductor and Artistic Director of the Suisse Romande orchestra in succession to Wolfgang Sawallisch.

WILLIAM STEINBERG
1899–1978

German conductor. After studying with Abendroth in Cologne he became Klemperer's assistant at the Cologne Opera House (1920). He was Musical Director of the Prague Opera (1925–29), and the Frankfurt Opera (1929–33). He was then conductor of the following orchestras: the Israel Philharmonic (1936), the San Francisco Symphony Orchestra (1944), the Buffalo Symphony Orchestra (1945–52), the Pittsburg Symphony Orchestra (1952), and the Boston Symphony Orchestra (1969–72).

LEOPOLD STOKOWSKI
1882–1977

American conductor born in Britain of Polish descent. He studied at the Royal College of Music and began his career as organist of St James's Piccadilly (1900–05), and then of St Bartholomew's Church, New York. In 1909 he became conductor of the Cincinnati Symphony Orchestra, and in 1912 he succeeded Carl Pohlig as conductor of the Philadelphia Orchestra. He remained with it as Principal Conductor until 1936, building it into an orchestra of great character and renown. There-

Leopold Stokowski

after he worked more independently, appearing in films (including Walt Disney's *Fantasia*, 1939) and on radio. He founded the All-American Youth Orchestra (1940), and the New York City Symphony Orchestra (1944). Later he was Guest Conductor of the New York Philharmonic Symphony Orchestra (1946–49) and then co-conductor with Dimitri Mitropoulos (1949–50). Though somewhat eccentric and always a great showman, Stokowski was nevertheless a remarkable musician. His rather romantic orchestral 'transcriptions' of the classics (in particular Bach keyboard works) have been much frowned upon by purists, but admired by the general public.

WALTER SUSSKIND
1913–1980

Czech conductor. After ·studying at the Prague State Conservatory, he began his career as a concert pianist. He was appointed conductor at the Prague Opera (1934–37), but emigrated to England in 1939. He was Principal Conductor of the Carl Rosa Opera Company (1943–45), and conducted at Sadler's Wells and Glyndebourne. He was Principal Conductor of the Scottish Orchestra (1946–50) and of the Scottish National Orchestra (1950–52). He also conducted in Australia, Canada and, with the St Louis Symphony Orchestra, in the United States.

GEORGE SZELL
1897–1970

Hungarian – born conductor. He studied in Vienna and Leipzig and appeared as a child prodigy pianist. He was appointed first conductor of the Strasbourg Opera in 1917, and thereafter worked in a similar capacity in opera houses in Prague, Darmstadt and Düsseldorf. He was Principal Conductor of the Berlin State Opera (1924–29). He then conducted orchestras in most parts of the world, particularly Great Britain, where for a time (1937) he directed the Scottish Orchestra. He settled in America in 1942 and was Principal Conductor of the Cleveland Orchestra from 1946 until his death.

VACLAV TALICH
1883–1961

Czech conductor. Studied the violin at the Prague Conservatory and played in the Berlin Philharmonic Orchestra under Nikisch. In 1904 he became conductor of the Odessa Municipal Orchestra. After further study in Leipzig and Milan he became chief conductor of the Plzeň Opera (1912–15). In 1919 he was appointed Principal Conductor of the newly reorganized Prague Philharmonic Orchestra, and under his guidance (1919–41) it grew to greatness. He directed the Prague National Opera (1935–45, and 1947–48), but fell victim to political in-fighting and ended his remarkable career as head of the chamber ensemble of the Bratislava Slovak Philharmonic Orchestra.

ARTURO TOSCANINI
1867–1957

Italian conductor. He studied the cello at the Conservatories of Parma and Milan. While playing in the orchestra of the Rio de Janeiro Opera House he stepped in for a missing conductor with such success that other engagements soon followed. He became chief conductor at La Scala, Milan (1898–1903, and 1921–24), and of the New York Metropolitan Opera in 1907. In 1928 he quarrelled with Mussolini's Fascist government and went to America to become conductor of the New York Philharmonic Symphony Orchestra (1929–36). In 1936 he formed his own orchestra, the National Broadcasting Company Orchestra, which he conducted until 1954. He worked also in Europe, directing opera at Salzburg and Bayreuth, but left in disgust at the rise of the Nazi Party. He settled in America in 1939, returning to Italy for a few months in 1946 to give concerts to help with the rebuilding of La Scala. His electric personality and phenomenal memory made him one of the most remarkable conductors of his generation.

EDO de WAART
b.1941

Dutch conductor. After studying at the Amsterdam Conservatoire he

Edo de Waart

came to prominence in 1964 when he won the Dimitri Metropoulos competition for conductors, which gave him a one-year apprenticeship with Leonard Bernstein and the New York Philharmonic. In 1966 he became Assistant Conductor to Bernard Haitink and the Concertgebouw Orchestra, and Conductor and Artistic Director of the Netherlands Wind Ensemble. In the following year he shared the conductorship of the Rotterdam Philharmonic with Jean Fournet, and in 1972 became its Permanent Conductor and Artistic Director. In 1968 he worked with George Szell and the Cleveland Orchestra, and in 1970 became Conductor of the Netherlands Opera. Since then he has appeared with most of the world's leading orchestras, including the Royal Philharmonic (1969), the London Philharmonic (1973), and the BBC Symphony Orchestra.

BRUNO WALTER
1876–1962

German conductor. He received his training at the Stern Conservatory in Berlin, and after several years experience in German opera houses (including the Royal Opera in Berlin) he became director of the Vienna Court Opera (1901–12). From 1912 to 1922 he was general director at Munich. He first appeared in England in 1909 at a Royal Philharmonic Society concert. In 1925 he became director of the Charlottenburg Opera, Berlin, and from 1930 directed the Leipzig Gewandhaus concerts. But after 1933 the rise of the Nazi Party made him concentrate his activities in Austria, where he helped to found the Salzburg Festival. He became Artistic Adviser to the Vienna State Opera in 1936. In 1938, because of the Nazi takeover, he left Austria altogether and went to live in Paris. The war drove him from Europe in 1939 and he settled in America, appearing as guest conductor for a great many orchestras. In 1949 he was appointed Music Adviser to the New York Philharmonic Symphony Orchestra, often appearing with them as a conductor.

FELIX WEINGARTNER
1863–1942

Austrian – born conductor and composer. He studied at Graz and Leipzig, and with Liszt at Weimar. He began to make his mark from 1884 with various Kapellmeister posts – first at Königsberg, then Danzig, Hamburg, Mannheim and Berlin (where he directed both opera and orchestral concerts, 1891–98). After working in Munich for several years he succeeded Mahler as conductor of the Court Opera in Vienna (1907). In the meantime his reputation spread internationally. He visited London for the first time in 1898, returning often to conduct Royal Philharmonic Society concerts and the London Symphony Orchestra. He visited America in 1905 to conduct the orchestra of the New York Philharmonic Society, and in 1906 toured with the New York Symphony Society's orchestra. His own music includes eight operas and seven symphonies, but is seldom played nowadays. Weingartner was also known as a writer on musical matters.

WALTER WELLER
b.1939

Austrian conductor. Became leader of the Vienna Philharmonic Orchestra in 1960, and also made a considerable reputation with the Weller String Quartet (formed in 1957). He studied conducting with Joseph Krips and George Szell and became known as a conductor in 1968 when he took over a Vienna Philharmonic concert from Karl Böhm, and a Vienna Volksoper performance from Josef Krips: on each occasion through the illness of the respective conductors, and, also on each occasion, at a few hours' notice. In 1969 he signed a long term contract with the Vienna State Opera. Since then he has conducted orchestras throughout Europe and America, and has been Principal Conductor of the Royal Liverpool Philharmonic (1977–80). He is now Principal Conductor of the Royal Philharmonic Orchestra.

Sir HENRY WOOD
1869–1944

He began his career as an organist, and studied at the Royal Academy of Music with a view to becoming a composer. His first conducting engagements were with various small opera companies. In 1895 he was invited by the impresario Robert Newman to conduct a series of Promenade Concerts at the newly built Queen's Hall. Together they founded the New Queen's Hall Orchestra for the purpose. These concerts proved enormously successful and placed him on the map as a conductor. Thereafter he was invited to conduct at most important musical events in Great Britain. He was knighted in 1911. His work with the Promenade Concerts continued well into the Second World War, by which time he had become a legend – the present Proms are named after him. Wood introduced new music by a whole range of different composers and was remarkably catholic in his sympathies. He was a strict orchestral disciplinarian and produced results of extraordinary vitality – even if not always of great sensitivity.

Sir Henry Wood (**right**).
Arturo Toscanini **(facing page)**.

Index

Figures in *Italic* denote photograph or illustration

Credits

t indicates top; *b* indicates bottom; *l* indicates left; *c* indicates center; *r* indicates right.

Picture credits: *cover photo* Erich Auerbach FRPS. **6** Museum für Geschichte, Leipzig. **7** *tl* Bildarchiv Preussischer Kulturbesitz, Berlin; *c* British Library; *b* Erich Auerbach FRPS. **8** *t* Germanisches Nationalmuseum, Nuremberg; *b* Mary Evans Picture Library. **9** *c & b* The Mansell Collection. **10** *t & b* Mary Evans. **11** *c* Mansell. **12** *t* Mansell; *cl* Mansell; *bl* Barnaby's Picture Library. **13** Mansell. **15** *t* Germanisches Nationalmuseum; *c* Mansell; *b* Mansell. **16** *br* Royal College of Music; *bl* Bildarchiv Preussischer Kulturbesitz. **18** Mansell. **19.** *t, c & b* Bildarchiv Preussischer Kulturbesitz. **20** *t* Mary Evans; *bl* Mansell; *cb* Mary Evans; *br* Mansell. **21** *t & bl* Osterreichische Nationalbibliothek, Vienna; *br* Mansell. **22** Illustrated London News. **23** *tl, tr, cl, cr* Royal College of Music; *bl* Mary Evans. **24** *t* Mansell; *bl* Mary Evans; *cb* BBC Hulton Picture Library; *br* Royal College of Music. **25** Bodleian Library, Oxford. **26** *l* Scala, Florence; *r* Mansell. **27** *bl* Mary Evans; *br* Mansell. **28** *t* Mansell; *b* Royal College of Music. **30** Topkapi Saray Museum, Istanbul. **32** Museum fur Geschichte, Leipzig. **33** *r, from top*: Royal College of Music; Mansell; Mansell; Mansell; *bl* London Symphony Orchestra. **34** *t* Decca; *b* David Redfern Photography. **35** *t* Royal College of Music; *cl* London Symphony Orchestra; *cr* Royal College of Music; *r* Mary Evans. **37** *t* BBC; *c* Landeshauptstadt München, Stadtarchiv; *b* Osterreichische Nationalbibliothek. **38** *tl* BBC; *bl* BBC; *tr* Mary Evans; *cr* Illustrated London News; *br* Mary Evans. **39** *tl* BBC; *bl* Mary Evans; *tr* Mary Evans; *br* BBC. **40** *t* Auerbach; *b* Universal Edition (London). **41** *bl & br* Covent Garden Archive. **42** *l* Auerbach. **43** BBC. **44** Universal Edition. **45** *c* Auerbach; *bl* Decca; *cb* Deutsche Grammophon; *br* Decca. **46** *tl* Greater London Council; *tr* Barnaby's. **47** *l* IBM, Bell Telephone; *tr* Mary Evans; *c* BBC; *b* Imperial War Museum. **48** Decca. **51** *t* Harry Weber/EMI. **54** Barnaby's. **55** *tr* Mansell. **56** *l* Scala; *r* Barnaby's. **61** *l* Reg Wilson. **62** *br* London Symphony Orchestra. **64** *tr* Decca. **65** *tr* Decca. **66** Harry Weber/EMI. **67** Clive Barda. **68** Buffet Crampon UK Ltd. **69** *b* Reg Wilson. **70** Mike Fear. **71** Auerbach. **72** *t* Auerbach. **73** *bl* Bildarchiv Preussischer Kulturbesitz. **74** *tr* Harry Weber. **77** *br* Mary Evans. **78** *tl* Decca. *br* Harry Weber/EMI. **80** Mary Evans. **82** *tl* Mary Evans; *tr* Mansell; *cr* Mansell; *br* Decca. **84** *br* Harry Weber/EMI. **86** Clive Barda. **89** Clive Barda. **90** *bl* Barnaby's; *cb* Barnaby's **91** Barnaby's. **92** Premier Ltd., Leicester. **93** *br* Mary Evans. **95** Clive Barda. **96** *br* Reg Wilson. **98** *t* Clive Barda. **99** *tl* Clive Barda. **100** *tl* Novosti. **101** *l from t*: Barnaby's; J Allan Cash; Barnaby's; *b* Barnaby's; *cr* J Allan Cash; *r* Barnaby's. **102** *t* Clive Barda; *b* Mary Evans. **103** *(box)* Barnaby's; Syndication International. **105** Mansell. **108** Richard Holt. **110** Gerald Drucker/Philharmonia. **113** *t, bl & br* London Symphony Orchestra. **114** BBC. **116** *t* Royal Philharmonic Society; *b* Mary Evans. **117** Royal College of Music. **118** Royal Philharmonic Orchestra. **119** Royal Philharmonic Orchestra. **120** *t & b* London Symphony Orchestra. **121** London Symphony Orchestra. **122** *l* National Maritime Museum, Greenwich, London; *r* London Symphony Orchestra. **124** *l & br* London Symphony Orchestra; *tr* Stanley Castle/LSO. **125** *t* Philharmonia/Clive Barda; *bl* Philharmonia/G Macdomnic; *br* EMI/Reg Wilson. **126** *t* Clive Barda; *b* Reg Wilson. **127** *t, c & b* BBC. **128** *tl* London Philharmonic/Colin Busby; *tr* London Philharmonic; *b* London Philharmonic/Tom Bradley. **129** *tl* London Philharmonic; *bl* Neville Graham; *tr, cr & br* London Philharmonic. **130** *t* Royal Liverpool Philharmonic Orchestra; *b* Mary Evans. **132** *tr, tl, br & bl* Royal Liverpool Philharmonic Orchestra. **133** Halle Concerts Society. **134** Halle Concerts Society. **135.** *tl & bl* Halle Concerts Society; *cl* Halle Concerts Society/Len Stirrup; *r* Reg Wilson. **136** *t, bl & br* City of Birmingham Symphony Orchestra. **137** *t* Reg Wilson; *b* CBSO/Sophie Baker. **138** *l* Reg Wilson; *tr & br* Scottish National Orchestra. **139** Concertgebouw Orchestra, Amsterdam. **140** Siegfried Lauterwasser. **142** *t* Deutsche Fotothek, Dresden; *remainder* Bildarchiv Preussischer Kulturbesitz. **143** Lauterwasser. **144** *t & c* Deutsche Fotothek, Dresden; *b* Dresdener Staatskapelle/Hermann Koenigs. **145** *t & c* Museum für Geschichte, Leipzig; *b* Bildarchiv Preussischer Kulturbesitz. **146** *t & c* Museum für Geschichte, Leipzig; *bl* Auerbach; *br* Phonogram. **147** Phonogram. **148** Harry Weber/EMI. **150** *tl & bl* Osterreichische Nationalbibliothek; *r* Lauterwasser. **151** Lauterwasser. **152** *l* London Symphony Orchestra; *c* Bildarchiv Preussischer Kulturbesitz; *br* Berlin Philharmonic Orchestra. **153** *bl & br* Bildarchiv Preussischer Kulturbesitz. **154** *tl, bl & r* Lauterwasser. **155** *br* Concertgebouw Orchestra. **156** *t* Concertgebouw Orchestra; *bl* Auerbach; *br* Concertgebouw/Godfried de Groot. **157** Richard Holt. **158** Auerbach. **159** *t* Czech Philharmonic; *b* Auerbach. **160** *t* Orchestre de la Suisse Romande/François Martin; *bl* OSR/Festspiele Bayreuth/Wilhelm Rauh; *r* Decca. **161** *t* Harry Weber/EMI; *b* Mary Evans. **162** *t & bl* Israel Philharmonic Orchestra; *br* Decca. **163** Novosti. **164** *t & b* Novosti. **165** *t* Auerbach; *b* Novosti. **166** Keystone. **167** *t* Mansell; *b* Royal Philharmonic Orchestra. **168** *t & b* New York Philharmonic. **169** *bl* Bettman Archive; *br* New York Philharmonic. **170** *all except cl* Boston Symphony Orchestra; *cl* Bettman. **172** *tl* Boston Symphony Orchestra; *r* Chicago Symphony Orchestra. **173** *t* Bettman; *b* Chicago Symphony Orchestra. **174** *tl, bl & c* Chicago Symphony Orchestra. **176 & 177** Philadelphia Orchestra/Louis Hood. **178** Philadelphia Orchestra. **179** *tl, cl & bl* Philadelphia Orchestra; *br* Detroit Symphony Orchestra. **180** *t & b* Detroit Symphony Orchestra. **181** *t & b* Detroit Symphony Orchestra. **182** *l & r* Cleveland Orchestra. **183** *t & b* Cleveland Orchestra. **184 & 185** *all* Cleveland Orchestra. **186** *l & r* Los Angeles Philharmonic. **188** *inset & main pic* Bettman. **189** *t & b* Los Angeles Philharmonic. **190** National Broadcasting Company. **191** *t & b* Keystone. **192** Decca. **198** Auerbach. **199** Clive Barda **206** Reg Wilson. **207** *t* Auerbach. *bl* Clive Barda; *c* Decca; *r* Godfrey Macdomnic/EMI. **217** Keystone.

Instruments: color photographs of instruments by Mike Fear. All instruments kindly loaned by Boosey and Hawkes Ltd., London, except timpani, bass drum, Chinese gong, glockenspiel, cocktail drums, talking drums, bongos and timbales, loaned by Chas. Foote Ltd., London.

Illustrators: Ken Stott (conductors); John Woodcock; Aziz Khan; Gerard Brown.

Reproduced scores supplied by: OUP (Gabrieli); Boosey and Hawkes (Bach, Stravinsky); Eulenberg (Debussy); Universal Edition (Stockhausen); British Library (Haydn); Novello (Parry).

Acknowledgements: the publishers are most grateful to all the featured orchestras for supplying information and photographs. They also wish to thank: Donna Sturm (USA picture research); University of London Library; Covent Garden Archive; Clive Barda; Don Kennedy and EMI Records Ltd; John Kehoe, Graham Turnbull and the Decca Record Company; Novosti Press Agency; Robert Morley; Roger Daniels; Victoria Funk.